S0-ACB-871

The McCloskey Challenge

Books by Lou Cannon

Ronnie and Jesse: A Political Odyssey

The McCloskey Challenge

Lou Cannon

The McCloskey Challenge

E. P. DUTTON & CO., INC. | NEW YORK | 1972

First Edition

Published simultaneously in Canada
by Clarke, Irwin & Company Limited, Toronto and Vancouver

Library of Congress Catalog Card Number: 73-179-860
SBN 0-525-154329

To Ginny,
who helped

Contents

Foreword

The idea for *The McCloskey Challenge* took conscious root in April 1971 when Pete McCloskey and I were en route from Washington, D.C., to San Francisco, the jumping-off point for what would become a controversial visit to Laos and to the northernmost provinces of South Vietnam. The book would, hopefully, be an insightful study of McCloskey as man and candidate, showing him, as I tried to depict Ronald Reagan and Jesse Unruh in a previous book, with all his warts. What did McCloskey think of such a book? "Fine," he said. "You've already written that I'm an egomaniac, and all us egomaniacs like to have books written about them." I had not called him an "egomaniac," of course. But I had written a column quoting McCloskey's reply to Elizabeth Drew of WETA-TV in Washington when she asked him why he was in politics. "It's hard to say how much is vanity and how much is ambition and how much is desire to be in the public limelight, and how much is patriotism, wanting to serve the country," McCloskey had answered. This book is about that vanity and that ambition and that desire for limelight. It is also about that patriotism, a word that McCloskey is not afraid to use to describe his own conduct.

Congressman Paul Norton McCloskey, Jr., the subject of this book, was candid beyond call in subsequent interviews and gave generously of his time and of his opinions. He understood that my intention was to write as balanced a book as possible, and he made available information and documents that lesser men would have withheld. *The McCloskey Challenge* is a better book because of it. It is also better than it otherwise would have been because of the assistance of his lovely wife, Caroline (Cubby) McCloskey, and their eldest daughter, Nancy. I appreciate also the useful interviews given by Pete McCloskey's parents, Paul N. McCloskey, Sr., and Vera McCloskey, and, especially, the information supplied by Mrs. Virginia McCloskey Hartzell, the congressman's sister.

McCloskey's friends matched McCloskey in their candor. Most helpful were Charles McClung and his wife, Charlotte, the twin sister of Cubby McCloskey, plus Lewis Butler, Charles U. Daly, Mr. and Mrs. Ryland Kelley, Mr. and Mrs. David Lennihan, Dayton Reinke, and Mr. and Mrs. Robert Thede.

Numerous political figures in the White House, in Congress, and in California granted interviews and insights. I particularly am indebted to John Ehrlichman, President Nixon's adviser for domestic affairs; Putnam Livermore, the California Republican chairman; and Congressman John Rousselot, a boyhood friend of McCloskey's. Others who helped included California Governor Ronald Reagan; Ned Hutchinson, the governor's appointments secretary; Robert Finch, special counsel to the President; Senator Robert Dole, the Republican national chairman, and Franklyn Nofziger, the Republican national committee's director of communications. Other congressmen who assisted, in large ways or small, included Charles Gubser, Donald Riegle, and Jerome Waldie, plus John Anderson, Larry Ashley, Phillip Burton, James Cleveland, Don Edwards, Chet Holifield, Andrew Jacobs, Jack Kemp, Henry Reuss, and Charles Wiggins. Several staff mambers of these congressmen provided assistance, especially Ellen Mae Gospodnetich, Alan Parker, Ailsa Stickney, Vyonne LeMasters, and Patrick Rowland.

McCloskey's staff, more than any other, patiently responded to half-a-hundred queries with answers and documents. Constance M. Bethray, McCloskey's personal secretary, bore the brunt of these inquiries, and Paul LaFond, the former Marine officer who is now a McCloskey staff assistant, helped in myriad ways. Others among the many who assisted, included Michael Brewer, David Brown, Janet Brune, Arthur Bushkin, Anne Canby, Lucy Homans, George Murphy, David Niklaus, Jan Pearson, Barbara Ramsay, Anne Sherwood, and John Wilson.

Walter T. Ridder, my employer, made *The McCloskey Challenge* possible by graciously allowing me time to do the book. I am indebted to William Broom, the Washington bureau chief of Ridder Publications, for his consideration and his work in my absence, and indebted, also, to my good friend Albert Eisele, another Washington-bureau colleague, for his encouragement, cigars, and helpful suggestions about my manuscript. A number of colleagues in the Washington press corps and on various California newspapers made my task easier. Among them were Larry Allison, editor of the Long Beach *Independent Press-Telegram,* and Gilbert Bailey, a contributing editor of the same paper; Dennis Britton and Thomas Foley of the Los Angeles *Times*; Adam Clymer of the Baltimore *Sun*; Harry Farrell, political editor of the San Jose *Mercury-News*, and Larry Stammer, state-capitol bureau chief for the *Mercury-News*; Mercer Cross and Wayne Kelley of *Congressional Quarterly*; David Broder of the Washington *Post*; Matthew Storin of the Boston *Globe*; and Ben Shore, Washington correspondent for several California newspapers. My special thanks goes to Jeff Littleboy of the Stanford News Service for a useful story and for other information.

Sally Rugaber and Margo Kline competently transcribed numerous interviews from tapes; Karen Hanson, with some help from Martha Campbell, capably typed the manuscript; Cheryl Klein effectively performed both of these time-consuming chores. Judson Clark, the president of *California Journal*, was kind enough to read my manuscript with his usual care and perception.

I especially appreciate the permission of Rodney G. Minott to quote from his book on McCloskey's first congressional campaign (*The Sinking of the Lollipop*, Diablo Press, 1968), and I appreciate also a helpful interview with him and his wife, Polly, and subsequent letters.

And I also wish to thank: Janet Adams, Patricia Allison, Shirley Temple Black, Sheana Butler, Mr. and Mrs. Charles Cherniss, Murray Chotiner, Cecily Clover, Senator Alan Cranston, David Dahle, Michael Deaver, Alexander Donald, Gael and Marilyn Douglass, Janet Farley, David Gosselin, Paul Haerle, William Hecht, Al Hederman, Edward Hunter Hurst, Grant Kenyon, Herbert Klein, James Leeds, Allard K. Lowenstein, Karen Matthiesen, Barbara Leh Maxwell, Terry Maxwell, Charles McClung, Jr., Edwin Meese, John Miller, Roger Mosher, Roderick O'Connor, Mark Pratt, Robert Reno, Gretchen Schmidt, Al Schreck, Lois Christensen Seidel, DeVan Shumway, Forrest Shumway, Carl Spaeth, Rusty van Bronkhurst, John G. Veneman, Casper Weinberger, Sanford Weiner, and Elaine Walker Whitmore.

Last, and decidedly not least, I want to thank the two persons who helped the most. The first is my wife, Virginia Cannon, who served as research assistant, counselor, critic, and friend and to whom this book is dedicated. The other is Robin Schmidt, McCloskey's campaign manager and understanding advocate, who opened every door and combined total loyalty to his employer with a scrupulous regard for truth. My own conclusions are defined by a different compass than Robin's, but we share a concern that the ship shall reach the shore.

It goes without saying, but I shall say it anyway, that all responsibility for the accuracy of quotations, the determination of facts, the value of observations, and the relevance of conclusions are my own. I began this book in the belief that I should tell all of which I was aware and in the hope that an account as unbiased and wide-ranging as possible would be of the greatest value to the country, to McCloskey, and to my readers. What follows is an attempt to define the nature of the McCloskey challenge and the character of the man who makes it.

LOU CANNON

Vienna, Virginia
August 1971

The ability to be cool, confident, and decisive in crisis is not an inherited characteristic but is the direct result of how well the individual has prepared himself for the battle.

—Richard M. Nixon

1. Thanksgiving 1970

Start with the presumption that it is difficult to pick the day. I say difficult because not even Pete McCloskey himself knows when the challenge began, much less when or where it will end, and those around him believe it began on different days in different places deep within McCloskey. They, also, do not know where it will end, though they are conscious of its beginnings and concerned about its destination. Start with that. Start with the presumption of difficulty, as McCloskey himself might do, and begin in Washington, that great, troubled city that is the focal point of the McCloskey challenge. Begin in Washington, at the White House, and drive down Seventeenth Street to Constitution Avenue and follow Constitution to the Theodore Roosevelt Bridge. Cross the bridge and proceed north on the George Washington Memorial Parkway. Go back in time to the Thanksgiving before last, to Thanksgiving 1970. Go back in time and stay on the parkway until it reaches the McLean off-ramp, then turn west along the Chain Bridge Road. Turn off at Old Langley Farms and follow the road onto a tree-shaded lane a half-mile from the home where Robert Kennedy once lived. Turn left on Langley Lane. Turn left and drive slowly, for the road is narrow and there are children about. Stop before you reach the Georgetown Pike. Stop at a once-faded white frame house with a basketball hoop on the garage, a house converted by Cubby McCloskey into a western home complete with wooden sundeck. Walk inside, invisible, and smell the odors of turkey and fresh oysters and pecan pie. Stop here. It is as good a place as any to begin.

Thanksgiving Day 1970 should have been a feast of home-coming and celebration for the McCloskey family. The Mc-Closkeys were together again after the long campaign, together in Langley, Virginia, except for the eldest daughter, Nancy, who was in school in California and spending the holiday with her aunt. The election was three weeks past, and Paul Norton McCloskey, Jr., who answers among friends to "Pete" and "Peter" and other names, had for the third time been elected to the House of Representatives. He had received 77.6 percent of the vote, and he should have been happy about it. Cubby McCloskey was happy. The McCloskeys had gathered around them their friends and their family for what some of them thought was the best Thanksgiving dinner of all. The friends were Robin and Gretchen Schmidt and Lewis and Sheana But-ler and Richard Borda, he an assistant secretary of defense, and Pete Morton, a cousin of Cubby's who had brought fresh oysters with him from New England. There were also thirteen children, even though not all of the children were there, and what Gretchen Schmidt remembers most about the day is that the children ate forty pounds of mashed potatoes.

What her husband, Robin, remembers is that it was a fine Thanksgiving of talk and feasting. Butler, then the assistant secretary for program planning and evaluation in the Depart-ment of Health, Education and Welfare and a former Mc-Closkey law partner, had brought the wine, and Sheana had baked pecan pies. Morton had brought a pie, too, a mincemeat pie that some of the guests remember as the best they ever tasted. Cubby had roasted the turkey and prepared homemade cranberry relish, and Gretchen Schmidt had contributed a shrimp aspic. The children ate turkey and mashed potatoes and peas. "It was one of those lovely Thanksgiving dinners you have, where everybody is really enjoying themselves," recalls

Robin Schmidt. "And the Bordas were really very pleased; it was their first Thanksgiving away from home, and they were pleased to be included, because they felt at home. And the Butlers and the Schmidts and the McCloskeys were all kind of celebrating the fact that we had a unit away from home that was happy and cohesive. The children were happy, and it was a nice beginning for a holiday season, where we really were in kind of an alien land, but together. We had several toasts, I remember. I wrote a funny little jingle about what we were doing, and everybody was in kind of a laughing mood. And sometime during the dinner the conversation sort of turned to more serious things because Dick Borda was deep into Defense Department affairs, and Butler was struggling with things at HEW, and Pete and I, of course, had just been through the elections, which saddened us because the Republican party had gone the route it did. It seemed to be so contrary to what was needed in the country; rather than unifying, they were pushing it to polarization. And so at some point in the dinner there was a kind of somber note which especially struck Pete. And he went away from the table and got a pad of paper and started scrawling."

It is like McCloskey to start scrawling on a yellow legal notepad while others are eating and drinking. It is like him, too, to finish dinner ten minutes ahead of everyone else, for McCloskey eats rapidly when he remembers to eat at all. He wrote for a long time that Thanksgiving evening, and he continued writing later when most of the guests had gone. He talked about what he was writing only a little, saying at one point the next day that "maybe we ought to write the President another letter." He worked on it over the weekend. The scrawl became his thirteenth letter to President Richard M. Nixon, his fifth on the subject of Vietnam. The letter was dated November 30, 1970:

Dear Mr. President:

Most Americans have just enjoyed a bountiful Thanksgiving and we now look forward in a few weeks to a national exchange of gifts and good wishes at Christmas time.

All of this seems a little hollow, however, when we reflect on the fact that we have just completed seven straight weeks of daily bombing of Laos, and that American troops and firepower are continuing to kill people in Cambodia, Laos, and Vietnam.

At this season of the year it is an American tradition for our more powerful and affluent citizens to stop and give thanks, as well as to share some of their wealth with those less fortunate.

As commander-in-chief of the armed forces of the world's most powerful nation you are the only person capable of ending our part in the killing in Southeast Asia. If we cannot end the conflict, we can at least end American participation in a type of warfare which is inconsistent with our national goals, and our leadership in the cause of peace.

For this reason I would like to suggest your consideration, as commander-in-chief, of the issuance of an order to stop the killing, or at least to order Americans to cease participation in the killing, as America's gift to the world this Christmas.

If Vietnamese wish to continue this conflict, let this be their choice, not ours. The two Vietnams are at least equal in population and weaponry, and there are far more South Vietnamese trained and armed today than there are North Vietnamese.

There are too many good things to do for others in this world of the 1970s for the world's most powerful western nation to be setting an example of leadership in the art of destroying Asian people and villages.

It seems also that we are doing a disservice to those who have suffered the most, our prisoners of war and their families. To reunite them, we ourselves must first do what is right—complete the withdrawal of our troops from Indochina at the earliest practicable date. I suggest that your goal of a generation of peace better can be served by withdrawal of all U.S. troops within six months than by withdrawal within the several years apparently contemplated by your present policy.

Once our troops are withdrawn, should our prisoners not be returned in good health, Mr. President, *then* let us consider going in to get them, with whatever forces as may be necessary, and with Members of the Joint Chiefs and Congress in the assault wave. This war might not seem so easy to condone if we ourselves were living less safely and comfortably in Washington and were instead exposing ourselves to the hardships and choices we ask our 19-year-olds to endure.

Respectfully,
Paul N. McCloskey, Jr.

The letter, sent with the handwritten signature "Pete McCloskey," was acknowledged in a two-sentence reply by White House legislative liaison William Timmons. Old Stanford Law School classmate John D. Ehrlichman, the assistant to the President for domestic affairs, had more fully responded to two earlier letters, both of which McCloskey describes as "unanswered," but neither the replies nor the Nixon policy in Vietnam satisfied McCloskey. "We must do something," he told friends, "we must do something that Nixon will understand." On December 20, 1970, he talked about it before four hundred persons, most of them opponents of the war, in the Palo Alto (California) First Presbyterian Church. "I suspect if a grassroots organization was formed in this state to deny the President the Republican nomination, it might affect his thinking," McCloskey said. "It will probably take a massive outpouring of public opinion to accelerate troop withdrawal to the point where all Americans are out by the end of next year and not to resume the bombing."

Pete McCloskey talked for a long time that Sunday evening, standing ramrod straight and jabbing his points home with a forefinger, speaking in that resonant staccato voice which is like water flowing over hard gravel. It was five days before the Christmas gift of peace that never came, and McCloskey said he was fearful that the United States would expand its "destructive" efforts in Vietnam. He predicted that the South Vietnamese government would collapse as soon as U.S. forces withdrew. And he said that the American people had changed their goals, while the government had not. "We see our government as the protector of individual freedom, but our policy in Vietnam has led to a way of making war that is repugnant to the ideals of democracy," he said. "We executed war criminals at Nuremberg for the same crimes we are committing in Vietnam—destruction of civilians and villages."

The Palo Alto speech was a logical extension of the Thanksgiving Day notes that became a letter to the President. But it would be too easy to fix the date of either the letter or the speech as the time when a particular flame ignited within McCloskey that enabled him to launch his challenge to the President. "There really was no precise moment," said Senator Eugene McCarthy in 1968 when announcing his own challenge to President Lyndon Johnson. "It was nothing like Saint Paul being knocked off his horse." Pete McCloskey is even less likely to be knocked off his horse than Gene McCarthy, and McCloskey also is unaware of the precise moment when it all began. Certainly, "it" began sometime before Thanksgiving, though how much before is hard to say. The day before that Thanksgiving celebration, McCloskey, Schmidt, and I had lunch together at the Rotunda, a Capitol Hill restaurant that informs its congressional diners of pending votes and quorum calls. Two things stand out in my notes, made afterward. One is the mere presence of McCloskey at the Rotunda—usually he dines with constituents, reporters, or other congressmen at the House restaurant, or, by preference, wolfs down a liverwurst sandwich at his desk, because, as his staff would have it, he has run out of K-rations—and the other observation, more significant, is that McCloskey said some things which he asked not to be written about at the time. What he talked about was the presidential challenge, and I remember being more struck by his secrecy than by his statements. This is partly because one becomes used to any sort of statement from McCloskey, but mostly because he is a reporter's model of on-the-record utterance who rarely asks anything withheld from publication. In a world where "background" lunches are a rule of being, and off-the-record confidences a commonplace, McCloskey has bluntly and correctly attacked the Washington backgrounder as a device permitting government officials to anonymously float trial balloons disguised as news stories. So it seemed to me significant that when McCloskey talked about what a presidential challenge might accomplish within the Republican party he viewed the challenge as sufficiently "unthinkable" that he did not want it published. He clearly had been thinking long and hard about that challenge and about the course and character of the Nixon administration, particularly about a political campaign based upon the suggestion that the Republicans favored "law and order" while the Democrats opposed it. "What are we coming to in this country?" he said at one point. But he was unready to declare an open break with the commander-in-chief of the American armed forces. Schmidt, eating quietly and occasionally participating in the discussion, did not seem at all surprised by what McCloskey said, only by the fact that he was saying it to a reporter.

McCloskey had talked about the challenge before, to Schmidt and to Lew Butler, and, of course, to Cubby. Butler, who then lived on Turkey Run Road a little more than a mile away from the McCloskey home, remembers him coming over for dinner earlier in November, soon after the campaign. "Both Sheana and I commented about it," Butler remembers. "He was just like a caged lion. He really had a wild look in his eye. He was pacing around here—I attributed it just to being so keyed up, having been campaigning so hard. I saw him get like that in the first campaign, where he'd just keep going on nervous energy; he gets intense and exhausted, and you can see it in his eyes. Sheana was very disturbed by the whole thing. He just kept talking about the war. He said we've got to stop it, we've got to do something. Seems to me like he said: 'I think the only way to do it is to run. Really threaten the President politically.' He just kinda went on like that, and he said: 'What do you think?' I said: 'Pete, I think you ought to take two weeks or a month to wind down and have some perspective. You're just out on your feet.' Well, I forget. We organized a bunch of football games with the kids and started going canoeing; he really did wind down."

There are some of McCloskey's friends and supporters, some

of his enemies, too, who think that he never really does wind down. They look for an inner reason to the challenge, one which they are not certain that even McCloskey can define.

"The McCloskeys raised Peter as if he had a destiny," says Dayton Reinke of San Marino, California, Pete's closest friend in high school and the best man at his wedding. "And I think he feels he does have a destiny, like Patton had a destiny to become a great general. Perhaps one reason why he was a hero in the Korean War is that he felt this was an opportunity, subconsciously, for fame and recognition. I think he feels that he wants to leave something, an edifice or something. I think he wants to make an imprint on history." Others who have come to know McCloskey later in life also have perceived this destiny quality. "He makes up his mind subconsciously," says Rodney Minott, a history professor who wrote a book about McCloskey's campaign against Shirley Temple Black. "He lives in such a way as to create a self-fulfilling prophecy. The presidency is a classic example. He burns his bridges behind him, and then he does what he wants to do all along."

Perhaps. "As much as I've lived with him, as long as I've known him, I don't know that anyone will really capture what it is that makes him react," says his wife, Cubby. "Some things that you think are going to make him react, he doesn't react to. Other things you think he would react normally to, he gets very unhappy about."

"I don't understand his motives, and he doesn't either," maintains Butler, who in some ways knows McCloskey better than other men. "They're complex. Sheana's always understood this better than I; she was in college with him. She says Pete has always been on stage, even in athletics. He had a kind of stage manner and loves to be on stage."

There are other explanations, other touchstones, other checkpoints on the road to Damascus. Ned Hutchinson, a onetime neighbor and still close friend who is now appointments secretary to Ronald Reagan, remembers jogging across the Stanford golf course with McCloskey in 1960 at a time when both men ran to work. McCloskey was then thirty-three, Hutchinson not quite thirty. They were both of them Republican activists who were supporting Richard Nixon against John F. Kennedy, and Hutchinson remembers McCloskey as saying: " 'You know, Nixon puts his pants on just the same way as you and I, and I think I could do a better job running for President than he's doing.' And it wasn't a boastful thing." This happened more than eleven years ago, and Hutchinson is not certain of the precise accuracy of the quotation, but it is exactly the sort of thing that McCloskey would say to a fellow Republican in the midst of a presidential campaign. "He always said things to shock people," Reinke remembers. "It's part of his mystique. He did things [in high school] for the show business of it, the glamour. He's done that sort of thing all his life."

It has, by any standard, been quite a life. It is a life that led Pete McCloskey from high-school stunts and athletic challenge to the U.S. Marine Corps and the challenge of combat, and, further, to the even more exacting challenge of law. It is a life ruled by many inner laws, not the least among them the pre-nuclear belief of Oliver Wendell Holmes that McCloskey loves to quote: ". . . Perhaps as long as man dwells upon the globe, his destiny is battle and he has to take the chances of war." That is what McCloskey always believed. He took the soldier Holmes as literally as the lawyer Holmes, and he still wants his sons to be Marines. Now he takes his chances in the name of peace and against a war that he has long opposed. "The way we change policy in the United States is when the voters choose between two alternatives," he told me in a Hong Kong hotel room at the conclusion of a 1971 Easter congressional recess trip to Laos and Vietnam. "I want to focus this issue and fight it through and get a decision by the voters of the United States as quickly as we can. And if the only way to do it is for me to run for the presidency of the United States, I'm going to do it. And I'm starting now."

Part One
The Adventurer

We, the class of '45, have been told many times in our three years of high school that we would be leaders in the postwar world. Most of us will be just ordinary citizens, but a few perhaps will someday literally hold positions of high responsibility. If so, their actions then will be the results of the beliefs they are forming now. . . .

—South Pasadena High School
senior Paul N. McCloskey, Jr.,
in his graduation address

2. *Irish Rebel*

John Henry McCloskey, as adventurous as the family from which he sprang, arrived in New Orleans in 1842, an orphan and an immigrant. He came from County Derry, in the north of Ireland, where the McCloskeys ("son of Bloskey") traced their lineage back to Bloskey O'Kane, a famous chieftain who in 1196 slew Murtaugh O'Laughlin, heir to the throne of Ireland. John Henry, despite his orphan status, was a fortunate Irishman, one of those who reached the United States before the murderous potato famine of 1846 that Irishmen still refer to as the Great Starvation. He learned the trade of carpenter in New Orleans. In 1853, at the age of twenty, he made the long journey to San Francisco, where his life and the lives of the McCloskeys who came after him read like a history of California. San Francisco in those days was the supply center of the California gold rush and the wellspring of what would become a century-long population boom. It had been a village of fewer than 1,000 persons in 1848, but the population was pushing 40,000 by the time McCloskey arrived. John Henry lingered in San Francisco for only two weeks, then pushed northward to Yreka, where he intended to find work as a miner. He never did. Carpenters were in short supply and on high wages in the gold country, and John Henry stayed on as a carpenter and prospered.

Irishmen were no novelty in California in the mid-nineteenth century. By the 1860s the European nationals—English, Irish, Germans, Scandinavians, Eastern Europeans, some Portuguese and Italians—outnumbered the native Californians and were only slightly less numerous than the American nationals from other states. The gold fields had played out, for the most part, and the Old World settlers and the farmers from Ohio and Illinois and New England had begun to settle the cities and till the virgin soils of the California valleys. John Henry McCloskey bought a two-thousand-acre ranch near Livingston in Merced County in the lee of the great central valley that slashes through the heart of California and separates the Sierra Nevada from the Coast ranges. It was a land of vast ranches in the late nineteenth century, and, sometimes, of vast floods. Later, Merced was one of the counties where the farmers rose in revolt against the power of the Southern Pacific Railroad political machine.

Henry Harrison McCloskey, born in Yreka in 1858, was a young boy when his father came to Merced County. His mother had died during his early childhood, and John Henry remarried, taking for a second wife a woman who his son would not accept as stepmother. Barely fourteen, Henry Harrison ran away, leaving behind both his family and the Catholic faith that his father had brought with him from Ireland. Paul Norton McCloskey, Sr.,* the son of Henry Harrison, vaguely remembers attending a cathedral as a young boy. "But my mother was a Presbyterian, and there never was a question of religion in our household," he recalls. ". . . I don't recall my father ever acting as a Catholic in religious matters." Henry Harrison's indifference to formal religion has extended to son and to grandson. In its place the grandfather established a legal tradition and a skepticism, both of which are symbolized by the near-worship that Pete McCloskey extends to his soldier-lawyer hero, the great skeptic, Oliver Wendell Holmes. It was not easy for Henry Harrison McCloskey to become an attorney, however. He worked as a reporter and then a Southern Pacific Railroad telegrapher in

* The "senior" is not actually part of his name. Mr. McCloskey, now past eighty, says he has adopted it in recent years to avoid confusion between father and son.

Merced, but he wound up at Hastings Law School in San Francisco, passed the California bar in 1900, and practiced law until his death in 1914. His son, Paul Norton McCloskey, became a lawyer, too. Pete's father was one of the upwardly mobile San Francisco Irishmen of his time, and attended Lowell High School, which then, as now, was known for academic excellence. Paul Sr., who became "Pete" in high school, was a superb athlete who went on to win four consecutive baseball letters at Stanford. It was also at Stanford that Pete Sr. met Vera McNabb, the daughter of Samuel McNabb, an illustrious and politically active Southern California attorney who was three times elected mayor of San Bernardino and served as U.S. attorney during the Coolidge and Hoover administrations. Vera McNabb, now seventy-eight, still sparkles when she talks of her father, but then she is a sparkling person about almost everything, and a vigorous and effective campaign worker for her son. She maintains that she wasn't too interested in studies at college. "I'm a people person who just sort of danced my way through Stanford," she says. "It was a good time."

Paul Norton and Vera were both members of the class of 1915. They became engaged while at Stanford, and married in 1917, the year that America finally entered the war to end all wars. Afterward, Paul Norton would talk with regret about missing that war and would try to sign up for the next. The McCloskeys settled in San Mateo in the congressional district that their son represents today, and Pete Sr. passed the bar and moved south to San Bernardino to practice law. They brought with them a daughter, born Virginia McCloskey in 1919 but known from infanthood to family and friends as "Ginna." She was the only child for eight years. Paul Norton Jr. was born on September 29, 1927, and his father was elated at the arrival of a boy. "Daddy sent a telegram up north to friends in San Mateo saying we had a re-Peter," Ginna remembers. "The telegraph girl thought he didn't know how to spell, and she changed it to 'repeater,' and they thought for some time we had another girl."

Young Pete McCloskey was four years old in the autumn of 1931 when the McCloskeys moved forty-eight miles northward from San Bernardino to South Pasadena, where Pete McCloskey, Sr., joined a law firm based in Los Angeles and Washington, D.C. The Depression touched everywhere in America, but few places were as unscathed by the economic upheaval as South Pasadena and its richer neighboring community of San Marino. The poisonous smog that today blights life throughout the entire Los Angeles basin was a rarity in the early thirties, and Pasadenans were shielded from the clear, dry California sun not by a curtain of dirty fog but by elms and maples and palm trees. The streets were broad and the traffic light, the houses white and well kept, the churches numerous. The people, like the houses, were white and well off. They were of English, Scots-Irish, and German stock, for the most part, with a sprinkling of Scandinavians. Most were successful men—successful doctors and lawyers and architects and businessmen—whose belief in the American dream outlived the economic ravages of the time. They lived in communities of mutual success and tree-lined parks and a few famous homes. Perhaps the most lavish, near the borderline of Pasadena and South Pasadena, was the estate of chewing-gum magnate P. K. Wrigley, the man who owned Catalina Island. San Marino boasted the famous Huntington Library with art treasures that included Gainsborough's *Blue Boy*. Norman Chandler, the strong-minded publisher of the Los Angeles *Times*, lived in San Marino, then as now one of the wealthiest communities in the United States. South Pasadena was wealthy, too, but with enough difference that at the high school which both communities then shared they would say, kidding on the square, that South Pasadena was "the other side of the tracks." Both communities were solidly and irretrievably Republican. It is historically appropriate that the John Birch Society today maintains its headquarters in San Marino, for the world the members of that secular faith seek to recapture came as close to existence in the San Marino and South Pasadena of the thirties as it ever did anywhere.

But those unrecoverable years were not pleasant for Pete McCloskey, a curious and active child who was adventuresome and different from the first. He was difficult for his mother to control, particularly in his early years of school. In the second grade another boy pushed him off a school porch on his head, and young McCloskey was knocked unconscious. Soon thereafter, he fell ill with a serious kidney disease, described by Ginna McCloskey (now Mrs. Walter J. Hartzell) as "a kind of nephritis . . . that left him with a great nervousness." The family was self-sufficient, rather than close-knit. "We were like two only children," recalls Ginna. "I think you have to know a family that has only two children eight years apart to know what we were like. Peter was terribly busy and interested in everything. He was hard to manage if he wasn't occupied with things that interested him. He was fine if he was occupied." Vera McCloskey was the lively, outgoing sort of person she was at Stanford and is today. Pete McCloskey's father was more reserved and withdrawn, a fine athlete who golfed in San Bernardino and took up tennis in Pasadena, and who, according to Ginna, "always retreated into books when he was relaxing." Both parents were worried about their son, particularly after his illness. "He spent a couple of months in a kind of rest home where he could be totally controlled," Ginna recalls. "When he came home, with the normal schooling, which I don't think was perhaps much of a challenge for him, and not too much after-school activity, he was bored and getting into small difficulties looking for things to do. Finally the family put him in Southwestern Military Academy on a temporary basis. They gave him controlled athletics, and he loved it and thrived on it. Even after he was well, he stayed there. He was busy all the time."

Southerwestern Military Academy, founded in 1924, was two blocks from the McCloskey family home at 2777 Fleur Drive. It was operated by Major Maurice Veronda, and is in business at the same location today, now owned by Major Veronda's son and with the word "military" removed from the title. In the 1930s, Southwestern was very military, with flags and sabers and rifle practice and marching drills. Its rituals and programs favored outings and songs and self-reliance and "The American's Creed" —"It is my duty to my country to love it; to support its Constitution; to obey its laws; to respect its Flag; and to defend it against all enemies"—and it seemed the perfect place for Pete McCloskey, who excelled there as athlete and as scholar. In 1937, when he was ten, young McCloskey was one of only four Southwestern cadets to win a gold medal for scholarship while also winning silver medals for deportment (no cadet won a gold medal) and rifle marksmanship. He looks straight ahead, smiling confidently, in the school photos of those years, and *The Confab,* the academy yearbook, reveals participation in an astonishing array of activities: baseball, football, track, the philatelic society, the yearbook, and the Christmas pageant, in which he played Santa Claus. He was credited in a note signed by Captain William J. Veronda, the present-day owner of the academy, with being "a fine Spanish pupil." But it was in athletics that he won the affection and respect of his classmates. "I remember the football games we played against Southwestern," says Grant Kenyon, who attended Huntington Grammar School in San Marino and is now a Sacramento lobbyist. "We hated to play against McCloskey, because he was just so tough."

McCloskey was small for his age in his first years at Southwestern, but his physical condition improved rapidy. Significant in his development were the well-planned summer excursions that Southwestern then took around the state in covered wagons. The Southwestern caravans, with McCloskey along, toured the California redwoods, the Oregon caves, Mount Shasta and Mount Lassen in 1936, Lake Tahoe and portions of Nevada in 1937, the Sequoia redwoods and Yosemite in 1938, the World's Fair and the redwoods again in 1939, and the fair and Mount Lassen in 1940. McCloskey has never forgotten the camaraderie of those outings, the songs around the campfires, the dank, rich smell of the redwood forests. "I've been a conservationist all my life," he said once, simply, and perhaps his love for the out-of-doors and the special blessings conferred upon Californians began on these Southwestern Academy summers. The family did not see much of him in those days. Vera and Pete Sr.—he was "Mr. Mac" to many of his son's friends—had put down roots in South Pasadena. They spent many of the summers at the beach, which Ginna loved, and saw their son mostly on weekends. Young Pete lived in Southwestern barracks during the school year and was away many weeks of each summer on the covered-wagon tour. He owes, and acknowledges, a large debt to Southwestern, the place where Pete McCloskey learned self-reliance and leadership and found himself.

South Pasadena, undeterred by the Depression, also responded slowly to the impending war. The alarm, after all, had been sounded by Franklin Roosevelt, who never carried either South Pasadena or San Marino. "I always was a Republican, and I used to do a certain amount for the party in San Marino, but I was always too busy with my family in those days," recalls Vera McCloskey. "I used to say to Pete: 'Well, we didn't know anybody who was voting for Mr. Roosevelt, but he has won with a great majority, so Pete, we respect the flag and we respect our President.' Three terms I told him that." Young McCloskey was more interested than South Pasadena in both Roosevelt and war, although not necessarily in the conflict his nation was slowly, too slowly, preparing for. As a Southwestern student (on the wall of one classroom was a Lincoln motto: "I will study and get ready and my chance will come"), Pete McCloskey became absorbed in Mathew Brady's pictorial history of the Civil War. His heroes were Robert E. Lee and Stonewall Jackson and Jeb Stuart. Years later, the first books he would buy with his own money would be the three volumes of *Lee's Lieutenants.*

"My heroes have always been men that fought," says McCloskey now. "John Marshall, the first chief justice, was also a second lieutenant at Valley Forge. Oliver Wendell Holmes, who is my idea of what a man should be, was wounded three times in the Civil War."

But it is probably misleading to infer from this that McCloskey as a teen-ager was obsessed by the notion of war and fighting. His classmates of that era, at least, do not remember him that way. What they remember, as expressed best by John Rousselot, is "a boy who was never part of a set path and who was always on the go, always on the move. He was a true adventurer, and you never knew exactly what to expect. Part of the reason you were attracted to him was because there never was a dull moment."

Rousselot, the son of a successful chemist and businessman, was a close friend of Pete McCloskey at South Pasadena–San Marino High School, known to everyone simply as "South Pas." He reached the Congress before McCloskey, and preceded his once and present friend as a figure of public controversy, chiefly on the strength of his position as public-relations director for the John Birch Society in the mid-sixties. When the South Pas class of 1945 held its twentieth reunion, Rousselot was voted the school's "most controversial" graduate, a distinction that the class in 1971 passed on to McCloskey.

Acceptance did not come easily for John Rousselot. He came from an athletic family and was an outstanding athletic prospect at Huntington Grammar School until stricken in the eighth grade and then in high school. "I think this group of guys was remembers that it left him depressed and somewhat belligerent. But Schmidt and Rousselot, after a bad beginning, became fast friends and leading members of a clique of ten South Pasadenans and San Marinans who banded together in the ninth grade and then in high school. "I think this group of guys was good for all of us in really significant ways," says Schmidt, looking back on it. "I think it helped make Pete and me feel very much like we belonged in that adolescent period when you really want to belong. It did great things for John, in pulling him back into not being an object and very much accepted for being John Rousselot and nothing else. There was a very hard period, when John was really the butt of a lot of jokes that might have seemed cruel to an outsider but which essentially made him feel very secure, being a full member and giving no quarter and asking none. We used to play football every Sunday afternoon, and nobody ever gave John a nickel. He played just as hard and got hit just as hard and tackled just as hard as anyone. And he was as tough as or tougher than anyone else."

If there was a touchstone to the group, it was the independence of every member in it. "The guys didn't want to become part of the athletic clique or the motorcycle-car clique or any other clique," says Dayton Reinke, who became Pete McCloskey's closest friend in high school. "They just kind of liked each other's varied interests. But there really wasn't a head or a tail to the thing. They were just a lot of imaginative guys that were together."

The imagination showed itself when this anticliquish clique decided to choose a collective name for itself. The name selected, at the suggestion of Jim Leeds,* was the Amalgamated Federation of Virgins, known from then on as the AFV. Among other things, the AFV spoofed the school's leadership clique, and, to a lesser extent, the whole idea of social exclusivity. Donald (Bud) Vance, one of the members, made cards in the school print shop that pronounced each AFVer "an immaculate untouchable member in good standing, in the eyes of his fellow fraternity brothers." The name was also appropriate in other ways. "The AVF crowd didn't smoke, drink, or chew, but they made out with girls," recalled a non-AFVer at the class's 1971 reunion. How much they "made out" is a matter of individual evaluation and selective memory. "At high-school age you always like to think of yourself as having great prowess with girls," says Rousselot. "We didn't take ourselves too seriously."

* Leeds, described by Rousselot as "quiet, a good writer, and a thoughtful person," went on, like McCloskey, to Stanford and the law. He also became a law partner of McCloskey's.

But the girls always took Pete McCloskey seriously, and he returned their interest. His first love, says McCloskey, was Elaine Walker (now Whitmore), who lived in the house behind him. Southwestern Cadet McCloskey came calling one day and left behind his saber, which was returned to him at the academy amid merriment from his fellow cadets. McCloskey had a string of girl friends throughout high school, the most devoted of whom was Marjorie Wardwell, the daughter of a Navy captain. Winifred Hadden, now Winky Lennihan and the wife of one of McCloskey's closest supporters, claims the distinction of being the first girl McCloskey ever kissed. McCloskey's senior-year girl friend was Lois (Christy) Christensen [now Seidel], who recalls him as "very independent, a lot on the ball" and who shows her devotion for him in a thoughtful, well-composed message in his senior yearbook. "He usually had several girl friends," recalls Rousselot. "His great problem was that he liked them all, and it was difficult for him to make choices. He'd make problems for himself sometimes, and we used to kid him about it. He'd probably get more upset with us kidding him about his girls than anything else. He'd maybe have two or three girls, and he'd have a date with one on the beach in the afternoon and with another that night. He liked so many of them he'd have a hard time making up his mind."

Winky Lennihan became the girl friend of Rousselot, known to the AFV group as "Baldy John." Rousselot taught her to drive, and sometimes vacuumed the house for her so they could go out together. "They protected each other in that gang, and if I wasn't nice to Baldy, they were mad at me, and they let me know," she remembers. "It was a great gang. Peter was known at the time as the intellectual of the gang, which wasn't particularly a compliment, because it wasn't an intellectual group. We had a marvelous time. Robin was the wildest, the absolute wildest."

Robin Schmidt recalls that McCloskey had a claim of leadership within the group, but often went his separate way. "He did a lot of thinking for himself, always, and he had a habit of picking at his chin, which he still has," says Schmidt. "One of my most vivid memories is McCloskey sitting up in his window picking at his chin when we came to take him to the beach. He was completely tuned out. We finally left without him, realizing that he was doing other things, thinking other things."

It was this habit of doing and thinking "other things" that made Pete McCloskey a special person within the AFV, where the word most frequently associated with him was "unpredictable." "He said things to shock, mostly for effect and mostly verbal," recalls Reinke. "I first heard the word 'concubine' from Pete and didn't know what it meant. He had a sort of Victorian view of things, imposed, I would say, by his mother, but he liked to say things for their shock value. He felt he was more Errol Flynn, more dashing that way, than if he had been straight down the line. If, as a reporter, you would mark down that a man had bitten a dog, Pete might say it was eight feet tall when it was only two and a half and that the gash which hardly broke the surface required eight stitches. It was all imagination and glamour. That was Peter's charisma."

McCloskey's propensity for verbal effect revealed itself in the nicknames that the AFVers called one another and sometimes use among themselves to this day. Pete was "Salt" (or Saltpeter), and later "Snark" or "Snayhead," sometimes "Madman." Schmidt was "Chicken," Rousselot "Baldy John," and Vance, who worked hard throughout high school, "Sweatshop Sam." Reinke, fortunate enough to possess a nickname before he joined the AFV, was and remains "Dumpy" to his friends. He also remains devoted to McCloskey, with whom he played varsity baseball in three seasons at South Pas and two on a middling-to-good semipro baseball team. McCloskey's chief qualities as a baseball player were desire and a fine batting eye. He played second base and right field, wherever, said some of his friends, "he'd do the least damage." "He was not a good fielder," said Rousselot, the team manager. "We used to kid him about putting his knees together. He'd stop the ball in the most unbelievable ways. But he was a competitor, and he had a competitive spirit he'd pass on to others. He would talk to other players and encourage them by saying, 'Damnit, we're not going to accept defeat.' That sort of thing was catching. Only he'd kind of kid others and encourage them to do better without putting them down."

Reinke, who played third base and was the captain of the high-school team, remembers McCloskey as a "seeing-eye singles hitter" who batted very well in the clutch. "His main problem at second base was his lack of speed and inability to cover the territory," recalls Reinke. "But he was a hitter who could see the ball as well as anybody, or better. He just watched the ball and flicked his bat at it." McCloskey led the South Pasadena team in hitting in both his junior and senior years, batting .320 in his final season. He and Reinke, the two members of the AFV who preferred baseball to the beach, also played on the San Marino Merchants, a semipro team that wore discarded Los Angeles Angels uniforms because of the largesse of Sid Cherniss, attorney for the team and father of Charles Cherniss, a South Pas classmate of McCloskey. The San Marino team was a traveling team, playing at Burbank and El Segundo and Lincoln Park in Los Angeles with the assistance of Cherniss, who transported them in a big Packard automobile with whatever spare gasoline ration stamps he was able to obtain.

There was, after all, a war on, and many of the young men in the South Pas class of 1945, including McCloskey, hoped for a chance to participate before it ended. The call to arms had also reached Peter McCloskey, Sr., who had just missed World War I, and who had tried, without success, to enlist in the Army Air Corps after Pearl Harbor. Fifty-one years old when the war began, the senior McCloskey possessed the appearance and physical condition of a man ten years younger. He was respected by young Pete's friends, who delighted in a photograph showing the two McCloskeys and the boy's schnauzer dog,

Moxie, all with remarkably similar wire hair. ("Sometimes we called the dog 'Peter' and called Pete 'Moxie,'" says Reinke.) Charles Cherniss remembers McCloskey Sr.'s "strong, gentle voice," and David Dahle, the star pitcher of the South Pas team, credits "Mr. Mac" with influencing him to attend Stanford, where he won three letters before turning pro. But Pete McCloskey, Sr., was not at home during most of his son's high-school years. Rebuffed in his attempts to enter the service, he finally talked the Army Corps of Engineers into accepting him, and served as head of the contract and claims section in Costa Rica from November 1942 until April 1943. Some of young Pete McCloskey's friends say this long absence destroyed whatever chance remained for father and son to form a close relationship. "I think it was very difficult for mother, who had grown up as an only child," recalls Ginna Hartzell. "I had been 'easy,' a girl, didn't have wild ideas, did what I was supposed to do. Raising a boy was difficult for mother by the very nature of it, and more so with my dad gone, because she felt the responsibility very keenly. I don't think Peter ever gave her any trouble, but she worried about it all the time." Vera McCloskey does not recall that her son ever expressed concern about his father's absence. "I suppose it bothered him, but he didn't say anything," she says. She does remember that Pete sent his father a driving-license application for signature when he turned sixteen, adding in his letter the words, "Now, I am a man."

He was not yet that, though he was a leader among boys. In addition to baseball, McCloskey participated in such student-body activities as Hi-Y, and was elected school commissioner of finance. He earned Bs or better in most of his courses with a minimum of study, received a scolding from the San Marino police after he and other AFVers squirted water from a stirrup pump into a parked car, and attended Boys State, the mock government sponsored each year by the American Legion in the state capitol at Sacramento. It is probable, if McCloskey's own recollections are any guide, that he also spent more time reading and thinking about the world than even his AFV friends realized. The best indication of this is McCloskey's performance at his high-school graduation, where he was one of four commencement speakers. As always, McCloskey was unpredictable. His refusal to write out a prepared text like the other speakers reduced his teacher to tears and anger, and so upset his mother that she thought about not attending the graduation.

When the class of 1945 graduated, the war was over in Germany and the end in sight in Japan. However, the atomic bombing of Hiroshima was still nine weeks in the future, and many in the graduating class looked forward to a long war and the invasion of Japan. McCloskey's speech began with a reference to the vanquishing of Germany and declared that Japan, "her partner in crime, is just beginning to feel our vengeance as her cities, one by one, are burned and destroyed. We have proved to these peoples," he said, "that in war, democracy is not soft and decadent, but perfectly able to take care of itself. In peace, we must do the same."

McCloskey's speech went on to warn that the Germans would try to blame the "fatal mistakes" of their own leaders rather than Allied strength for their defeat. The Germans remained unconverted to democracy, he said, and it was up to the United States to prove that democracy was indeed a superior way of life. Reflecting the hopeful internationalism of his time, McCloskey predicted that the United States would take an ever-increasing role in world affairs. The nation must show tolerance of the ways in which other people live and must practice what it preaches at home and abroad. "As we want our country to stand for fair play among the nations of the world, then we, the people, should stand for fair play in our dealings with one another," he said. Cultivation of these attitudes would also create leaders who "will someday lead the country as we would have it led."

Vera McCloskey had sat with her head down throughout the early portions of the speech, but she was beaming by the time it was over. Afterward, the citizens of prosperous San Marino and South Pasadena crowded around her in praise of her son, who had outshone the other speakers and demonstrated an interest in world events which he had previously kept to himself. It would not be the last time that Pete McCloskey would surprise those who thought they knew him best.

3. *Romantic Interlude*

Pete McCloskey's commencement speech had addressed itself to what Americans then called the "postwar world." McCloskey, however, still thought about the war, and he enrolled in the Navy V-5 pilot training program and was sent to nearby Occidental College the same month that Japan unconditionally surrendered to the United States. After the war ended, V-5 went through a series of consolidations, and McCloskey divided the semester between Occidental and Cal Tech, with a final month at the University of Southern California. At that point V-5 cadets were informed that their one-year college training program was being extended to two years, with a three-year service obligation to follow. "We were given the option to go into the regular Navy, and I took it," says McCloskey. "I didn't want to stay in the program for five years." McCloskey was sent to Great Lakes Naval Training Station for a ten-week boot camp.

The summer of 1946 was a desperate time for the armed services. Everyone who could get out of the service seemed to be getting out, and all branches were devising programs aimed at attracting young men to military careers. One of these programs was known as "hobby craft," and commanders at naval installations across the country were ordered to construct special buildings at which enlisted men could engage in woodworking, metal shop, ceramics, and other hobbies. The floor plans for these hobby-craft buildings were prepared at the Naval Annex in Arlington, Virginia, during the summer of 1946, and McCloskey, who had taken mechanical drawing, and another seaman were assigned to do the layout. The result gave McCloskey an impression of the workings of "government" that was reinforced by his experiences as a lawyer and has never left him since. "Neither of us was competent," McCloskey says. "And there were no instructions on these floor plans where, for instance, the electrical outlets were to go. I used to wonder about it. You don't put welding equipment next to the oxygen tanks." But McCloskey and his fellow novice were now considered experts in hobby-craft layout. In July 1946 they were transferred to Camp Allen, at Norfolk, Virginia, and stationed in abandoned barracks that had previously housed German prisoners of war. There they sent out the lathes, bandsaws, and other equipment intended for use in the hobby-craft installations. It was easy duty. Every day Seaman McCloskey would walk a half-mile or so to a nearby naval prison for his chow and spend the rest of the time shipping out the equipment for hobby buildings he had designed. "I left the service with an absolute disdain for the federal bureaucracy," he remembers.

McCloskey returned home for Christmas 1946, uncertain about the future. Both his parents wanted him to go to Stanford—"We never thought of him going anywhere else," says Pete Sr.—but his father maintains that Pete made up his own mind about the law. Vera McCloskey, usually influential with her son, says she "kind of wanted him to be an engineer, because we'd had so many lawyers in the family. I thought Pete would make a good engineer." Nonetheless, she accepted her son's interest in the law, perhaps because she worshiped the memory of her father, Samuel McNabb, who had become a referee in bankruptcy after his Republican loyalties cost him his U.S.-attorney post under the New Deal. "Pete's a good deal like his grandfather," she says. "He combines his father's fine, legal, articulate mind and my father's qualities. My father was a good lawyer, and he loved everybody. When he passed away there was a stack of IOU's in his safe-deposit box owed him by widows which he had made his children promise never to collect. He did things for people all his life."

All this was in the future. In the early months of 1947 Pete McCloskey gave no indication he would follow in the footsteps of his father or his grandparents on both sides. He talked vaguely of playing baseball or of being a mechanic. But he applied for admission to Stanford at his parents' urging, and he and they were pleasantly surprised when he was accepted as a GI-bill student with credit for his work at Occidental and Cal Tech. That summer, while awaiting the opening of the fall quarter at Stanford, McCloskey and Dayton Reinke took jobs on a garbage truck. "Those two carried the garbage, and all the girls on the street would hang out the windows laughing and talking to them, and I just nearly died," says Vera McCloskey. "And, oh, he would smell. We had a laundry on the back porch of the house, and I'd have him take off his clothes there and have a shower. He laughed and kidded me about it. He'd say, 'Well, everybody's eating cantaloupe this week,' or 'Everybody's having tomatoes.' He was a clown, you know. He's kidded me all his life."

It was on a weekend at the Corona Del Mar beach during his tenure as a Pasadena garbageman that Pete McCloskey made his most important discovery. She was Caroline Wadsworth, an identical twin who early in life had been dubbed "Cubby" by an older sister attending the University of California, where the school nickname is the "Golden Bears." The Wadsworth twins were the daughters of William Henry Wadsworth, a well-to-do, Kentucky-reared attorney from nearby Altadena who lived in an elegant old English house known to AFV members as the "mausoleum" because of its stained-glass windows. Cubby had dated Reinke and Peter Meyn, two members of the South Pasadena high-school group, and she had heard the stories about McCloskey. "I was dying to meet him, because they referred to him all the time, not as a joke, but as part of their conversation," recalls Cubby. Pete and Cubby were attracted to each other instantly—"I just knew she was the one," he says—and he recalls proposing to her on their second date. The recollections of Cubby and Vera McCloskey are only slightly less romantic. McCloskey's mother, then president of the Stanford Club in Pasadena, remembers that the club was having a tea for the freshmen who would attend Stanford, and her son came in and told her to "meet the Wadsworth twins, because I may marry one of them." There was not much doubt among Pete's friends that the "one of them" was Cubby. For that matter, there wasn't much doubt with Charlotte, who in the first year of Pete McCloskey's courtship was sometimes unhappy at the disruption of the close relationship she had always enjoyed with her twin sister. "He sees what he likes and zeroes in," says Cubby's twin, now Charlotte McClung. "He zeroed in on sister, and that was all she wrote." Charlotte's husband, Charles McClung, a sensitive and thoughtful attorney who also graduated from Stanford, believes that Pete is one of the few men who actually immediately fell in love. "I think most of us, like Shaw says, could mate up with anybody," says McClung, "but not McCloskey."

If Pete McCloskey knew what he wanted, Cubby McCloskey thought she wanted something else. "The thing that first attracted me to Pete really isn't Pete at all," she says now. "The thing that attracted me was that he seemed to be more mature than a lot of his compatriots. And he projected a quiet, gentlemanly demeanor around other people. Now that I know him, I know that's not him. My children call it 'playing the role,' and they say, 'Dad, you're playing the role.' He really had that side to him, but he's very much a rollicking kid in a lot of ways; I mean, he really is. The thing I really began to love about him was that he was far ahead of his time in poking fun at a lot of phony things, a lot of phony inhibitions on sex and other things that don't mean anything at all, things like parking your crummy car in front of my house, what will the neighbors think? He had this marvelous irreverence for all those fake values. This really was the Peter that I didn't see when I met him. I guess I was looking for someone like my dad, somebody who was gentlemanly and mature. I was fooled. He really wasn't that way at all."

The irreverence perceived by Cubby was a fact of life to Pete McCloskey's friends in Pasadena and at Stanford. "He didn't care what he wore or what the weather was or who your family was or where you came from," says a friend who knew him at college. "All that unessential stuff which is so very essential to most people just sort of passed him by." Jack Miller, a fraternity brother of McCloskey at Phi Delta Kappa and now a Long Beach attorney, remembers that McCloskey's eating habits were incredibly deficient. "They were just awful," he says. "He wouldn't eat vegetables, and sometimes he forgot to eat at all. He would stop when traveling somewhere and buy peanut butter and saltines for dinner and eat them in the car." McCloskey, despite an occasional drinking bout at Stanford, didn't and doesn't care for either tobacco or hard liquor. "I've never seen him snockered," says Miller, and adds with a smile: "He doesn't have to. He's unreliable sober." The words "unreliable" and "undependable" are used frequently by McCloskey's friends of that era. "He's absentminded as hell," says Forrest Shumway, a Phi Delt buddy who is now president of the Signal Oil Company. "For instance, he'd take you down to the cleaners or down to the drugstore and drop you off and forget to pick you up. That kind of thing. He forgot to bring his wife to my engagement party."

The other side of the "undependability" coin was an abnormal power of concentration that would serve McCloskey well in politics. Miller remembers him concentrating on an assignment amidst noise and horseplay, then abruptly slamming his book shut and racing out to an athletic contest or a date with Cubby. "He seemed to have a total ability to shut out others and forget about them," Miller recalls.

Cubby Wadsworth and Pete McCloskey went north by different routes in the autumn of 1947 to begin their studies at Stanford. They were already serious about each other, although Cubby remembers that "Peter was very ambivalent about it. He kept saying, 'You're just a freshman at school; you shouldn't let yourself get tied down.' But when I even looked like I was going to go out with someone else, he was there with his Irish up, looking at me with great anger."

McCloskey did not, by every account, and especially his own, do well in his first year at Stanford. Charles McClung believes that Pete was a "bad test-taker" and, despite a high aptitude and an ability to concentrate, never realized "that what you have to do to get the grade is to do what the guy standing up there thinks you should do. Most of us who got fairly good grades realized that right away." McCloskey also had other interests, among them Cubby, athletics, and the Phi Delts.

The Phi Delts, dominated by returning GIs and Marines who had little interest in fraternity ritual, were something special. "They were a good outfit, a bunch of jocks," says Miller, who was one of them. "That was the big attraction for Pete. He's a frustrated jock." Being an athlete of any kind was something demanding in the Phi Delts, who staged bone-wearying athletic contests just for the hell of it. David Dahle, the star pitcher at South Pasadena High, whom Pete McCloskey, Sr., had induced to attend Stanford, remembers best the games of "knee football" played in the fifteen-by-twenty-four Phi Delt living room. The games usually ended when someone was hurt. McCloskey endeared himself to his fellow Phi Delts, as he had the AFV, by his intense competitive desire and his lack of speed. John Rousselot, crippled by osteomyelitis, had regularly beaten McCloskey in dashes across the width of a football field. At Stanford, McCloskey raced against the late Vern Percell, a 275-pound football tackle, who, according to a Phi Delt legend, beat McCloskey by three yards while running backwards.

But there was an element to McCloskey's competitiveness that counted for more than either his desire or his lack of speed.

This was his consistent sportsmanship, a quality that rarely combines with competitiveness in such high measure. "Many people who are confused with being good sports are winners," observes Charles McClung. "They win all the time, so naturally they're good sports. McCloskey's not necessarily a winner, and yet he has to be the best sport there is."

At Stanford, McCloskey was a substitute outfielder behind Lloyd Merriman, an outstanding baseball player and an All-American halfback. Unlike his father, a four-time letter winner, McCloskey never lettered. But he delighted his father on one occasion, Paul Sr. recalls, by telling him that half of the hits he made trying out for the varsity were bunts. Bunting is the one baseball skill that Peter Sr. takes credit for imparting to his son.

McCloskey always pursues multiple interests, and it was at this time that he became deeply interested in the Marine Corps. The Marines, with their ruggedness and elitism, appealed to his nature and his sense of history, and he readily joined the reserves under a program that provided several weeks of training and a commission upon graduation. Several other Phi Delts joined, too, but neither they nor McCloskey expected to employ their military training in combat. Wars were something that were over, and it was primarily the physical challenge and the military romanticism of the Marines that lured McCloskey and his friends.

Cubby seemed more important than either baseball or the Marines. She was pinned in January—"Peter really didn't want me to play the field, and I really didn't want to play the field, either"—and they saw each other constantly after that. "Sister got mononucleosis and was totally shot down from trying to do too much," recalls Charlotte. "Peter got it, too. The first year was just kind of a get-through-it." There were times, in 1948, when it was uncertain whether either of them would get through. On one particularly rainy day, as McCloskey recalls it, baseball practice was canceled so he drove over to pick up Cubby to go for a ride. "As we were rounding a corner I kissed her, and we made eighty-eight degrees of a ninety-degree turn and hit a tree," he remembers. "We were both knocked out. She had a cut on her forehead, and I had a severe head injury. We both woke up in the hospital, and after that her parents agreed maybe it was a good idea that we got married." One magazine account in 1971 gave a spicier account of the events leading up to the marriage, declaring that McCloskey had suggested to Cubby's father that it might be a good idea if they got married because Cubby might be pregnant. McClung, the source of the account, says it apparently resulted from a misunderstanding of what he meant to convey. "Pete said that he and Cubby had to get married, that they couldn't wait," says McClung. "It meant the opposite of saying that she was pregnant. He was saying that he couldn't continue to maintain his celibacy because they were so much in love." Charlotte agrees. Peter, she says, drawing a rectangle in the air with her forefinger, was "a Victorian and the squarest guy you ever knew."

In any event, the Wadsworths gave their consent after extracting a promise from the young lovers that Cubby would finish school. They were married August 6, 1949, in the Wadsworth garden in Altadena, with Charlotte Wadsworth the maid of honor and Dayton Reinke the best man. Reinke remembers that the minister misled them on "The Lord's Prayer"—"It was what you would expect, with McCloskey involved"—but the wedding, complete with a chrysanthemum-filled fountain, was a featured newspaper social item in Altadena. The McCloskeys honeymooned at Lake Arrowhead and returned to Stanford, where Cubby was starting her junior year and Pete his second year in law school.

"We had made a deal with Cubby's father that he would pay her tuition at Stanford but we would take no other money," says McCloskey. "I was on the GI bill and received $110 a month. I had three jobs that paid another $130 a month. We lived very comfortably in a tool shed in the back of a guy's farm for a year. We had a pet sparrow hawk that used to drive

Cubby wild. The countryside was green and smelled good, and we were happy."

Then, on June 25, 1950, the North Korean Army rolled over the thirty-eighth parallel and attacked the Republic of Korea.

4. *The War Lover*

He had always loved war and fighting and the out-of-doors, and he welcomed the opportunity to test his soldier's faith in combat. Cubby did not welcome it. She became pregnant the same June that the war began in Korea. McCloskey was commissioned a second lieutenant in the Marine Corps on June 2, 1950, and trained at Quantico, Virigina, from October 1 to December 20. He was then transferred to Camp Pendleton, California. Cubby continued at Stanford during this fall quarter, and in December came down to Pendleton to visit her husband. On January 27, 1951, Pete McCloskey embarked for Korea aboard the USS *Breckinridge.*

New experiences have always stimulated McCloskey, and the Marines who knew him in those days remember a happy man, absorbed in learning and the Corps and Korea. "For the first few months of that time it was a real privilege to live out of doors with a pack on your back and to climb all those mountains," recalls McCloskey. "We started out with extremely long-range exchanges of fire and a lot of patrolling. This was a great enjoyment for me. I had followed World War I and the Civil War. I'd studied military tactics all my life. The ultimate was a platoon leader in Korea where you had your sixty-one men, your forty-five-man rifle platoon and your sixteen-man machine-gun sections. Occasionally, we'd have tanks or aircraft. We ranged pretty much to ourselves. At night we'd tie into company perimeters. Most of the time a rifle platoon was a separate command. Map reading was one of the essentials. You were trying to know where you were going and what you were doing, trying to keep men warm and fed and make sure that you looked after your troops and that your people didn't straggle. Your first opinions were wrong half the time. Good men turn out to be weaker than you thought; weak men turn out to be far stronger than you thought. These are all great lessons. I never felt, the entire time I was in Korea—and our unit probably had as much sustained combat as any—that what we went through measured up to what men had to face fighting in the Civil War, for example. A platoon leader just didn't survive in the Civil War. If he led his men in Pickett's charge at Gettysburg or the Bloody Angle at Spotsylvania, he didn't survive. And he didn't have great medical attention or anesthetics. Any American that's alive today is privileged to be living in peace and tranquility that's been earned through a lot of hardships. The Marine Corps is one of the means, hopefully, by which you put back a little of what you've gained by other people suffering far worse problems than we have today."

How much of this was on McCloskey's mind at the time is hard to say. His emergence into politics as an antiwar candidate and congressman and his present challenge to President Nixon have prompted him to codify his attitudes into a logical structure that accepts the necessity for warfare but rejects United States involvement in Vietnam. However, his high-school commencement speech, his absorption in the Civil War, and his readiness to join the Marine Corps all bespeak a concern with country and a sense of duty quite consistent with this present-day recollection. And the testimony of his own comrades confirms that McCloskey possessed a sense of mission in Korea, a country where the Marines suffered 26,000 casualties, including 4,262 dead.

It was exactly one week after the North Korean invasion that Marine Commandant Clifton B. Cates cabled General Douglas MacArthur, then the Far East commander, volunteering U.S.

Marines for combat duty. MacArthur readily accepted, and a Marine brigade soon became heavily involved in defensive fighting around Pusan. Afterward, the brigade was absorbed into the First Marine Division, which spearheaded the successful landing at Inchon. The Marines, the U.S. Eighth Army, and South Korean troops fought their way steadily northward, and victory seemed at hand. Then, in November 1950, Chinese Communist troops entered the war in great numbers. The First Marine Division, operating in subzero weather, participated in a historic withdrawal—"attacking in another direction," said the commanding general—that cost 4,400 Marine casualties and claimed many more Chinese soldiers. Pete McCloskey arrived in Pohang, Korea, on February 16, 1951, and was assigned to C Company, First Battalion, Fifth Marine Division. Five days later, C Company moved north from Wonju and led a counteroffensive against the Chinese Communist forces. The division remained in contact with the enemy in a long series of marches to Hwachon Reservoir, where, on April 25, it was isolated by the first Chinese spring offensive. "On the night the Chinese counterattacked, I had the northernmost United Nations position in North Korea as far as we know, just west of the reservoir," says McCloskey. The First Division blocked the offensive and began to move north again in a series of attacks that McCloskey and the others who survived them would never forget.

"I first knew of him when I was in battalion headquarters as a lieutenant and he was a lieutenant and platoon leader in Charlie Company," recalls Charles (Chuck) Daly, who became and remains one of McCloskey's closest friends. "In January the division had been run out of the North and was kind of putting itself back together in the South. I think we were the first replacements to join them after that debacle in the North. There was a lot of patrolling and guerrilla hunting, and then we gradually started moving up on an offensive. I remember one time we came to a valley where there was a large number of American dead. I think it was the Second Army Division, and it had obviously been poorly trained. There were no holes, and people had been surprised, killed in their sleeping bags and the rest of it. Pete was very indignant about that."

Daly believes that McCloskey was different from other Marines. "Very few of us thought about anything other than how to get by today on this patrol or whatever. But there was something different about Peter. There was a lot of courage, of course, but there was something more there, just some undefinable thing. I think it was partly pride, and partly devotion to his commanding officers, who also came to rely upon him."

That reliance was put to the test on May 28 at Hill 566 near the valley of Yanggu. McCloskey remembers the hill. "The North Koreans [he, like most U.S. military personnel, called them "gooks" then] had these eight machine guns mounted along the front of the hill covering that bridge on the left side that ran from our hill over to theirs, with a big steep abyss on the left side. We had a gentle rice-paddy ravine going up between us and the hill." First Lieutenant Richard (Spike) Schening, the recently appointed company commander, ordered one platoon to take the hill from a flanking ridge. But the platoon leader sent to do the job found himself pinned down by enemy machine-gun fire. "What do you intend to do about it?" Schening asked over the radio. The trapped officer gave a noncommittal answer, and Schening relieved him, placed the platoon sergeant in command, and ordered McCloskey to rescue the men. "And what he's saying," recalls Daly, "is go get an outfit that's surrounded and bring them back." McCloskey started off, accompanied only by a corpsman named Dixon who had come down the hill earlier to give medical aid to a straggler. "I started angling up toward the place that I'd last seen the platoon," McCloskey remembers. "Dixon, luckily, was short and fat, and he'd been running. He must have been fifty yards behind me and was angling to try to cut the corner and catch me. So I started up that ridge line, and I thought I knew where the platoon was, and I kept seeing that I was getting higher on the hill all the time, until finally I could look over. And I thought, 'Goddamnit, I'm almost up to where our people are on the hill, and it seems awful quiet up here, and Jesus Christ, where's the goddamned Marines?' Well, what had happened was that the platoon sergeant had said, 'Let's get the hell out of this machine-gun fire,' and had pulled back a couple of hundred yards. I angled up the ridge line and came to a little clearing, not more than fifty feet across, and there's all this leafy spring foliage around, and kind of a dappled sunlight in the late afternoon with the sun and the shade. And Jesus, all of a sudden this little clearing looks kind of dangerous to me. For some reason, I stopped at the edge of that clearing. It was silent, it was quiet, I was up high on the hill—a little higher than I thought. I hadn't seen any Marines, and I suddenly got a little kind of cold, clammy feeling. 'My God, why am I here?' Luckily, I stopped. I was sort of shielded by the last row of bushes before it broke out into the clearing, and I stopped. Down below me, to the left, about twenty yards down the slope and twenty yards to the rear, I can hear this heavy breathing. And it's old Dixon, panting to catch up with me. I stopped and looked across this clearing, and all of a sudden I see the bush move, and here's a Korean rifleman wearing a padded jacket. He's got a rifle at port arms, and he's starting to point it to where Dixon is making all this racket coming up the hill. And I see him turning—he's got a bayonet on that rifle that honest-to-God looked to me like it was two feet long—it looked like a big needle. And the rifle was about four feet long, and this guy's turning that rifle, and luckily his attention was diverted from me by Dixon. He's got greasepaint on his face, he's got twigs on his shoulders and a net on his helmet, and he looks like a goddamned bush, and I never would have seen him. I was trembling. If I had moved a muscle he'd of seen me. So I kinda took the carbine and tried to swing it around, and I'll never forget it, I think it must have taken me five seconds to get that carbine zeroed in on that guy. I was absolutely scared shitless. And it wasn't the fear of being killed. It was the fear of being captured. I finally pulled the trigger on the carbine, and nothing happened. I had it on safety. I finally got the safety off, and I squeezed off three rounds and knocked that sonofabitch on his back. I turned around, and I must have been four feet off the ground. I went past Dixon flying. I said, 'Dixon, get the hell out of here.' "

McCloskey went back up Hill 566 the next morning, leading the once-trapped platoon that had been extricated by its sergeant after Schening relieved the officer in command. A morning mist clung to the hillside, and McCloskey took his men up a narrow, spiny ridge that approached Hill 566 from the left. Most of the North Korean machine guns faced down the hill across the rice paddy, protecting against a frontal assault, and only a single emplacement guarded the ridge up which the Marines crept under cover of the sheltering mist. McCloskey took out that machine gun. "I did it with a grenade," he remembers. "I hurled that fuckin' grenade farther than I've ever thrown anything in my life, and then the platoon was up the hill and started cleaning out the bunkers." While one squad took out the machine guns, McCloskey raced across the top of the hill with another, yelling and firing his carbine at the now-retreating enemy. Suddenly, like a pheasant whirring up before him in the grass, a pony with a Chinese astride rode up and galloped down the hill. "I had never seen anything like it," says McCloskey, who has often relived the assault of Hill 566 in his mind. "Here was this shaggy Genghis Khan of a pony with an equally shaggy Chinese on it. I thought he was a Mongol from two thousand years before. He rode that pony down the hill with forty Marines firing at him. No one came close to hitting him. He rode out of sight down the ravine, a horseman from the past. I never saw another pony in Korea."

It was May 29, 1951, and Hill 566 was taken. McCloskey, wounded in one hand, was awarded the Navy Cross, the second highest decoration for which a Marine is eligible. The citation accompanying the decoration singled out McCloskey for "daring initiative, aggressive determination, and inspiring leadership responsible for the success of the attack." But the day's fighting was not over. The North Koreans had preregistered mortars on the hill, perhaps in anticipation of losing it, and the vulnerability of the victorious Marines worried Schening. "He had been company commander for about a month, which is a long time in that business," says Daly. "He was a tough, sharp-faced Marine in his thirties who seemed very old to us and who really believed in that adage about taking care of your men and they will take care of you. He used to carry a walking stick he took from one of the shell-ripped trees that were everywhere in Korea." Schening was watching from the next knoll, and he didn't like what he saw. Four companies of Marines had participated in the assault, and three of them were bunched up on the hill, smoking cigarettes and talking to their buddies amid the ruined bunkers and the enemy bodies. "There's this great herd instinct in human beings, and you lose people when you herd together in combat," says McCloskey. "The guy over on the next hill, looking through his glasses and deciding whether it's worth disclosing his position by dropping in a few rounds, won't do it if he sees ten men spread out over a hundred yards. He won't try, because he knows his weapons won't do that. But if he sees ten men in a group, there's a target, so he'll fire. I can see that great man, Spike Schening, yet, standing atop the hill and bellowing in a voice that could be heard a quarter of a mile: 'You fucking Marines, quit bunching up. Spread out!' He talked like that for about thirty seconds, and people did start moving, looking up from their ration cans and adjusting their packs on this nice comfortable little hill with all the bodies on it. They moved off, grumping about Schening, and all of a sudden the enemy drops in five 122-millimeter mortar rounds on the top of the hill, one after another, and by the time anybody looked up, we'd taken about fifty casualties. Spike had been hit, his radioman had been hit, his executive officer had been hit, the mortar officer had been hit, the mortar section had been wiped out. My platoon, which had taken maybe four or five casualties in an assault that killed forty and captured twenty-two, lost more men from those five rounds than from the entire attack. All of us were out on the perimeter, but I'd sent one squad back to get their packs, and those yahoos, thinking the war was over as far as they were concerned, were walking along one yard apart. Eight men, and I think five of them got hit in that crazy mortar barrage. But the great act there was Spike Schening's. Nobody gave him a medal for it, even though his yelling moved men out of the area and saved a lot of lives. That was the great act of professional competence that whole day. Later that day, Daly's platoon overran the regimental command post where these mortars were mounted; it was only about half a mile away. He gets the Silver Star, I get the Navy Cross, Schening gets four months in the hospital. But *he* performed a great professional Marine act."

It is this concept of professionalism and leadership, rather than the question of individual courage, that obsessed McCloskey in Korea, and that concerns him still. While there are conflicting evaluations about McCloskey's performance as student, lawyer, congressman, and political candidate, the testimony speaks with one voice on his performance in the life-or-death reality of Korea. An enlisted man who sometimes fell behind and who describes McCloskey as a "fucking mountain goat" remembers that he always made stragglers keep up with the platoon but never chewed them out after the march. An officer from another company who participated in the Hill 566 assault believes that McCloskey, in battle, "was the best possible guy to have around." A corpsman who was severely wounded alongside McCloskey in another action told me: "Just believe everything he says about combat. I can't talk about it myself, after all that's happened, but you can believe McCloskey and know that he's telling the truth."

The touchstone of McCloskey's performance in Korea appears to be the professionalism he respected in Spike Schening and in his previous commanding officer, Major Jack Jones. "The finest organization that exists in the profession of soldiering is the Marine Corps," he says today. "If you go down to Quantico and look at the graduating class from the officers' candidate school, they're the most beautiful guys you've ever seen. And I suppose it's basically because man has a desire to test himself against the toughest challenge of his time. . . . You like to do a little better than you think you can otherwise do, and I think this is the thing that probably holds the Marines together in some respects, sort of a common understanding that if you're going to have to stand somewhere with one guy on your left and one on your right, you hope it's a Marine." It is a characteristic of McCloskey that he is capable of carrying the best of his beliefs to an extreme. This extends even to his view of military professionalism and prompted him, on one occasion when he was appalled by the poor security of a U.S. Army regiment, to mount his machine guns facing into the Army positions as a precaution against nighttime infiltration by the Chinese. His professionalism was also evident June 11, thirteen days after the capture of Hill 566. McCloskey's platoon, operating in conjunction with Republic of Korea troops that he says "sometimes were two miles ahead of you and other times five miles behind," entered a narrow river valley. On this day the Marines were operating with tanks and advancing slowly up the valley under fire from Chinese mortars. "The men were lying low in the rice paddies, and the mortar rounds were coming in, hitting the guys in the ass," says McCloskey. "We took four casualties that way. Finally, we had to go back. I piled the men on the tanks to cross the river, because we didn't have any sleeping bags and I didn't want them all wet and cold during the night. The last tank hit a mine in the river, and the driver lost both feet. He was screaming with pain, but we got him across the river and blew up the tank with a grenade so the Chinese wouldn't get it." But there was to be no rest for the patrol. The Chinese had sighted an artillery piece to fire directly down the hill where the platoon took cover. This is how McCloskey remembers it: "There was no trajectory and no warning. The rounds came right down on us, and we were all scared shitless. Thomas Burchik, the corpsman beside me, was hit bad. He took the round that would have killed me. I got it in the leg from the same round. Both our corpsmen were casualties, and I went around giving morphine. We finally got our wounded out of there. I didn't do anything that anyone else wouldn't have done, and they gave me a Silver Star for it. I didn't deserve it."

What, in fact, McCloskey had done that many other men would not have done was to refuse evacuation for treatment of his own wound. The round that severely wounded Burchik, a courageous nineteen-year-old whom McCloskey had once seen perform a tracheotomy on a fallen Marine under fire from the Chinese, shattered McCloskey's leg and cut a tendon. ". . . He disregarded the intense pain and loss of blood and continued to treat the casualties," says McCloskey's Silver Star citation. "When a stretcher party was able to reach the area, he directed the evacuation of casualties and returned to his platoon. Only upon the direct order of his battalion commander and senior medical officer did he allow himself to be evacuated for treatment. Second Lieutenant McCloskey's alert actions and courageous devotion to duty undoubtedly saved the lives of four critically wounded comrades." Daly, who was hit by a stray bullet the next day and began thirteen months in a series of military hospitals, is convinced that McCloskey was sufficiently wounded to require evacuation from the battle zone. But after McCloskey was finally treated, he volunteered to rejoin his officer-short unit. Two days later he was again at the head of his platoon, preparing to lead his sixth bayonet charge against a fortified hill.

There comes a time when even the most fearless men are afraid. McCloskey, weary from weeks of battle, and with fresh shrapnel in his leg, remembers the time before that sixth bayonet charge as his own time of fear. "I didn't think I was going to get killed in the next charge," he said. "I knew it." But he once more prepared to lead an assault, this time across three hundred yards of grassy meadow up a heavily fortified ridge line. The odds seemed more formidable than ever before to a unit that had lost most of its platoon sergeants and too many of its officers and men. McCloskey remembers that the company requested air strikes on the hill but was unable to obtain them. He also remembers that "colonels and generals were screaming that their reputations depended on the hill being taken at a certain hour." Finally McCloskey persuaded regimental command to order three artillery barrages on the hill. He led his men across the meadow as the barrages began, certain that the charge would be his last, only to discover that no Chinese fire was coming from the hill. The Marines cleared the crest just in time to see the backs of the retreating Chinese, who had inexplicably been given orders to abandon their positions. "We felt we were living on borrowed time after that," McCloskey says in retrospect.

McCloskey talks well, but not easily, about the war. Sometimes on long trips he will tell friends about it, talking for hours in his low, resonant voice, with a curious blend of passion and objectivity that contains almost no personal coloring. It is almost as if he has recorded it all, on a camera somewhere in the back of his mind, and is playing it back as it really happened, without the tricks that one's memory usually plays on mind cameras. And there are other stories, about which McCloskey talks more rarely. One is about a time when he and other Marines watched, laughing and joking, as a support force that had largely been spared the rigors of war came under heavy fire from the Chinese. "Here we're laughing at our fellow Marines who are getting hit," he says. "It shows you what combat can do to normal human feelings." In recent years McCloskey has also taken to telling reporters about a time when he marked a Korean village for an air strike after his platoon was fired on by two Chinese riflemen. The riflemen fled before the planes arrived, and the bombs killed or wounded some two score villagers, mostly women and children and old men. In opposing United States involvement in Vietnam, McCloskey has used this story to illustrate the devastation that modern warfare causes in a rural Asian land. But the story does not appear in any early McCloskey war accounts, and there is no evidence that he felt any sense of remorse about the killing of civilians when he returned from Korea. What evidence there is instead points to a genuine pride in his own role in that war. "My first impression of McCloskey as really being quite different from other people was when he said it was just a great honor to fight in the first world peace force and he was obviously very serious about it," recalls Lew Butler. "He was very pleased to go to Korea." John Ehrlichman, the presidential assistant and onetime Air Force navigator whose wife took Cubby McCloskey in while Pete was fighting in Korea, also finds no evidence of secret guilt. "He got a great relish out of those wartime experiences, and he found them, at least from conversations I've had with him, very exhilarating and not at all disillusioning," says Ehrlichman. "And he's remained an honorary Marine all this time."

Still, despite these recollections and McCloskey's own evident pride in his Korean performance, it is not beyond the realm of possibility that the air strike he ordered worked inside of him somewhere and in some remote way helped influence his present course. All of us have stored experiences which mysteriously reappear years later in unexpected contexts, and McCloskey, perhaps more than others, draws deeply from his past. He also possesses the special sense of war's horror that seems to be peculiarly reserved for lovers of war. It is well that we know how terrible war really is, else we should grow too fond of it, Robert E. Lee said before the slaughter at Fredericksburg. It is a perception that Civil War student Pete McCloskey shares in our time.

Whatever the effect of the air strike on McCloskey's present position, it is almost certain that another incident that McCloskey rarely discusses influences his attitude toward political participation and helped form his notion of the Congress. Despite his loyalty to Schening and Jones and the leadership concept of the Marine Corps, McCloskey's frequent attitude toward some of his superiors is revealed in his statement that "colonels and generals were screaming that their reputations depended on the hill being taken at a certain hour." One such colonel, virtually a taboo subject because he was subsequently killed in action, was particularly despised by McCloskey, who thought him responsible for the death of many good men. McCloskey remembers one time in the bone-chilling cold of late Korean winter when this officer, in defiance of the Marine Corps tradition that officers never eat before their men, hoarded biscuits for himself when his troops were short on rations. The climax came when a biscuit rolled into the snow and two Marines scrambled for it while the officer, laughing, watched them fight. Soon thereafter, however, the unit was pulled out of line for an investigation that McCloskey subsequently learned had been triggered by a Marine's parent's complaint to a congressman. "It was the first time I had any realization of what a congressman could do," says McCloskey. But it was not to be the last time. He has told that story privately through the years, and it clearly symbolizes for him the kind of representational authority that congressmen should exercise.

Pete McCloskey's experiences in Korea partake of the courage and honorable burdens shared by young men of all nations in all wars. However, they go beyond a mere assumption of duty to something resembling the soldier's faith of his hero, jurist-soldier Oliver Wendell Holmes, who thirty-seven years before the Korean War told a Harvard graduating class: "If it is our business to fight, the book for the army is a war-song, not a hospital sketch. It is not well for soldiers to think much about wounds. Sooner or later we shall fall; but meantime it is for us to fix our eyes upon the point to be stormed, and to get there if we can."

Part Two
McCloskey Civilian

Peter has a sense of the law and a respect for the influence of the law on history that is very unusual, even for fine lawyers. He has a great sense of the continuity of the law with the past and of the evolution of the law.

—Lawyer David Lennihan

5. *Conservationist Lawyer*

The war had not been an easy one for Cubby McCloskey. Expecting her first child, she wandered about the rustic Stanford campus in the fall before her husband went off to war. Sometimes, young men who met Charlotte Wadsworth on campus were nonplussed on a subsequent day to encounter Cubby, six months' pregnant. "My twin sister was dying to get me off campus," Cubby recalls. "There were no pregnant women on campus at all." Cubby petitioned Stanford to allow her to graduate by correspondence from the University of California. Stanford, a proud and private institution, frowned on the practice of giving up its potential graduates to rival UC, but the university took cognizance of the special circumstances in Cubby's case and granted her petition. She returned home and gave birth to Nancy McCloskey on February 16, 1951, the same day her husband landed in Korea.

Despite Stanford's leniency, graduation-by-correspondence did not work out for Cubby. "I did nothing except play with my baby and didn't really get into studying," she remembers. Finally her father said, "I don't know why you're so worried; you still have a quarter. Go back and finish." Cubby promptly returned to Stanford, bringing her six-week-old baby with her. John and Jeanne Ehrlichman, also the parents of a small baby, invited her to stay with them until she got settled. Married students were a rarity on the Stanford campus, and they tended to band together. The McCloskeys and the Ehrlichmans, married about the same time, had become close friends in the year before Pete went off to war. Today Ehrlichman is disappointed by McCloskey for the sometimes personal character of his attacks on President Nixon, but he and his wife retain an affection for Cubby and a warm memory of those 1951 days at Stanford. Cubby lived with the Ehrlichmans until she found a place of her own, and she took her finals at Stanford during the same two weeks in which her husband assaulted Hill 566 and was twice wounded.

The McCloskeys held a joyous Christmas reunion in 1951, but the course that McCloskey faced as a prospective civilian was troubled and uncertain. He loved the Marines and considered staying in the service, until he was informed that he would be transferred to the judge advocate's office when he graduated from law school. "He didn't want that at all," recalls Cubby. "He loved the infantry. The thing that really appealed to him about the service was the men." McCloskey also considered an offer to join the Central Intelligence Agency, a position that conceivably could have led him into making policy in Laos today rather than in opposing it. But the CIA offer, though intriguing to McCloskey, was completely unacceptable to Cubby. "I said, 'That's fine,'" she recalls, although the language she used undoubtedly was stronger. "'You make the decision, the decision being whether you want your wife and your marriage or whether you want to go over to the CIA.' I just lowered the boom. Really, I was only twenty-one. I didn't wish to spend two more years of my life by myself, having just spent a year alone. I felt he had to make the choice." Put that way, McCloskey quickly abandoned any idea of joining the CIA. It would not be the last time, however, that McCloskey's adventuresome spirit and passion for public service would conflict with the needs of his marriage.

Apart from the indecisiveness, the six months after McCloskey returned from Korea were among the most idyllic of his adult life. He was stationed at Pendleton, and Cubby came down to live with him at what McCloskey calls "a honeymoon cottage on the beach." McCloskey served as a tactics instructor, a job for which he was well suited. But the kind of singularity that has always made McCloskey seem different from other people continued to afflict him at Pendleton. A few days before his discharge in June 1952 he went to the dentist. "I was trying to get a free cleaning of my teeth before I got out," he remembers. What he got instead was a deep gash and a permanent scar when the dentist's sandpaper disk slipped and ran down his chin. "Everybody thought it was pretty funny," he says. "I was the most highly decorated officer on the base, and here I survive Korea fine and was marked for life by a goddamn dentist."

McCloskey returned to Stanford Law School after the Marines, mindful of his poor academic showing before the service, and possessed of a new determination. McCloskey's father thinks that the difference was Korea, which had matured his son; others believe that McCloskey's belated performance in the classroom was nothing more than the typical showing of a highly motivated returned veteran with a family to support. But it was not easy. At best, he was a mediocre student in law school, and Sam Thurmond, the assistant dean, sent Pete a concerned letter suggesting that he consider some profession other than the law. Cubby believes that this suggestion may have spurred her husband to work harder in law school. In any event, McCloskey flung himself into his law-school studies and performed better than ever before. And he also passed up a chance to take the easy—and wrong—way out. When a friend brought over a copy of a test and left it, McCloskey tore it up without looking at it. He was determined to get wherever he was going on his own.

Stanford Law School in those days prided itself on the high percentage of graduates who passed the difficult California bar examination on the first try. McCloskey, who was slowly forging ahead in his studies, surprised everyone ("Thurmond was damn sore," he says) by applying to take the bar while still in law school, an event that was highly unusual even for good students. It seemed especially dubious for McCloskey, who wasn't required to take the examination at all. California law at that time permitted returning veterans to become lawyers "on motion," a procedure that required no test of any kind. "The bar exam is something you really sweat out, and there is a tremendous social stigma if you flunk it," observes Charles McClung. "Everybody coming back from the war was going in on motion. You walk up to the Supreme Court, raise your hand, and you're in. Many of us assumed that this is what Pete would do. He had a wife, a child, he was not a smashing student, he had been out of it for a while. We thought sure he'd pass on motion. And the suggestion that he would do it this way made him mad. He was going to take the test, and he was going to pass, or else he wasn't going to be a lawyer." McCloskey surprised everyone except himself and Cubby by passing on his first try. "I was trying to prove a point," he says. "And, of course," adds Cubby, "we needed for him to pass it, because we needed him to get out and support two children at this point. By George he did, and he picked that phone up and called Sam Thurmond. He said, 'Sam, I made it!' And they've been close friends ever since."

McCloskey set out immediately to make a living as a lawyer. He took a $300-a-month job with the district attorney's office in Alameda County, across the bay from San Francisco. Under the leadership of Frank Coakley the Alameda County office had won a national reputation for prosecuting ability, and McCloskey found the professionalism to his liking. He served four months in on-the-job training at a branch office in Hayward, and then, in January 1954, moved into the Oakland municipal court branch and a world of minor crimes. "It was kind of a fun job," recalls McCloskey. "Some really tough criminal lawyers came into the municipal court occasionally in Oakland. We'd try one or two jury cases a week, and then a whole lot of little misdemeanor cases just before the judge. You'd go into court at ten o'clock and maybe try half a dozen cases by noon, and maybe three or four in the afternoon before the judge, and then every third or fourth day a jury case. This was the best trial experience you could get, because the public defenders were excellent and the private attorneys were tough." McCloskey fit right in with the young, aggressive crew of prosecutors that Coakley had assembled. "He was a very squared-away guy, pleasant, and well-spoken," says Al Hederman, then the number-two man in the Oakland office and now the chief assistant district attorney. "He was a gung-ho prosecutor, the way he must have been a Marine, and we were very sorry to see him leave." The McCloskey temperament proved ideally suited for the criminal courtroom. McCloskey was an avid investigator, and he responded to the challenge of an adversary proceeding. Above all, the courtroom appealed to his sense of the dramatic. One case concerned an oversized hoodlum named Big John who used to knock money off the bar in Skid Row taverns and then stare down the drunk who sought to reclaim it. McCloskey, whose own witness made a poor showing, labored to convince the jury that the victimized drunk, rather than the defendant, was worthy of belief. "But just think, ladies and gentlemen," he told the jury, "if you're in this situation, and you're sitting at the bar and Big John walks up behind you and knocks your money off and you get down and all of a sudden you reach down into the sawdust under your bar stool and pick up the money and you look up. And you look into the eyes of Big John and he's looking at you just like—like he's looking at me right now." The jury turned as one when McCloskey said the final words, and Big John, too late, wiped out the look of hatred that he was bestowing upon McCloskey. The jury convicted Big John in thirty minutes. These staples of everyday petty crime were the kind of cases McCloskey tried during his invaluable apprenticeship in Alameda County. Once he spent a week monitoring a burlesque house. On other occasions he prosecuted various minor offenses in behalf of the Contractors Licensing Board, an assignment that landed him an invitation to the contrators' annual dinner. McCloskey attended, but his introduction as a deputy district attorney was greeted with groans. "Then the evening entertainment started," says McCloskey. "She was a stripper who immediately stripped down to the buff and pranced around. Guys were trying to get her to pick quarters off the table, and I was looking at this, wondering, 'My God, what happens if the police raid this place with this going on and the young D.A. is here?' So I quietly excused myself and left, to the relief of everybody there."

Despite his fondness for the prosecutor's role, McCloskey was restless again. Peter McCloskey, their first son, had been born on December 24, 1952, while his father was still at Stanford Law School, and Cubby was pregnant with their third child. McCloskey wanted to get into private practice and earn a better living for the family, and both he and Cubby preferred the suburban area south of San Francisco to Alameda County. He submitted his resignation and prepared to become what he has always called a "country lawyer." But he faced one troublesome case to try before he left. This was a malicious-mischief prosecution arising from an incident in which a bucket of red paint had been thrown over a statue of Jack London shortly before the annual "big game" between Stanford and California. Such events are normally dismissed as pregame pranks, but the Oakland newspaper management was incensed that the London statue had been singled out for the paint dousing. The paper's concern stirred an investigation which resulted in the arrest not of Stanford students but of two UC grads, one a famous ex-athlete. The prosecution was a touchy one for the Oakland office, which numbered many UC grads on its staff. McCloskey was a Stanford alumnus, and he was leaving anyway. He agreed to stay an extra week and prosecute the case.

The evidence against the accused paint wielder turned out to be dependent upon the testimony of two newspaper reporters who supposedly had overheard the planning of the crime. The reporters had told the police investigators about it, and had said that it was intended by one of the accused, owner of a nearby restaurant, as a publicity stunt. McCloskey called the reporters, only to be told that their editors didn't want them to testify. Newspaper reporters in California enjoy a statutory protection against disclosure of news sources, but this privilege does not normally extend to withholding information about a crime. "It was squarely a case where these guys were witness to an act which constituted a crime, and it had nothing to do with their refusing to reveal a source of news," said McCloskey. But this argument made no impression with McCloskey's superiors, who informed him he would have to try the case without calling the reporters as witnesses. McCloskey felt this decision was based on pressure from the newspaper management. He withdrew from the case and left Alameda County on December 31, 1954, a week before the trial. "They tried the case and lost it, as I said they would," he remembers.

The Alameda County experience had been valuable, but Cubby believes that the final incident left a bad aftertaste. "It was a disillusioning thing to Peter to find that the press had such immunity," she says in looking back on it. "He was very idealistic then, and he believes in the law."

McCloskey's passion for the law soon became evident in private practice. He joined a well-established firm in Palo Alto, the community adjoining Stanford. But the association was a brief one. He quarreled with one of the members of the firm and longed to be out on his own. "What it amounted to was that he just wasn't happy working for somebody else," says Cubby. "He always has been his own man. When *his* firm became the biggest in Palo Alto, he became unhappy with it. He just doesn't like a big, unwieldly thing."

McCloskey went into business for himself in June 1956. He

was unknown and poor. The McCloskeys had settled in Ladera, a tree-shaded hilly San Mateo County suburb where John McCloskey, their third child and second son, had been born on March 25, 1955. McCloskey drove a red Model-A Ford to work and shared a $50-a-month office space in a ramshackle former home in Palo Alto that also housed an insurance broker, a travel agent, and another lawyer. Cubby painted the office and put a rug down. Lew Butler, the able attorney who many years later would join McCloskey as a law partner, remembers those early days. Butler was then a member of Pillsbury, Madison, and Sutro, one of the most prestigious of San Francisco law firms. "I'd go down and see him every once in a while," recalls Butler. "In his first office Cubby was doing the typing. And Pete took every kind of case in Palo Alto that no one else would take, just to keep going. I was in the opposite kind of law practice—you never worried about a client. I thought at the time, all this great prestige. It was kind of sickening. Anyway, Pete was at the opposite end of the spectrum, and he was just hustling like mad. But I guess it never occurred to me that he wouldn't make it. Somehow he's been doing these things all the time I've known him."

He really did take every kind of case. He represented clients in repossession cases, divorces, business disputes. He represented alcoholics, mentally unbalanced persons, criminal clients who had no hope of paying a fee. "He used to say that one-third of his time would be devoted to charity or to public-interest cases, and we had to work hard enough on the other two-thirds to pay for the one-third," recalls Janet Brune, his longtime legal secretary. "When people came to the door at home soliciting, I used to say that I gave at work." McCloskey delighted particularly in bizarre or attention-getting cases, or characteristically, in those cases that posed particularly difficult challenges. In one case he won acquittal for a defendant accused of the indecent-exposure offense known as "lily-waving" by drawing on an old common-law precedent which held that the offense requires at least two witnesses. And in dozens of unpublicized cases he demonstrated a love for the law and a capacity for hard work that commended him to clients and to fellow lawyers. He also, like many good attorneys, excelled at cases that never came to court. "He's a tremendous arbitrator between parties," says Janet Brune. "The challenge of getting people to see the ridiculousness of their situations appealed to him. He didn't try to prevent divorces when the parties had made up their minds, but he worked assiduously to keep from having the divorce bitterly contested in court. He would do almost anything to keep cases from going to trial. He had more physical stamina and could exhaust other people. He never tired of working with them."

Carl Spaeth, then the dean of Stanford Law School, says McCloskey could be briefed on a case as he walked down the hall and then successfully argue it in court. "Pete's practice was of that character," says Spaeth. "His batting average was higher than Willie Mays could ever aspire to. He'd win case after case, and it was another notch on his rifle. He was an advocate. But through it all ran an inclination to take the case of the underdog."

Not everyone shared this positive view of McCloskey's legal performance. Some of those who do share it register significant qualifications. One attorney who worked with McCloskey cites "a certain impulsiveness and a tendency to jump into things without quite enough background." Another, while complimenting McCloskey's ability as a trial lawyer, says that he "goes from peak to peak and lives on the crest of the wave. The law's very pedestrian at times, and that drives Pete up the wall." Charles McClung, who is a McCloskey admirer as well as his brother-in-law, believes that McCloskey's enthusiasm for a cause sometimes led him to take cases that he ought not to have taken. "It's like a doctor who opens a guy up and wanting to cure his cancer so bad, says, 'I can cure your cancer.' Now, Pete wouldn't mislead people, but his very enthusiasm and the fact that he'll jump in with the full force of his efforts might lead a client to believe he has a chance where he doesn't. I've seen clients of Pete's who've lost cases in the long run that I could have told them they were going to lose in the beginning. And some lawyers would have. Pete wouldn't give up, which can be a drawback. It's also an experience of youth." By the early sixties, recalls Janet Brune, McCloskey was averaging 1.2 new files each working day and had a constant caseload of four hundred. This sometimes led to a belief by clients and attorneys that he didn't finish what he started or pay enough attention to detail. Ned Hutchinson, a friend and neighbor, contends that McCloskey misadvised him that he couldn't marry his Danish fiancée within the United States without jeopardizing her visa. McCloskey also provoked some dismay among his law associates by representing a pair of clients who skirted the edge of the law with a series of land deals. McCloskey, in a comment he would make about the Berrigan brothers, defended his representation on grounds that every person is entitled to counsel.

One quality of McCloskey's that was in some circumstances a virtue and in others a defect was his inability to perform when he couldn't believe his client or his opposition. He gave up the defense of Dr. Geza de Kaplany, who was subsequently convicted of the torture-murder of his wife by corrosive acid, because he couldn't accept the defendant's claim that an alter ego was responsible for the crime. "If I didn't believe in a case, I couldn't sell it to a jury," says McCloskey. And he did poorly in some cases where he believed that an opposing attorney was misstating the facts. "I get emotionally handcuffed dealing with someone I don't trust," he says. "I used to have very grave difficulty practicing the law when there was an attorney on the other side lying and I knew he was lying."

"Every single virtue that a man has is accompanied by a corresponding defect," McCloskey once told me in making the point that tactics which are militarily sound in one situation are disastrous in others. The converse is also true. The same lawyer who finds McCloskey "impetuous" praises him for his trial ability and a "real feel for the law." The attorney who says he goes "from peak to peak" lauds his willingness to challenge any injustice. David Lennihan, a San Francisco attorney who is at the same time one of McCloskey's most dedicated supporters and severest critics, sees his friend as a kind of general practitioner of the law who addresses himself to the whole range of human problems. "In terms of dealing with humans and human problems and the fabric of the law as a whole, a good country lawyer is a really admirable person," says Lennihan. "McCloskey impresses me as being that kind; he's not a specialist. He has a capacity for thoroughness and patience which overcome any lack of brilliance he may have. I don't particularly admire the brilliant lawyer—he's quick to make up his mind. If he's wrong, he's arrogant. Now, the good ones are more patient, and Peter's one of those. He's a damned good lawyer."

He is also an attorney who became a success without any concern for amassing wealth. Butler believes that McCloskey's lack of concern for money borders on the "irresponsible." And McClung says that when McCloskey was elected to Congress he not only gave up his law practice but walked away from his accounts receivable. "He didn't want anything to do with people that owed him money from before. Money means nothing to Peter. Nothing."

McCloskey more than compensated for any lack of acquisitiveness with a sure instinct for the kind of people's case that has become commonplace in these days of government-supported legal services but was uncommonly rare in the mid-fifties, at least in suburban California. The case that started him on his way arose in the Green Meadows subdivision, a small enclave of Palo Alto which possessed a telephone exchange common to the neighboring community of Mountain View. The exchange was sometimes troublesome during emergencies; telephone operators asked to summon the fire department, for instance, would usually call Mountain View rather than Palo Alto. On one occasion, a house burned down because of the delay. A certain suburban snob appeal also was involved. Roger Mosher, an attorney with the McCloskey firm for several years, believes that many Green Meadows residents preferred a Palo Alto exchange to a "less prestigious" Mountain View number. McCloskey had represented the subdivision's homeowners' association in negotiations with the developer for a swimming pool. The association collected a dollar from each subdivision family that wanted a Palo Alto telephone number and from other families in the surrounding area who also wanted their numbers changed. They then hired McCloskey, for $750, to take their case before the State Public Utilities Commission (PUC). Despite attention from the local newspapers, few attorneys gave the case any chance at all. The telephone company was represented by Pillsbury, Madison, and Sutro, and the PUC was historically favorable to the utility's position in such cases. The moving of trunk lines to accommodate Green Meadows would be a six-figure expense for the telephone company. But McCloskey mobilized the whole area in behalf of his petition for a new exchange. Families pooled baby-sitters and paraded more than a hundred witnesses before the commission to tell of their difficulties in obtaining ambulances, fire trucks, and police cars. McCloskey also spent two months researching precedents and came up with one favoring Green Meadows. To the astonishment of nearly everyone, McCloskey won the case—and the gratitude of 750 potential clients. "This is really what launched my law practice," says McCloskey. "It's been the basis of my practice ever since."

The Green Meadows case had been ahead of its time, and McCloskey was also out in front on environmental issues. "He didn't have a comprehensive view of the environment at first," says Carl Spaeth. "He loves these hills, and he was just thinking about protecting his own backyard." Nonetheless, McCloskey became identified early as a conservationist, and there is some merit to the contention of George Murphy, his press secretary, that "Pete was for conservation when most copy editors couldn't spell 'ecology.'" In the late fifties and early sixties a latent conservationist movement sought to save San Mateo County from the urban sprawl that had already become the central feature of San Jose to the south. McCloskey associated with this movement in a series of conservationist challenges that ultimately changed the political map of San Mateo County and provided the springboard for his own political career. His most famous effort, which dragged out over a four-year period in the early sixties, concerned the attempts of the picturesque community of Woodside to save its skyline from the scar of a high-tension power line sought by Stanford for its new nuclear accelerator. The enemy was more powerful than in the Green Meadows case. On one side were the citizens of a well-heeled but vote-poor Woodside; on the other, the combined forces of the Pacific Gas and Electric Company, Stanford, and the U.S. Atomic Energy Commission. McCloskey was not in on either the start or the finish of the battle, and this time he lost the decision before the Public Utilities Commission. But he played the key role in twice carrying the case to Washington, and, according to Alexander Donald, a leader in the fight to stop the power line, effectively presented the case for the community. Eventually, Woodside lost its fight to put the line underground, but did win a special pole design and emplacement of the poles by helicopters with no destruction of foliage. McCloskey also gained political attention, partly because of the nature of the case and partly because of the slashing attack he waged on Joint Atomic Energy Commission Chairman Chet Holifield, Democratic dean of the California congressional delegation, and Representative Craig Hosmer, another Californian who was the ranking Republican committee member from the House. In his testimony before the AEC, McCloskey charged that the two congressmen had shown "clear bias" by supporting a court fight against a Woodside ordinance requiring underground power lines. "Pete's challenge was never personal," says Holifield in looking back on the hearing. "He was representing his clients, and representing them well."

The Woodside case also gave McCloskey a taste of Washington politics. "He wasn't at all awed by what he saw," remembers a friend. "But he wanted to be part of it." Janet Adams, a San Mateo County conservationist who was active in the Woodside affair, remembers that the power-line foes worked out of California Senator Thomas Kuchel's office on one of their trips to Washington. "Some of us were in a meeting, and Kuchel said, 'When you're through the power-line fight, get that man to run for office.' "

McCloskey was flattered, but he didn't need the senatorial advice. As it turned out, he had already reached the same conclusion on his own.

6. *Citizen Politician*

California's best politicians have always distinguished themselves by proclaiming their antipathy to politics, and Pete McCloskey is no exception. It is a legacy of the "star system" produced when the Progressives united behind Hiram Johnson in 1910 to smash the power of the Southern Pacific Railroad, the force that thoroughly dominated the state's political and economic system in the final decades of the nineteenth century and the first decade of the twentieth.* Briefly stated, the star system that is the hallmark of nonpartisanism in California came about when the victorious Progressives wreaked their legislative vengeance not only upon Southern Pacific but also upon the entire political apparatus that it dominated. Political parties were reduced to impotence by a series of laws and state constitutional amendments, the most far-reaching of which established a cross-filing system allowing candidates to run for the nomination of every party—and without any partisan designation on the ballot. Political programs emanated not from the Legislature or the parties but from a popularly supported chief executive who was envisioned by the Progressives as created in the image of Hiram Johnson. Johnson's successors matched neither this image nor

* For a more complete account of the effects of the nonpartisan legacy in California politics, see the "Political Setting" chapter in the author's *Ronnie and Jesse: A Political Odyssey* (1969). Readers interested in the rise and fall of the Progressive movement are also directed to George E. Mowry's excellent account, *The California Progressives,* published by the University of California Press, in 1951.

the Johnsonian reality, and the Progressive movement faded into decay after the enactment of far-reaching social reforms. Left behind was an enfeebled party system and a political structure in which officeholders appealed to their constituencies almost entirely on a personal basis. "The man, not the party" became the touchstone in California four decades before its celebration as a cornerstone of modern politics. The great California politicians who came after Johnson in almost every case made their reputations outside of partisan politics and appealed to the voters as candidates less narrow than their parties. Republican Earl Warren was a crusading district attorney who eventually became an overwhelmingly popular governor and an object of GOP mistrust. Democrat Pat Brown, like Warren, was a district attorney and a state attorney general before he was a governor. Brown had started politics as a Republican, and at the time of his first gubernatorial nomination in 1958 was considered the most "nonpolitical" of California Democrats. Republican Ronald Reagan, whose rhetoric in some instances much resembles Hiram Johnson's, came to public life as an actor and celebrity with an expressed and actual contempt for politics and politicians. "I think politics is a fairly dishonorable profession now," said Pete McCloskey in a 1971 comment similar in all essentials to a remark that Reagan had made during an interview less than three years before. "It brings out the worst in people instead of the best. There are so many temptations. It's very difficult to be honest and be a politician."

This purist view of politics as a profession that has to be rescued from the politicians is perfectly in harmony both with McCloskey's personality and with his California upbringing. It is also in tune with the passions of San Mateo County suburbanites, many of whom became aroused by the loss of trees and open space that their homes and freeways had displaced. The issues in the sprawling California suburbs—schools, conservation, highway routings—are truly nonpartisan, and they are the stuff of which antipolitical politicians are made.

Pete McCloskey slowly drifted into this type of issue-oriented political involvement. As Rodney G. Minott puts it: "He did not enter politics directly so much as he stalked along a variety of paths which eventually led him to his candidacy." Many of these paths were orthodox enough for a young lawyer. McCloskey was president of the Palo Alto Bar Association in 1960–1961, the Palo Alto Junior Chamber of Commerce's "Young Man of the Year" in 1961, the president of the Conference of Barristers of the State Bar in 1961–1962. He lectured on legal ethics at Santa Clara University and at Stanford, and in 1964 authored an unusual "programmed" text for grade-school students that consisted of 922 questions and answers about the United States Constitution and was conceived by McCloskey as "an answer to the narrow view held of the Constitution by the John Birch Society." But these outlets were insufficient to satisfy McCloskey's yearning for public service. In the summer of 1963, after racial demonstrations in Birmingham, Alabama, President John F. Kennedy convened the White House Conference on Civil Rights. Chuck Daly, McCloskey's friend and fellow platoon leader from Korea, was then a Kennedy aide, and he put McCloskey's name on the list of invitees. It was just what McCloskey had been waiting for. He attended and listened with fervent attention as Kennedy issued "a humble appeal" to the assembled lawyers to return home and form biracial committees. "I walked out of the room three feet in the air thinking I'd been asked to do something big," remembers McCloskey. "It was a great example of leadership. By making his pitch in this kind of humble way, the President had caused a lot of doubters and people who opposed him philosophically to actually do something. That really is what leadership is all about, to get a guy to do something a little more than he would otherwise do. This seemed to me a great example of what politicians should be about." After the conference McCloskey walked over to Daly's room in the east wing of the White House and told him of his political enthusiasm. "What Republicans do I talk to?" he asked. "They're all assholes," responded Daly, an ardent Democrat who has never supported any Republican except McCloskey. But McCloskey persisted in his questioning, and Daly finally suggested that he visit John Lindsay, then the troubled House maverick that McCloskey is today. McCloskey chatted briefly with Lindsay and visited his own congressman, J. Arthur Younger, to ask for advice on preparing for a public career. Younger, a congressman since 1952, advised McCloskey to subscribe to *U.S. News & World Report.* Either Younger or Lindsay or both of them (McCloskey is unsure at this late date, and he has told the story different ways) also suggested that McCloskey subscribe to *Congressional Quarterly.* McCloskey returned home and promptly dragooned half a dozen friends into sharing the $300-a-year *CQ* subscription with him.

But Pete McCloskey became more than a magazine subscriber as a result of his participation in the White House Conference on Civil Rights. The President's speech had fallen on fertile ground—and not just because of McCloskey's mounting desire for public service. While not initially knowledgeable about the problems of Negroes and other minorities, McCloskey judges people on individual qualities, and his innate sense of fair play led him to detest racial prejudice. In 1964 he lined up with the opponents of a statewide ballot initiative, Proposition 14, that was intended to repeal the state open-housing law. The proposition was attractively worded as a "freedom-of-choice" amendment that allowed homeowners to sell their property to whomever they wished. Opponents complained that it actually deprived Negro buyers of the right to live where they wished, since repeal of the housing law would ratify discriminatory practices by real-estate agents. They also contended that the housing law, which actually had been of limited benefit in opening up suburbs to minority buyers, stood as an important antidiscrimination symbol to Negroes. The California Real Estate Association (CREA) was singularly unimpressed by these arguments. Frustrated by the refusal of the Legislature to repeal the law, the CREA brushed aside moderate opposition within its own ranks and sponsored an initiative that went far beyond the original intention of repealing the open-housing law. Proposition 14, which purported to give all power to the property owner, also forbade the Legislature from passing any other open-housing law. The issue aroused McCloskey and Lew Butler, who was between Malaysian and African tours as a Peace Corps administrator. Butler believes that McCloskey regarded President Kennedy's statement at the White House conference as "something like a direct order from a commanding officer to go take a hill." Proposition 14 was an opportunity to respond to that direct order. McCloskey put up $300 of his own money to print "NO On 14" bumper stickers complete with a picture of Abraham Lincoln, and Butler started to organize San Francisco lawyers against the initiative. One lawyer who responded and afterward became chairman of the Northern California committee opposing Proposition 14 was Putnam Livermore, a softspoken and thoughtful outdoorsman who today is the Republican state chairman in California. Another was Howard Nemerovski, a bright young San Francisco attorney who was already preparing briefs to be used against Proposition 14 before the State Supreme Court. The four men set out to get the state bar of California to do what it had rarely, if ever, done before—take a position on a political issue.

"That was when I really became aware that Pete had this enormous interest and kind of talent for publicity," says Butler. "He really liked being out there in front." Butler and McCloskey organized a group called "Republicans Against Proposition 14" and persuaded the Palo Alto Bar Association to go on record against the initiative. On behalf of the Palo Alto bar, he then introduced a resolution condemning Proposition 14 for decision by the state bar convention in October. "He had three votes out of five hundred, and we talked about it at great length," recalls Butler. "He said: 'I don't want to make a fool of myself, but I've introduced the resolution, and the one thing I'm sure of is it's going to give me the chance to stand up on the floor of that convention and make a speech to those lawyers about Proposition 14. That's all I ask.' I said: 'What about trying to win?' He said: 'Well, I want to do that, too, but we're probably not going to do that. At least I can make a speech and say what it is the President told me I ought to say.'" Armed with McCloskey's resolution, Butler and his San Francisco friends flew down to the state bar convention at Santa Monica. "By that time we had Pete's three votes, and by rigging the voting, we had seventy votes in the San Francisco bar," says Butler. "We swore me in as a delegate. We got all the young guys to come to the meeting and didn't tell any of the old guys, and they asked for the vote. We had enough young delegates lined up so we won the vote of the San Francisco caucus before we went to Santa Monica." The anti-Proposition 14 group, now numbering about half a dozen young attorneys, started in immediately at the convention to line up votes. "I remember being really surprised," says Butler. "McCloskey had a black book, and he had the delegations listed down and he had the number of votes after each delegation, and he was really going around counting." By the end of the day, some two hundred delegates had committed themselves to voting for the resolution.

On the morning of the vote, according to Butler, McCloskey decided that he would yield the floor to William Gray, a liberal Republican attorney who had been president of the state bar at the time of the White House Conference on Civil Rights. Gray had attended the conference, and, like McCloskey, had been impressed with President Kennedy's appeal. As Butler remembers it, McCloskey went to Gray before the convention and said: "You remember what the President told us; here's the time to deliver." Gray did. He and the president of the San Francisco bar made an eloquent case against Proposition 14 while McCloskey, content in his role of blocking back, kept quiet throughout the whole debate. The bar overwhelmingly opposed Proposition 14,* despite the arguments of attorneys who maintained that it was improper for the legal profession to become overtly involved in political issues.

Proposition 14 recalls a far less desirable characteristic to his present-day critics within the Republican party. Ned Hutchinson, who knew McCloskey well, accompanied him and a group of youngish Republicans to the state convention of the United Republicans of California (UROC). Statewide conventions of UROC in recent years have been reduced to little more than a recital of right-wing catechism, but UROC in 1964 was a vigorous California component of the conservative resurgence that developed behind the candidacy of Barry Goldwater. This was particularly true in San Mateo County, where the UROC organization was led by Hutchinson, then thirty-three years old, and by other relatively young men. "We all felt that the party had to mean something to young people," Hutchinson recalls. "If the Republican party and the conservative movement are worth a damn, they must be worth a damn for people in their thirties." Hutchinson was pleased at the participation of McCloskey, who even then was recognized as a prospective candidate capable of making an effective presentation. McCloskey chaired the policy-planning committee at the UROC convention, and Hutchinson remembers him returning jubilantly to their hotel late at night saying that he had convinced the committee to oppose Proposition 14 the next day. UROC had favored a Proposition 14 before there was a Proposition 14, and McCloskey's fellow San Mateo Republicans could not have been more surprised if he had convinced the Catholic bishops to take up a resolution on birth control. "We were very impressed," recalls Hutchinson. "It showed his persuasiveness in no uncertain terms." What

* And the voters overwhelmingly approved the initiative, which was subsequently ruled unconstitutional by the State Supreme Court. The "no" vote against Proposition 14 was significantly higher in white areas of Santa Clara and southern San Mateo counties than in most other similar areas in the state, perhaps because of overwhelming newspaper opposition in the region.

followed showed Hutchinson something else. Hutchinson says he awoke the next morning to find a note in which McCloskey informed him he was returning to San Francisco to appear on a panel with Justice Douglas, and asking Hutchinson to handle the resolution on the floor. "I was disappointed as hell," remembers Hutchinson, who lacked both McCloskey's boldness and any real capability on the issue. The resolution, accordingly, was never taken up. "This was an early lesson to me," says Hutchinson. "You've got to depend on people in politics."

McCloskey's "undependability" was already legendary with his family and friends. Cubby had learned to live with it long ago. Butler had experienced it as far back as 1955, when he made an appointment with McCloskey to visit Fall River, an out-of-the-way fishing spot at the foot of Mount Shasta, six hours' drive from San Francisco. McCloskey showed up two and a half hours late, with his son, not quite three years old, in tow. "Since I had no three-year-old son, I thought that was a hell of an imposition," recalls Butler. "But Pete had been with clients, and all of us who knew him well had come to recognize that you'd see Pete when he got there. He would do anything for you, but you just couldn't count on him. He always planned fifteen things more than he could possibly do, and when you understood that, you never worried about it."

To his friends McCloskey more than compensates for this undependability. He has a ribald, small-boy sense of humor which Cubby says "is the best thing about him and which I hope he never loses." He loves pranks and firecrackers and practical jokes, and his good friends vie with one another in recalling particular McCloskey escapades. At the McClungs' wedding the weekend after McCloskey's discharge from the Marines, he brought along a smoke bomb that Charles McClung calls "a clear violation of the Geneva convention." McCloskey on this occasion was outwitted by Charlotte Wadsworth's father. "Daddy knew Peter for what he was, and was positive he had something up his sleeve," recalls Charlotte. "He had it all organized for us to go over the back wall and into a neighbor's yard and take off from there. And sure enough, Peter had this terrible black smoke bomb, which, if he had thrown it successfully into our car, would have ruined us." McCloskey held the bomb in his hand waiting for the McClungs to depart. Finally the fuse grew so short that he had to drop it in the driveway, and the guests choked and ran from the smoke as the McClungs departed over the back fence. A group of Nevada Indians was not as lucky. En route to Marine training on the East Coast in his Stanford days, McCloskey hurled a cherry bomb in their car as he passed. The driver of McCloskey's car, according to a friend, didn't drive under eighty for the next five states.

The McCloskey boyishness is accompanied by a directness of language and expression that Congress has done nothing to curb. His favorite greeting was for years the extended middle digit (he intersperses it now with the peace sign), and he surprised a car full of GOP notables soon after arriving in Congress by responding to their waved greeting with the outstretched middle finger. Robin Schmidt, accompanying him on this particular day, suppressed an urge to slide beneath the seat. McCloskey also has a variety of expressions, of which perhaps "all good stuff" is the most printable. In part this behavior is probably a display of the attention-getting quality that so many have associated with McCloskey; in part it may be that "irreverence for fake values" which Cubby praises. Whatever the source, McCloskey's humor at its best can be marvelously deflating. When Butler was director of the Peace Corps in Malaysia, he wrote to McCloskey telling him his troubles, among them the difficulty of traveling through the jungle to provide medical service for the aborigines. In return he received a note admonishing him to "cut out that bullshit about snakes" and invitations to such athletic nonevents as the "Mud Bowl," a touch-football game organized by McCloskey, Chuck Daly, Ned Hutchinson, and their friends. McCloskey drew up a printed commentary on the line-ups for at least one such game, played December 31,

1961, at "Ladera Stadium." The comments are vintage McCloskey:

EAST	WEST

LER

Lennihan — Lawson

Princeton's great thinker against the last of the Armenian rug merchants; Lennihan is hard to move and slow afoot; Lawson is a lightweight but fast. *Edge: West.*

LGR

Hoyt (Big Daddy) — McDonnell

Both of these men are well past their prime; McDonnell was All-Tulagi in '44, Hoyt all-corn-belt in '34. *Edge: West (on girth).*

REL

McCloskey — Wells

East's fine end is finally approaching athletic greatness; Wells is in best physical condition of career after strenuous six weeks' training; wedge-headed approach gives him ability on line charge. *Edge: East.*

QB

Hutchinson (Captain) — Schreck

Hutchinson's competitive desire overcomes enormous lack of physical talent; Schreck slippery but has never been known to catch a pass. *Edge: East.*

WB

Borda — Mosher

These two hoary throwbacks to the Paleozoic age are of equal ferocity and IQ. *Edge: West (more teeth).*

BB

Altick — Iverson

Effectiveness of both men depends on being allowed to call signals, of which there is small chance in view of identity of their respective captains. *Result: Chaos. Edge: Even.*

TB

Kelley — Daly (Captain)

Kelley throws well out of the cup; Daly needs one badly. *Edge: East.*

Comment: This may be last in long series of bowl games, as players'

interests turn to Church or Birch. West's strength in line and oral discourse is matched by East's speed and slyness.

The Mud Bowl and half-a-hundred similar events demonstrate the "frustrated-jock" aspect of McCloskey's personality that has come to be well understood by his family. "I don't think he ever relaxes, really, unless he is doing something," said Nancy McCloskey, his twenty-year-old daughter, who is like her father in many ways. In those days when Nancy and her brothers and sister were growing up, McCloskey was an unreconstructed amateur athlete. He coached Little League and served as its legal counsel. Friends who visited him for a weekend would find themselves engaged in well-planned "septathalons" in which they ran, jumped, and threw the shot put. As the years went by, McCloskey also turned increasingly to the outdoors. He likes to fly-fish, particularly for trout and steelhead, and to camp. His Korean experiences made him an inveterate mountain climber. He and some fourteen other families fell in love with Fall River, and, led by Dave Lennihan, came up with $4,000 down payment apiece and bought a 500-acre ranch there.

He was a prosperous lawyer now, though he cared as little about money as ever. After building up his law business in downtown Palo Alto, McCloskey ignored the well-meaning advice of friends and local lawyers and moved out of downtown Palo Alto into the Stanford professional center where there wasn't a single lawyer. "He rented a vast amount of space which he couldn't afford, and that again seemed like a typical McCloskey move, which of course was enormously successful," says Butler. "Eventually he dragged eight more lawyers over there with him. But at the time it was a single building sitting out in the middle of a cow pasture, and McCloskey was the only lawyer around. But he liked it out there, because he liked being in the country, and it was near his house." McCloskey's one-man law firm, growing slowly at first, then swiftly, became McCloskey, Wilson, Mosher, and Martin, and the caseload became greater than ever before. At his new office he took to running to work and changing his clothes at the office. Cubby and Janet Brune, his secretary, were constantly trying to keep track of a wardrobe to which McCloskey seemed completely indifferent. Once he arrived at the office without shoes and socks and discreetly kept his feet under the desk while he interviewed clients. Another time he came to work in hiking shorts and boots and backpack, with an announcement that he planned to go camping later in the day. But he became absorbed in his work and threw his backpack in the corner. It stayed there for a week while McCloskey came into the office, each day intending to go on his backpacking trip. He never made it.

The McCloskeys had moved from Ladera to nearby Portola Valley and built what Cubby still calls their "dream home" there. It was a fine house, but McCloskey's thoughts were elsewhere. "Pete was never home much," recalls Al Schreck, his neighbor in Ladera and later in Portola Valley. "He was always in demand as an effective, colorful speaker. He was not as articulate as he is now, but he was always damn good." McCloskey spoke to women's groups ("Women should know their property rights"), to population-control groups (abortion reform was necessary), and to a state legislative committee considering mandatory blood-alcohol tests for drunk-driver suspects (drunk-driving laws are allowing "the most dangerous offenders" to escape punishment).

But none of it was enough. Pete McCloskey was driven onward, by some force that he seemed unable to identify, toward a public destiny that he could only dimly comprehend. Above all, he began to feel a sense of responsibility toward the Vietnam War in which the U.S. Marines, *his* Marines, were heavily engaged. McCloskey was already talking about the war in 1964, before the Marine commitment and at a time when the Gallup poll showed nearly two-thirds of Americans taking little or no interest in South Vietnam. Then, in 1965, McCloskey was offered, and accepted, a role in Exercise Silver Lance, the largest Navy-Marine training maneuvers since World War II.

Silver Lance was the brainchild of Marine Lieutenant General Victor (Brute) Krulak, an expert in counterinsurgency warfare. It was conceived first of all as a training exercise for a Marine aviator general who needed background in guerrilla warfare and planned with the developing Vietnam combat in mind. But reality outstripped the war games. The week before Silver Lance started, the First Marine Brigade that was supposed to benefit from the exercise reconstituted itself as the Ninth Marine Brigade and landed in Vietnam. The chore of running Silver Lance was dumped into the lap of Brigadier General Edward Hunter Hurst, who then was drawing up contingency plans for Southeast Asia and Guantánamo Bay. "I didn't expect to be exercising while we were fighting a war, and that's what Krulak made us do," recalls Hurst. "We had all assumed that Silver Lance was going to be canceled." Silver Lance seems in retrospect a tragic commentary on America's slide into the Southeast Asian war. Even the exercise's place names, inspired by the bullet-ended "Camelot" reign of President Kennedy, seem somehow a cruel historical comment on Vietnam involvement.

The focal point of Silver Lance, staged on three California offshore islands and ashore at Camp Pendleton, was the mythical community of Lancelot (Southern California), a small pro-American country threatened by a Chinese-type aggressor, Modred, and its North Vietnam-style "satellite," Merlin. McCloskey, outfitted in striped pants and a homburg that had been virtually his only payment from a destitute client, played the part of George Siboney, U.S. ambassador to Lancelot. He had been chosen for the role because Krulak wanted a lawyer and someone outside the regular corps who didn't mind being rude to generals. Ever the actor, McCloskey was perfectly matched for the part, which he had spent six weeks studying. "My whole job was to try to give the Marines a hard time and to require men to fight a war in accordance with rules laid down by the ambassador," recalls McCloskey. "In other words, you were trying to make each Marine into a diplomat. If you ran the artillery through a guy's house, you paid him damages. If you went into a graveyard, you didn't dig into the graves. You followed the customs of the country, and you tried to win the hearts and the minds of the people. My job, as the ambassador, was to force the Marines to live in ways different from the ways Marines ordinarily do. Marines assault hills and blow up everything in sight, then leave. In Silver Lance, the Marines were to come into the villages, live with the people, and try to get intelligence from them. So my job was to pose the Marine general a lot of frustrating problems, and I did." Krulak had written some two thousand incidents into the script, among them mob attacks on the Marines by natives speaking Spanish ("that being the only language other than English that many Marines knew," says Hurst), innumerable requests for food and medical aid, an appeal for textbooks, and a score of military and political problems intended to divide Hurst's understrength force. The script was a particular problem for Hurst, who was bone-tired from a full night of planning an exercise that he had never expected to conduct. "It was a terrible ordeal for me, and I wasn't even supposed to be in the thing," says Hurst, who in 1971 retired from the Corps. "Pete was playacting and doing a grand job of it. He never relaxed at any time, which is what gave me the greatest problem. If only he had shrugged or smiled when we were alone in private. But he didn't, and it kept the tension up." Krulak appreciated Hurst's ordeal, wishing him well on one occasion when they were alone, and on another passing him a note that said: "Hunter—Never get caught without your staff. Brute."

The denouement came when the Marines were unable to protect an oil refinery that the ambassador said was owned by a friend of President Johnson's. "George Siboney" saw the flames from the burning refinery and called Hurst at 3:30 A.M., threatening to have him relieved. Eventually, however, the Merlin-sponsored guerrillas overran Lancelot, the ambassador was withdrawn from command, and General Hurst's Marines routed the unfriendlies in a script that had a happier ending than Vietnam.

Both Hurst and McCloskey received commendations from General Krulak.

Silver Lance had been great fun for McCloskey, but reality was something else again. In 1965 a Marine friend lost his leg in Vietnamese combat, and McCloskey visited him soon after he was evacuated to the United States. He left that visit, McCloskey said afterward, feeling that he had to "do something" about the war. What he tried to do, characteristically, was to become a combat officer in Vietnam. McCloskey was now thirty-eight and the Marines, who again suggested a judge advocate's position, turned down his request for combat assignment. McCloskey kept trying. He applied to the State Department and was offered a job as province senior adviser in Vietnam under the program administered by the Agency for International Development (AID). This job application provoked the most intense family crisis since McCloskey's abortive attempt to join the Central Intelligence Agency fourteen years before. The McCloskeys now had four children (Kathleen, the youngest, was born on September 13, 1958, and Nancy, the eldest, was now in her mid-teens), and this time there was no talk of divorce. But Cubby, who had not been told about the application, was shaken by it, and she resisted both with her husband and with the State Department. "I thought the AID application was a mistake, because it was just a symptom of Peter's restlessness," she says. "His talents would have been buried in the countryside. It was just not the right place for him, and when the State Department people came out to interview me, I told them so. They took him despite me saying that, of course. I was no influence on them at all."

Confronted with his wife's opposition and that of Lew Butler and Charles McClung, McCloskey was uncertain about what to do. As he tells the story, he went to Aspen, Colorado, on a seminar with McClung, and decided, while they were fishing, to turn down the job. When he returned, he says, Cubby had decided to let him go if he wanted to. "The idea of my letting him go was a perfect joke," maintains Cubby. "He makes up his own mind, and I discuss it, but I don't have that kind of influence over him. I just don't. I figure he *has* to do what he wants to do, or he would make it miserable for all those around him. If he's not happy, it gets into diminishing returns for all of us."

What McCloskey clearly wanted at this point was a public career. He knew now that foreign service was fundamentally unacceptable to his family, but the urge to "do something" remained. Based on his successive applications to the Marines and the State Department, there is every reason to accept the assessment of at least two of his friends that his striking out at this point for a political career was in part a sublimation of his desire to serve in the war. "Before this became an immoral war, he was going over there and lick those sonofabitches single-handed," says a friend who talked to him soon after he visited the Marine amputee. But Pete McCloskey had been attracted to Congress at least as early as 1963, when he attended the White House conference. Not only had he subscribed to *Congressional Quarterly*, but he had read it, and he now thought of himself as the logical man to replace Younger. He broached the idea to several friends in 1966 and then went to Leland Kaiser, multimillionaire financier and one of Ronald Reagan's first Northern California backers. Kaiser knew McCloskey and Schreck and had, many years earlier, suggested to both of them that they become involved in politics. In McCloskey's early days as a lawyer, after Cubby stopped doing the typing and before the hiring of Janet Brune, Kaiser's daughter, Cynthia, had worked as McCloskey's legal secretary. But Younger was a loyal Republican incumbent, and the resurgence of the Republican party in California, then preparing for the Reagan landslide, was based on party unity. Kaiser bluntly told McCloskey that the party would oppose him if he ran, and for once in his life, McCloskey backed down. It was a strategic withdrawal, coming at a time of his life when restlessness, ambition, and desire to serve combined to make the course of service unclear. He talked about it to friends early in 1967, and reached a decision that he would seek the Republican nomination for Congress in 1968 regardless of what the seventy-four-year-old Younger did. The decision was typical McCloskey, for the state traditionally renominates all its incumbent Republican congressmen. Younger, however, was not renominated. He announced in April 1967 that he was seriously ill and issued regular progress reports for two months after that. Younger died of leukemia on June 21, and the same newspapers that carried accounts of his funeral also contained political speculation on the candidates who would attempt to replace him.

McCloskey was only one of these candidates, and Shirley Temple Black was not yet in the race. The talk centered on State Senator Richard J. Dolwig, who was regarded by conservationists as their archenemy for consistently supporting developers and industry against environmental claims. But Dolwig, unknown to his enemies, saw the changes that were all about him in 1967. He would actually support an important conservationist bill in 1969, the year before he abruptly decided not to seek reelection to the State Senate. Another possible candidate who was the center of early speculation was Caspar W. Weinberger, a long-time public figure who in many respects was probably the best qualified. Weinberger, a successful, Harvard-trained attorney who could be as restrained and aloof as McCloskey was impulsive, had made a mark in the State Assembly, where he authored legislation reforming the state's scandal-ridden liquor administration. In 1964 he wound up as a Republican state chairman with an inclination toward Nelson Rockefeller. Weinberger maintained an official neutrality in his state chairman's post, but there were no neutrals that year in the California presidential primary contest between Rockefeller and Barry Goldwater. The memories of that battle were still bitter enough in 1967 that the conservative millionaire backers of Governor Ronald Reagan quietly blocked Weinberger's proposed appointment as state finance director.* He entered the Reagan administration in a more modest capacity, first as the chairman of a government reorganization task force, then as the head of the bipartisan Little Hoover Commission. But Weinberger was indecisive in mid-1967. He was trying a complicated and drawn-out lawsuit, and he says he also was "doubtful as to whether anyone should run for Congress who was not a lot younger than me." Weinberger was then forty-nine. "I realized the importance of seniority and had a basic feeling that it's difficult to be terribly effective in the House until you had been there for fifteen or twenty years." McCloskey talked to Weinberger off and on, both before and after Younger's death, and at one point offered to support him if Weinberger ran. Weinberger remained noncommittal, and McCloskey pushed his own plans. On May 12 McCloskey attended a dinner at L'Auberge Restaurant in San Mateo that had been suggested and scheduled by Al Schreck. The purpose of the dinner was to discuss the proposed McCloskey candidacy and determine if he should run. The men invited by Schreck were close friends: David Lennihan, Ryland Kelley, Lew Butler, Roger Mosher, Hamilton Budge, Theodore Carlstrom, Alvin Calvin, and Schreck's business partner and brother-in-law, Albion Wells. "McCloskey was not at his most convincing before this group," writes Rodney Minott.* "He was humble to the point of irresolution; what he sought from them was confirmation and motivation." Butler remembers the evening as sort of a companionable prelude to the actual campaign. "We all got loaded and it was a very interesting

* A year later, when the finance directorship proved the weak point of the Reagan administration, the conservatives raised little objection to Weinberger. The governor appointed him, and Weinberger served capably until President Nixon named him chairman of the Federal Trade Commission. Subsequently, Nixon appointed Weinberger deputy budget director.

* From *The Sinking of the Lollipop* (Diablo Press, 1968), by Rodney G. Minott. Quoted by permission. All quotations attributed to Prof. Minott in chapters 6 and 7 are from his account of the campaign, unless otherwise identified.

evening," he says. "Everybody told off McCloskey, and he said: 'Any one of you guys would probably make a better candidate than I would.' We all said: 'Listen, that's probably true, but *you* don't believe it.' It was a very funny evening, and the next morning Schreck called me and said: 'Okay, Albie [Wells] and I are each chipping in five thousand, so that's ten thousand. You got to chip in one thousand bucks.' "

Schreck and McCloskey had talked together after the dinner and Schreck had been direct and critical about McCloskey's appearance. "Pete did not come on strong, and I told him that he did not come on strong," Schreck recalls. But McCloskey, either that night or the next day, must have reached an irrevocable decision to run. Two days later he was in San Francisco with Butler and Schreck, and the three of them stopped together to buy a bottle of wine for the birthday celebration of Len Kingsley, a business partner. McCloskey, as both Butler and Schreck remember it, kept saying that he had to call Weinberger. He did, and received an answer that Weinberger believed was noncommittal and that McCloskey interpreted as a decision to run. The three friends went from the wine store to an Irish whiskey bar on Sansome Street. "What the hell are we going to do?" says Butler. "First off, Pete had incurred ten thousand dollars in obligations and had the office and a campaign manager. So we sat in this bar and talked about it. We had a drink, and then we had another drink, and Schreck said to me: 'Lew, I gotta have a check for a thousand from you, 'cause we're not going to be able to pay the bills unless we collect these pledges, and you gotta come through.' I said: 'Are you kidding?' He said: 'Nope.' So after two drinks I wrote him a check for one thousand dollars. I hand him this check, and we have another round of drinks, and I said to Schreck: 'We're trying to launch the Planning and Conservation League; you'd better be a patron member. It'll cost you a hundred bucks.' So I collected a hundred bucks from him for my thousand. About that time, I don't know who said it, but we all agreed: 'Screw Cap Weinberger.' Seems to me that probably McCloskey agreed to that, and we agreed with him. After an hour and a half in this bar, it was clearly decided that Pete was going to run; and Cap Weinberger, if he was going to run—that was his business. Pete didn't have to honor that pledge. And that was that."

It had been a long time in coming. McCloskey had sought a public role in half-a-hundred minor ways ever since the Marines and Hill 566 and the Chinese who mysteriously ran away from the other hill on which he thought he was going to die. He had been unable to become a Marine again, and he had instead become a kind of citizen-soldier driven by a need for public action. He had become a politician now, and he would become a good one. Like most of the good ones in California, he would disdain politics all the way to the polls.

7. *Shirley and Pete*

San Mateo County, the once-green enclave where Pete McCloskey came to public office, occupies the northern and greater part of a peninsula that has San Francisco as its tip and San Jose as its base. Bisected by an offshoot of the Coast range and flanked on either side by the Pacific Ocean and by San Francisco Bay, it is a county blessed with a rich variety of terrain and vegetation and with a marvelous year-round climate. As late as the forties, San Franciscans used to go for a country drive down the deep peninsula to Redwood City ("climate best by government test") or to Stanford or San Jose. But the surging tides of population and unplanned growth overran the county after World War II. By 1968, in a book written during the McCloskey campaign, conservationist William Bronson could accurately declare: "San Mateo County, all of it really lovely country, has been half-wrecked by the developers, some of whom are thundering ahead to wreck the other half."* The McCloskeys lived in the unwrecked half, in the cradle of the Skyline ridge, but the edges of suburban blight crept in a steady offensive toward the hills. That blight most severely afflicted the long narrow sweep of land compressed between the bay on the west and El Camino Real, the king's highway, on the east. As Minott describes it: "While some attractive neighborhoods had been dropped into sections bordering the lower bay, it was for the

* From *How to Kill a Golden State*, by William Bronson (Doubleday & Company, 1968).

most part a thirty-mile-long swath of filled-in baylands, light industrial parks, a rail line, two major highways, a massive yet still overcrowded international airport, a county dump, a bay port, one of whose exports was napalm, and, in the north, a huge garbage dump serving the needs of San Francisco. Also in this north-south channel were masses of seedy ill-built low-cost housing units, rapidy deteriorating into suburban slums."

Pete McCloskey became a candidate for the House of Representatives almost at the precise time when substantial numbers of San Mateo County citizens were mobilizing to preserve what was left of their bay and their foothills. He was both an effect and a cause of this change, and many who were attracted to his candidacy had known him first in the Woodside fight or in some other conservationist endeavor. The conservationists, flexing their still undeveloped muscles in half-a-hundred small fights during the fifties and the sixties, were the spiritual descendants of the Progressives who had united against the tyranny and corruption of the railroad. But the forces they now fought were more durable, numerous, and malevolent than the "friendly Southern Pacific." Throughout most of the postwar period the developers held the upper hand in San Mateo County, where the governments were corrupt at worst and lackluster at best and where jurisdiction was fragmented among scores of cities, school districts, special-purpose agencies, and a usually complaisant county government.

McCloskey was a different kind of candidate than most of those who had come before him in San Mateo County, and his election campaign was different from the first. The most important difference, as it turned out, was a special election law that invited the kind of "nonpartisan" candidacy beloved by the Progressives. The law, like many others in California, had not been intended that way. Rather, it was a belated attempt by the Democrats to complete the partisan transformation that they had largely accomplished in 1959 by repealing the cross-filing law. The repeal left untouched a special election procedure allowing the candidate with the most votes to win regardless of whether or not he obtained a majority. The Republicans, on the way back to power in early 1960, and usually better disciplined than the Democrats, took advantage of several special election opportunities and won plurality elections in which a single Republican opposed several Democratic nominees. The Democrats in 1963 responded to this challenge by setting up a free-for-all special election "primary" with provisions for a runoff between the leading vote getters of each party unless one candidate received a majority of the vote. The new law restored the substance of cross-filing without retaining its form. Since voters, without changing their registration, could freely cross over in a "primary" election that followed general-election rules, they were in effect encouraged to participate in the other party's primary. Democrats in San Mateo County were particularly tempted to vote for the least objectionable Republican, since a Republican was almost certain to win the runoff election in any case. Only once in its history had San Mateo County sent a Democrat to Congress.

The differences between a normal Republican primary and a special election in which Democrats could help choose the Republican nominee were not immediately apparent to supporters of the woman who would become Pete McCloskey's major opponent. Conventional political wisdom in California during 1967 held that celebrities were virtually unbeatable, and Shirley Temple Black, whatever else she was, certainly was an established celebrity. The news accounts invariably compared her candidacy to those of former dancing partner George Murphy, elected to the U.S. Senate in 1964, and to ex-actor Ronald Reagan, elected governor of California in 1966. Mrs. Black was a member of the committee that had supported Reagan, and she was never reluctant to advertise their friendship. While Reagan and Murphy declined to breach party etiquette and openly support her against other Republicans, it was widely believed that they tacitly favored her candidacy. Murphy, visiting the state capitol in Sacramento during July, went a little beyond this tacit backing by declaring that Mrs. Black would "probably be a very popular candidate." But Shirley, petite and matronly and unsure of herself before any but the most friendly audiences, was not ready for a rough-and-tumble primary, particularly one in which Democrats could vote against her. Nor was her celebrity status of any real value in the kind of campaign that she faced. If analogies remain comparisons in which essential similarities outweigh essential differences, the analogy between the Shirley Temple Black candidacy and the Murphy-Reagan candidacies is, in fact, deficient in almost every respect. The first dissimilarity was the special election itself, an election in which the vote would become fragmented among a dozen candidates. Then, too, Shirley Temple Black was a woman in a state never particularly congenial to female candidacies. Despite her plea to become the only female member of California's congressional delegation ("One congress*woman* among thirty-eight congress*men* is *not* unfair, fellows"), there were many women supporters of Murphy and Reagan who were not about to vote for Shirley Temple Black. Mrs. Black was also far less prepared for the exigencies of political infighting than Murphy, who had been toiling in the Republican vineyards for years before his election, or than Reagan, a veteran of Hollywood union battles and an accomplished stump speaker. Most importantly, the celebrity-recognition factor that had worked for Murphy and for Reagan worked against Shirley Temple Black. Murphy and Reagan, candidates, looked exactly like Murphy and Reagan, actors, but Shirley Temple Black no longer looked anything like the dimpled little girl who had captured America's fancy in the Depression. When voters saw and heard Murphy (in 1964, not 1970) and Reagan, they recognized familiar and fundamentally reassuring personalities and listened to what they had to say. When they saw Shirley, if they were middle-aged, they were reminded of their own mortality and made inevitable inward comparisons between the golden-haired girl they had known on the screen and the dark-haired, somewhat nervous lady who was before them. Somehow, it seemed cruel even to allow her in the race, and the cruelty was not the less because of its self-affliction. Despite a distinguished record of social service in a myriad of health and charitable organizations and in the Junior League, she was a bad candidate from beginning to end.

The advantages of campaigning against Shirley Temple Black were not lost on McCloskey and his friends. Particularly, they were not lost on Sanford (Sandy) Weiner, an owlish-looking political professional who had helped engineer Murphy's victory over Democrat Pierre Salinger in 1964 and who had solicited and received a job with McCloskey in 1967. After Mrs. Black's announcement of candidacy late in August, Weiner commissioned a poll which showed her with a name-recognition factor of 76 percent, compared to 25 percent for County Sheriff Earl Whitmore, the second-best-known candidate. McCloskey had a 19-percent recognition factor. But the poll also showed that only 16 percent of the electorate intended to vote for Mrs. Black, a dramatic statistical confirmation of the gulf between her candidacy and the candidacies of Murphy and Reagan.* "The campaign represented a chance to win as soon as (a) the impact that it was a special election became clear and (b) the first poll indicated what it did," recalls Ryland Kelley, the lanky real-estate developer and artist who chaired McCloskey's executive committee. "Mrs. Black had all this recognition, and nobody was going to vote for her. And therefore, there was an opportunity for somebody. Looking over the rest of the guys, it was easy to see that Pete was the only probable alternative."

The probable alternative, though he sometimes seemed indecisive and misdirected to his friends, family, and newspaper editors, had long before the poll behaved as if he were operating on its premises. Among McCloskey's best moves were the hiring

* Eight percent of the voters indicated at this point that they would vote for McCloskey, a far more favorable percentage than Mrs. Black's, considering the differences in recognition.

of Weiner and his consultation, at the suggestion of Chuck Daly, with Representative Thomas Ludlow Ashley, a Democratic congressman from Toledo, Ohio, who had developed an effective precinct organization in a sometimes difficult district. Ashley, who could read polls and thought from the first that McCloskey would defeat Mrs. Black, gave some good technical advice on precinct organization and argued with McCloskey about the war, which Ashley, a former assistant director of Radio Free Europe, supported. The two men met during the summer at Daly's beach home on Monterey Bay, and Ashley was immediately taken with his prospective colleague. "Pete has enormous charm as a man to a man," Ashley observes. "He is direct without being abrasive, he's kind without being soft-headed, he's quite firm without being arrogant. These are qualities that most of us like in another man."

There is no endeavor, including war, where defeat is as much an orphan or where victory has more fathers than in a political campaign. The claims of parenthood are even more multiple than usual in Pete McCloskey's 1967 campaign, a rousing success in its middle and final stages. All campaigns start with the candidate, however, and Pete McCloskey was a superb candidate. He was direct and communicative, on television and in person, with a physical intensity and sense of purpose that attracted women and appealed to men. His wire-brush Marine haircut, his Stanford education, his war-hero background, and his clipped speech were all ideally suited to the well-educated suburban constituency he sought to represent. Perhaps most importantly, he inspired others to work for him and with him, thus ensuring the essential ingredients of political success. And he was blessed, going into the campaign and coming out of it, with friends whose affection for him prevented them from telling McCloskey what they thought he wanted to hear. "I have the best friends in the world," McCloskey says. "They all think the world of me, but none of them are afraid to tell me when they think I'm full of crap." Lennihan and Kelley and Butler and Schreck and the others on the tight-knit, largely amateur executive committee that gathered around him often had reasons to think that the candidate was full of something other than wisdom in the first months of the 1967 campaign. Sometimes they were right, sometimes not. But the give-and-take of early-morning meetings where they worked over McCloskey and each other was a valuable learning experience for all of them. It was the amateur component of a professional-amateur mix that has featured the best campaigns in California ever since Hiram Johnson campaigned against the railroad from the back seat of the then new-fangled automobile.

The professional side of the campaign was provided largely by Weiner, a Southern Californian who had shared ups and downs with various candidates but who had performed well for Senator George Murphy and was considered by many of his fellow professionals as a sound, sometimes brilliant idea man. "I think any good campaign that wins against odds has to be a blend and mesh of a whole bunch of things," says Weiner. "I was proud of the campaign from a professional point of view. But without the type of volunteer involvement that Pete had, it never would have made it. From the very beginning Pete attracted dedicated people that were willing to work all day and work all night because they believed in him. Their zealousness brought in a whole bunch of other people. At the same time a whole bunch of other people were brought in by early television and an otherwise strong use of media. In other words, it was a real meshing of everything that you set down on paper as an ideal campaign. The money came in. The volunteers came in. The other candidates performed, in my professional opinion, badly. Shirley's was a bad campaign professionally. Had it been a good campaign professionally, who knows what the result would have been? But you go on the facts that were there. The maze of candidates in the race, all spinning around rather recklessly, helped. I think it was one of the first campaigns in

California where you found dedicated Democrats working for a Republican that they could believe in. And we had moderate Republicans openly fighting the Republican establishment and not caring. I think this all blended into it."

Other things also blended in. A precinct organization that ultimately turned in one of the better California campaign efforts in recent elections was established, largely due to the efforts of Ted Carlstrom, Lee Langan, and Cubby McCloskey. Minott, subsequently the author of the campaign biography, prepared a voter-identification program that helped in concentrating the McCloskey forces on priority precincts. Butler and Bob Thede, another lawyer from Stanford, ran an efficient get-out-the-vote campaign. Geraldine Browning scheduled three hundred coffee appearances. McCloskey's intuitive news sense and the efforts of press secretary George Murphy, a plain-spoken San Francisco reporter whose talents and temperament were ideally suited to the candidate, kept McCloskey constantly in the news. And McCloskey made expert use of television. At Weiner's initiative the candidate had early in the going invited Shirley to a television debate paid for by the McCloskey campaign. She refused and in her reply said that McCloskey should use the time to explain his own positions. McCloskey did just that on a half-hour show preceded by drinks and lunch for the reporters at a Jack London Square restaurant in Oakland. Murphy knew that McCloskey was at his best under tough questioning. "I told them that if you guys ask easy questions I'm never going to buy lunch again," said Murphy. The reporters, none of whom were noted for asking easy questions with or without lunch, more than complied with the request. McCloskey was at his best. Money poured into the McCloskey headquarters in response to a solicitation approach at the end of the program, and the McCloskey campaign paid for a reshowing of the entire half-hour.*

* At least one of the reporters was distinctly unpleased by the subsequent use of the program as a McCloskey commercial. DeVan Shumway, then United Press International bureau chief in Sacramento and one of the state's

The other element in the successful blend cited by Weiner, perhaps the most important element, was the performance of the women. "The gals were fabulous," says Cubby McCloskey. "They're the ones who made it work. It was the thirty-five-year-old housewives who gave their life, blood, sweat, and tears." Cubby particularly credits Winky Lennihan, who headed the volunteer organization effort, and Fran Sherwood, who performed the difficult feat of scheduling the usually unpunctual candidate. While Pete McCloskey has always attracted women, it is worth observing that these ladies and dozens of others initially participated in the campaign because they knew Cubby socially and as a friend. Cubby herself played an important role in the campaign organization, as did two other McCloskeys, the candidate's sister, Ginna Hartzell, and his mother, Vera, who at seventy-eight is an effective and indefatigable precinct worker. "I've got all these old folks who can't get out, and they vote," she said after the 1970 campaign. "I say, 'I'm Mrs. McCloskey, your congressman's mother,' and they just eat that up, you know."

But the most important woman to Pete McCloskey in 1967 turned out to be neither wife nor mother, but his campaign opponent, Shirley Temple Black. Without Shirley no one outside of California would have noticed the campaign in the first place, but her services to McCloskey did not end there. Despite all her social work, Mrs. Black was still an essentially sheltered person with an almost total ignorance of partisan politics. Friends found her warm and charming, but a some-

---

best-known political writers, says he agreed to participate in the belief it was "a local television show." Shumway, now an assistant communications director for President Nixon, agrees that the program was a boost for the McCloskey campaign, but adds: "I just argue with the idea of doing that to a newspaperman. It put us in the position of being flacks for McCloskey, and unpaid flacks at that." Murphy says the newsmen were informed that the original program was paid for by McCloskey. There was no intention to rerun it at the time, he says, and the decision was made solely on the basis of the public response to McCloskey's performance.

times peremptory manner made her appear aloof and stand-offish to some women who had met her in Junior League. She had attracted press attention the year before the campaign by walking out on a San Francisco film festival that refused to ban the Swedish movie *Night Games.* While this earned her plaudits from some, it had also gained her the scorn and contempt of wealthy peninsula sophisticates who feared censorship more than sex. And then, also, Mrs. Black was a wealthy, very wealthy, woman conscious of her own material status. These qualities and circumstances combined in an almost chemical way to make working against Shirley the "in" thing for hundreds of women. Winky Lennihan put it best, in a comment that also reflects on the women's role in the McCloskey campaign: "The women did a phenomenal job. Starting on Thursday night before the election, we put out twenty thousand pieces of mail, all by hand. There were five processes for one mailing—signing, folding, stuffing, sealing, and stamping—and we always ran out of stamps, and we worked hard, and it was fun. Shirley was a beautiful candidate. She was beautiful to run against."

Sometimes it even seemed that Shirley was running against herself. In over her head from the beginning, and reading constantly that she was "supposed" to win a race in which she slipped steadily behind, she overreacted and said the wrong things. At one point she claimed the posthumous endorsement of Congressman Younger, a comment that offended his widow. (Norma Younger ultimately endorsed William Draper, an attractive moderate-conservative who conceivably might have beaten McCloskey in an orthodox two-way Republican primary.) Shirley also claimed the endorsement of former President Dwight Eisenhower, a move that backfired when the McCloskey staff obtained a disclaimer from Eisenhower's aide. Most importantly, Shirley consistently refused to debate, a position that McCloskey, with plenty of help from other candidates, successfully represented to voters as a sign of her weakness on issues. She *was* weak on issues, at least to the extent that she was unable to discuss them under verbal crossfire, and a supporter of Mrs. Black in that campaign is probably right when he says that "we were damned if we did and damned if we didn't on debates." Most of all, Shirley was damaged by the mistaken notion of her husband, millionaire businessman Charles Black, that he possessed the knowledge to run a political campaign. Black, who should have known enough to hire professionals from the start, went so far as to write a nasty letter to the boss of a woman wire-service reporter who attended a reception by invitation and started asking questions. By the time the Blacks and the San Mateo County Republican establishment turned to the veteran campaign management firm of Whittaker and Baxter, it was far too late.

The time, however, was right for Pete McCloskey, in part because of his attractiveness as war hero and conservationist, in part because his quality of "differentness" helped set him apart from the four other Republicans and seven Democrats in the race. He had already set himself apart from the county's cautious Republican establishment with typically McCloskey displays of independence that had little to do with ideological continuity. McCloskey entered Republican politics as a largely unformed conservative but his standards of support in the early and mid-sixties were entirely personal. He had backed conservative Republican Judge Tom Coakley for attorney general in 1962, largely because of McCloskey's respect for his brother, Frank Coakley, who had been his former boss, as Alameda County's District Attorney. In 1964 he had enraged establishment Republicans by contributing $300 to Democratic senatorial candidate Pierre Salinger and putting a Salinger bumper sticker on his car, but this action reflected more his friendship for Kennedy aide Chuck Daly than any espousal of liberal Democratic ideals. The same year that McCloskey supported Salinger he also backed Republican presidential nominee Barry Goldwater (thoughtful San Mateo County GOP activist Mike Deaver, now on Governor Reagan's staff, remembers that "the ladies went ga-ga for Pete" when he spoke to a group of Republican women on Goldwater's behalf), and the only thread common to the Coakley, Salinger, and Goldwater campaigns was that all of McCloskey's candidates lost. That, too, was part of McCloskey's differentness, because he has never been afraid to lose. He displayed this quality, as we have already seen, with his opposition to Proposition 14, the anti-fair-housing initiative. And though here, too, he lost at the ballot box, the cause for which he fought was won.

McCloskey's willingness to fight a housing initiative that seemed certain of passage had set him apart in 1964.* It was the war that set him apart in 1967, as in another way it sets him apart now. Shirley Temple Black, like many conservative Republicans at the time, was both a defender and a critic of the war, i.e., she supported United States involvement in the defense of South Vietnam while criticizing President Johnson and Secretary of Defense McNamara for purportedly tying the hands of the Joint Chiefs of Staff. McCloskey jumped on this statement ("It demonstrates a basic ignorance of a fundamental principle of civilian control of the military," he said a day after Shirley's entrance into the race August 29), but her position, except in depth of understanding, was in many respects indistinguishable from the views long held by McCloskey on the war. He was, after all, a Marine, and he had sought, unsuccessfully, both a military and a civilian role in the Vietnam conflict. The war had been on his mind ever since his friend had returned from it without a leg. But the emotion of "Win the War" is close to the emotion of "Withdraw," and McCloskey was gradually responding to the prodding of his antiwar brother-in-law Charles McClung. McClung, probably more responsible than any other person for McCloskey's shift from support of the war

* He set himself apart in the two following years, also, through participation in the California Republican League, a short-lived liberal Republican group that backed George Christopher for the gubernatorial nomination against Ronald Reagan in 1966 and soon thereafter disappeared from view.

to opposition, had questioned the legal precedents for U.S. involvement at a May 9, 1966, breakfast speech in Los Angeles, and his opposition had steadily deepened from that date. When McCloskey finally emerged as the Republican "peace candidate" on September 12, 1967, his arguments about the legality of U.S. involvement strongly resembled those made by McClung sixteen months before.

It is not, however, that simple. There was a strong pragmatic component to McCloskey's decision, and though it is often overlooked, there was also a military consideration that perhaps more than anything else led McCloskey to doubt the war in the first place. "I was skeptical of the terrain and the possibilities of winning the war," recalls McCloskey. "I had read [North Vietnamese General Vo Nguyen] Giap's book and believed that time and the terrain favored the North Vietnamese." McCloskey also knew that the war would be an issue in the campaign. This was guaranteed not by Shirley Temple Black but by the early presence in the race of *Ramparts* publisher Ed Keating, a superdove and an unsuccessful candidate for the Democratic congressional nomination in 1966, who had waged a suprisingly strong campaign on the war issue. Keating had little chance of winning in 1967, but he forced every candidate to discuss the war, a role that bears some resemblance to McCloskey's own position in the Republican party today. The importance of the war issue, as McCloskey remembers it, became apparent in early summer when he stopped for a beer at the Rat's Nest, a Stanford area bar, with Barbara (Barrie) Ramsay, the youngest daughter of a prominent Republican family. McCloskey wanted Barrie, now a Stanford law school student, to work for him, and she wanted to know his position on the war. "She was the first person to raise it with me, and I voiced some grave reservations but said I'd have to support the commander-in-chief," says McCloskey. "I'm not going to work for anybody who feels that way," Barrie replied coolly.

Conversations like this one made their mark on McCloskey.

So, too, did his hours of researching legal precedents in the Stanford law library and his growing belief that the United States was militarily trapped in Vietnam. Minott credits three persons—McClung, Stanford professor Carl B. Spaeth, and international law expert Herman Phleger—with playing a key role in McCloskey's transformation into an antiwar candidate, but makes a perceptive point in a parenthesis. During his research for *The Sinking of the Lollipop,* writes Minott, twelve people took credit for having done more to change McCloskey's mind on the war than anyone else. The same point could be made about a dozen other McCloskey actions, illustrating both the fundamental impenetrability of the man and his natural skill as a politician.

Perhaps McCloskey, confronted with questions both of principle and of pragmatism, simply saw, though it was not generally recognized at the time, that support for the war was slowly but steadily declining.* This changing atmosphere was sensed by McCloskey's executive committee, though many of its members didn't know what to do about it. "I had a nervous feeling about Pete becoming that identified in the [campaign] situation," says Ryland Kelley. "But it became clear after a while that identification made a hell of a lot of sense in providing him with a field to himself, or an issue to himself, among the other dozen candidates." Nonetheless, Kelley believes that the political component was the lesser part of McCloskey's decision. "It was a combination of things," he says. "Spaeth really worked hard to force that decision on him. And Charley McClung was ahead of the rest of us. Pete has great respect for his opinion."

One of the distinguishing qualities of McCloskey as a candidate is his willingness to share his reasoning as well as his posi-

* The trend of opposition to the war and a fascinating parallel between popular attitudes during two conflicts is examined in "Trends in Popular Support for the Wars in Korea and Vietnam" in the June 1971 issue of the *American Political Science Review*. The author is John E. Mueller of the University of Rochester.

tions with the voters. In two legal-size pages that Sandy Weiner called "the longest document ever issued in a political campaign," McCloskey on September 12 concluded that the United States was losing the political battle in Vietnam. The primary bar to successful negotiation of peace, he said, was American mistrust about Hanoi's motives, and he quoted from a North Vietnamese newspaper's contention that the United States intended to permanently maintain that country's division. "I am forced to agree that Hanoi has every right to conclude that the U.S.'s policy is to perpetuate South Vietnam as an independent nation government and that our negotiating posture thus far has been merely a means to achieve our end," McCloskey declared. "This, of course, flatly contradicts our announced position that the Geneva Accords of 1954 should be used as a basis for peace." Ho Chi Minh, argued McCloskey, in a statement then rare for Republican candidates anywhere, would have been overwhelmingly elected if we had stayed out of Vietnam, and would have "unified" the country without U.S. involvement in 1965. He contrasted Vietnam to Lebanon, where U.S. Marines put down an insurrection at the request of an "established government" and he went on, earlier than most Americans, to make a fundamental judgment on the U.S. involvement:

> The bitter lesson of Vietnam is that we appear to have made two serious miscalculations: first in the expectancy that the Saigon government, given our aid, would ultimately win the loyalty of a substantial majority of its people, and second, that those Vietnamese opposed to the Saigon government . . . would be unequal to the task of successfully opposing our massive military assistance. We underestimated what now appears to be a deep desire for independence rather than merely an attempt to expand communism in Southeast Asia.

McCloskey concluded his sometimes turgid, sometimes incisive brief against the war with a six-point program that called for negotiations with Hanoi on a "new basis" that agreed to reunification of the country. He urged a planned military de-escalation and termination of the U.S. commitment "as soon as possible." But he also said that the United States could not "precipitously withdraw," and he warned that if the administration refused to genuinely negotiate he would argue in the Congress for a gradual disengagement over a two-year period. When the time came, McCloskey proved as good as his word.

The antiwar declaration drew more volunteers and money into the campaign, particularly after McCloskey's successful exposition of his stand on television with the four reporters. Shirley Temple Black responded to the television program by declaring that McCloskey's position would lead to the abandonment of South Vietnam and the "butchery" of a million and a half people. "He has shifted position only to play upon the genuine fears and concerns of all American men, women, and children who truly want peace," her press release stated. She also compared McCloskey to Keating, who had agreed with McCloskey on the substance of the document but with Shirley about its political motivation. The McCloskey camp had long since stopped caring what Keating thought; their target was Shirley, and she remained obliging until election day.

Despite the shrillness and general ineptitude of Mrs. Black's press release, the McCloskey campaigners were sensitive about the notion that their man would abandon anyone to a "bloodbath," and they took pains in the campaign brochure—"McCLOSKEY is the man for CONGRESS; compare him with all others"—to advocate "refuge and sanctuary to those South Vietnamese who have relied on us. . . ." The brochure, possibly subject to professional criticism for its wordiness, was in every other respect a work of art. It reprinted McCloskey's six-point proposal from September 12, adding the provision for refuge and sanctuary and another point supporting a "firm military presence against Communist aggression in Southeast Asia when a country with a stable government and the loyalty of its people requests our aid." Thailand was given as the example of such a country. The brochure also contained seven McCloskey pictures, one of them of McCloskey receiving the Silver Star and another of his attractive family, and the complete citation that accompanied both his Korean decorations. The brochure's theme was that McCloskey was a highly decorated war hero who "knows both sides of war" and would fight for peace as a congressman. Better than any analysis of the often dreary campaign exchanges, the brochure demonstrates McCloskey's preoccupation with the war as his issue. The other issues mentioned, listed single column under the heading "a man with positive ideas" are: reduction of property taxes, involvement of private enterprise in welfare and employment, honesty in government, respect for the law, removal of discrimination in public places (California has had such a law for decades), support of the armed forces, conservation, and fiscal responsibility. There was also a provision on big government in which McCloskey declared, with Jefferson and Ronald Reagan: "The least government is the best government. Local dependence on federal handouts and regulations should be reduced whenever possible."

Did the election turn on the issue of the war? McCloskey retained some conservative support throughout the campaign, notably law associate Roger Mosher ("I'm the hawkiest of the hawks"), who has since broken with McCloskey for what he considers intemperate statements about "war crimes" and Laotian refugees. Some of McCloskey's support undoubtedly came then, as it does now, from people who admire his willingness to speak out on the issues even when they disagree with him. A Stanford Business School survey conducted after the campaign found that every respondent listed the war as the number-one issue, even though some 6 percent supported McCloskey while differing with him on Vietnam.

But the election did not depend upon that 6 percent. McCloskey received 52,882 votes, slightly more than one out of every three that were cast in the election. Shirley Temple Black, a distant second, polled 34,521 votes, and two other Republicans

–Draper and Whitmore–received more votes than Roy Archibald, the leading Democrat. Though Democrats outnumber registered Republicans in San Mateo County, the five Republican candidates received a total of 120,000 votes contrasted to 33,000 for the seven Democrats. An even more significant indication of the Democratic crossover–and the peace vote that surely went to McCloskey–is the paltry 8,800 votes received by Keating, who had polled 30,500 votes the year before in a primary election in which the Democratic turnout was less than half the total 1967 special-election vote. It is probably not going too far to say that Pete McCloskey's outspoken opposition to the war won the election for him, though the result might very well have been different in a closed Republican primary.

Any statement about an issue winning for a candidate presumes a professional campaign and enough money for a candidate to become recognized and make his views known. The McCloskey campaign was well financed from the first, thanks largely to the efforts of Al Schreck, who put in the first $5,000 and raised $40,000 single-handedly during the summer months. Schreck brought other wealthy businessmen into the financing committee as the budget grew to $100,000, then to $150,000. He is a scrupulous fund raiser, who raises money for Williams College and some favorite charities, and he gives of his own wealth to other causes. The McCloskey campaign was remarkably broad-based, drawing upon 1,967 contributors, of whom thirty-eight gave $1,000 or more. McCloskey raised and spent $150,961, compared to Shirley Temple Black's $98,148. Draper spent $79,645, even though he received only 19,566 votes. The reported totals for all candidates in the November 14 primary were $531,368. And McCloskey and Archibald, this time able to draw somewhat upon the resources of their political parties, started all over again the day after the election in behalf of their December 12 election campaign. McCloskey beat Archibald 66,000 votes to 44,000 in that runoff, considered an anticlimax by everyone. The final spending report submitted to the secretary of state showed that McCloskey's friends had in the two elections raised $197,704 to send him to Congress.

The Republican establishment in San Mateo County, unreconciled to McCloskey in the hour of his victory, continued to speculate on the sources of this money. Stanley Hiller, campaign manager for Mrs. Black, suggested that it was "Kennedy money," a contention that has been repeated many times since. In interviewing for this book, the "Kennedy-money" accusation frequently was made to me casually by anti-McCloskeyites as if it were a known truth. But nothing in the campaign record suggests that even a dime of Kennedy money came into the campaign, and McCloskey and all of his closest friends deny the charge.

McCloskey enjoyed the national publicity that came his way after the defeat of Shirley Temple Black, and he may also have enjoyed the after-the-fact talk about the Kennedy money. Soon after the second session of the 90th Congress convened, McCloskey sent Senator Robert F. Kennedy a one-line letter that said: "All right—where's the money?"

And Kennedy answered him:

> Dear Congressman McCloskey:
>
> Are you trying to tell me now that you didn't receive the money? You certainly didn't act that way when we met those few times in the hotel lobby.
>
> I remember you—a short, fat, swarthy-complexioned man with your goatee dyed red. When I gave you the $20,000 in cash you handed me that little card which had Johnson's name crossed off and said, "Kennedy in '68."
>
> Go ahead and deny it to your friends, but you and I know differently. YOU have to face yourself in the mirror every morning.
>
> Sincerely,
> Robert F. Kennedy

He added a personal postscript that summed up the feelings of thousands of volunteers who had walked precincts, licked stamps, and given time and money to the man they regarded as a different kind of candidate. It said: "P.S. I'm glad you won."

Part Three
McCloskey Congressman

I flew over miles and miles of area where the hamlets and villages had been totally destroyed. I have real reservations that this policy is anything but a war crime. If you look back at Nuremberg and our policy in 1946, we insisted that it was a war crime to wantonly destroy villages.

—Representative Paul N. McCloskey, Jr.,
after a 1969 visit to South Vietnam

8. *Tail Twister*

Freshmen are supposed to be seen and not heard in the House of Representatives, a legislative body that in 1968 still operated on the Sam Rayburn principle of "to get along, go along." McCloskey did neither. The publicity that attended the defeat of Shirley Temple Black made McCloskey far better known at the outset of his term than the typical incoming congressman. Most of McCloskey's subsequent actions built upon that base to rescue him from the anonymity that is the customary fate of first-termers in the House.

He was not, in any case, temperamentally suited to anonymity or to a fifteen-year watch in some committee where men in their sixties wait for their seniors to die. "He was always a loner, always a tail twister," says old Stanford and Phi Delt buddy Jack Miller, and neither McCloskey's friends nor his enemies would argue on that score. The attention-getting cited by Lew Butler, the Goliath-battling remembered by John Rousselot, came immediately to the fore in the House. So, too, did McCloskey's boyish capacity for shocking others, a quality he demonstrated anew at a Republican unity meeting soon after the defeat of Shirley Temple Black. The unity meeting, a kind of Republican love-in arranged by then state GOP Chairman James Halley, was intended to heal the wounds of the bitter special-election primary and assure victory over Democratic nominee Roy Archibald. The controversy over a supposed "homosexual scandal" involving some high Reagan administration aides was then at its height, and McCloskey, with the directness that his friends are accustomed to, sauntered in and said to old friend Ned Hutchinson, the governor's appointments secretary: "I know you're not queer, Ned. We used to chase girls together." Hutchinson relates McCloskey's proclivity for the "shocking" remark to a tendency to take the distinctive position on any political issue. "If there were fifteen people in the room and fourteen of them got up and said yes, there's some little trigger in Pete—it's just a compulsion—that he has to get up and say no," Hutchinson believes. "And if those same fourteen people got up and said no, I think there's a little trigger that says he's got to get up and say yes. And how that manifests itself, I don't know, but I've always seen it, it's always there. To conform to anything is absolutely impossible for him."

McCloskey's first display of nonconformity in the House for once did not shock the conservative Republican establishment in San Mateo County. It was, instead, the Democratic doves who had crossed party lines to vote for him who were probably most disturbed with McCloskey's initial reaction to the North Korean seizure of the USS *Pueblo* on January 23, 1968. The United States, declared McCloskey, should consider a declaration of war against North Korea. McCloskey's stand, though qualified by a statement that Congress should declare war only if the President thought it would be helpful in recovering the *Pueblo*, stirred letters of disapproval and bewilderment, but the Korean War hero stuck to his guns. He explained his position and the reasons for it in a February 16 letter to constituents. "I felt then, as I feel now, that we best preserve the peace by drawing clear lines as to when we will fight," said McCloskey. "In the case of the *Pueblo*, I was and am firmly convinced that the North Koreans would never negotiate except under threat to use force if necessary to recover the ship and its crew." He emphasized in the letter that he continued to oppose the Johnson administration's Vietnamese policy and referred to the war as "a conflict that only the South Vietnamese can win." But the *Pueblo* was a different matter, and McCloskey set forth, in his usual lawyer's style, the seven points he felt were relevant to his position:

1. The North Koreans will never negotiate if they feel we are unwilling to use force to recover our men.
2. We cannot *abandon* the crew of the *Pueblo*. We ask our best young men to risk their lives to preserve our security; at the very least, they are entitled to our risking ours to restore their freedom.
3. *Wherever* the *Pueblo* was, the retention of its crew is unlawful under international law.
4. The United Nations is of little help to us as a mediator, since it was against the U.N. that the North Koreans fought in 1950–53; the United Nations still has a nominal command of the forces which defend the Korean boundary lines.
5. Therefore, we have only the threat of force to back our negotiating position.
6. We should not use force again without a declaration of war.
7. From this experience, it is clear that we need a world court and world law to govern future incidents of this kind. Only then will we be able to have maximum security against World War III.

It is impossible to assess the effects of this explanation upon voters in San Mateo County, but it mollified some key supporters who were wondering if their "peace candidate" had become a hawk in office. Actually, the case can be made that McCloskey, rather than the ritual hawks and doves, was making a sensible distinction between American response to an act of international piracy and continued American involvement in a war that could not be won. His response to the *Pueblo* seizure, if anything, gave his opposition to the war greater credibility, but some Republicans would use the issue to impugn McCloskey's stability and judgment once he began his challenge to President Nixon.

Like most Northern Californians, McCloskey did not find the adjustment easy in Washington. He had difficulties putting together the kind of cohesive, issues-oriented staff that he required, a staff that could come up with the "true facts" on any issue upon which McCloskey took a stand. His first administrative assistant was a woman, a very competent woman, but McCloskey found it difficult to delegate responsibility to her. He has always had difficulty in delegation, and it is harder for him to delegate to women than to men. McCloskey is also the victim of his own enthusiasm in hiring. He accepts people at face value, and offsets this virtue in staff selection by cavalierly hiring those who impress him—sometimes for a job that does not exist. At the outset of his first congressional campaign McCloskey wound up with four persons—Weiner, Janet Adams, Thomas Page, and James Benedict—"each of whom," writes Minott, "had some reason to think that he would be the campaign's manager or director." Mrs. Adams, a knowledgeable San Mateo County conservationist with Democratic allegiances, ultimately assisted Weiner, while Benedict directed the advertising campaign. Page, who subsequently worked for Senators Eugene McCarthy and Robert F. Kennedy, returned to Washington after McCloskey, in effect, bought up his contract for $4,750. After this mixup, McCloskey's outspoken friends rode herd on him and curbed his hiring proclivities during the balance of the campaign. But his friends were not with him in Washington, and his staff organization and direction floundered.

McCloskey, as much as any man in public life, is able to solve problems by calling on old friends. The man he called on now was Robin Schmidt, the old South Pas High classmate whom Winky Lennihan had called "the wildest" of the AFV bunch around McCloskey. Schmidt, in his early forties, seemed anything but wild. He had grown up into a softspoken and inordinately thoughtful San Diego advertising executive with a passion for surfboarding. He responded to McCloskey's call for help * by changing his registration from Democratic to

* Schmidt says he was recruited for the job by Jim Leeds, the former South Pasadena High School classmate who was the "founder" of the Amalgamated Federation of Virgins and later a McCloskey law partner.

Republican, selling his share of his advertising business to his partners, and moving to Washington. However, the news that McCloskey had hired another administrative assistant was greeted skeptically by the old friends who had formed the McCloskey executive committee. "We figured that Peter was just spinning around in orbit and had brought back an old crony to Washington," says one of them. "But Robin turned out to be the best person he ever hired." Schmidt, like Butler and Lennihan and Ry Kelley, cared too much for McCloskey to lie to him. And McCloskey, whose great virtue in staff relations is his ability to hear unpleasant truths about himself, trusted Schmidt and paid attention to his judgments. "The first agreement Pete and I got was that he would not hire anyone else himself," Schmidt recalls. It was an agreement that McCloskey kept more often than he violated, and that helped him advance from the turmoil of those early days and build a staff that is now one of the most information-oriented in the House. And the positivism that sometimes served McCloskey poorly in hiring came to be a source of inspiration to his staff members, many of whom were given a responsibility to do "their thing" and who responded to the opportunity. This was particularly true with the young lawyers whom McCloskey hired or with those who had previous experience in politics. Among these were David Brown, a thirty-two-year-old attorney in the Department of Justice's antitrust division who became his legislative aide, and David Niklaus, a former administrative aide to Senator Thomas Kuchel, who became McCloskey's district representative. "One of the really admirable things about the guy is that he can be creative and accomplish things, but he's the closest thing to a free spirit in a very practical world that I've ever known," Niklaus believes.

Moving was a wrench, also, for Cubby McCloskey. The McCloskeys first of all had to give up their lovely home in Portola Valley, a home that was largely of their own design.

They left Nancy behind to finish the school year and brought her back the next, but the move was difficult for a teen-ager, and she never came to really like her new high school in Langley, Virginia. The younger McCloskeys adjusted well, but slowly. The memories of Portola Valley led McCloskey in the early weeks of his presidential challenge to say that he "couldn't lose," and to add: "If you lose an election and have to come back to California, you're not hurt too much."

McCloskey almost lost an election seven months after he went to Washington, at the Republican primary in June 1968. He made no secret of the fact that he didn't take the primary seriously. The sole candidate against him was a wealthy land developer named Robert Barry, who had served three terms as a New York congressman and, after his defeat, had moved to Southern California. He ran in Riverside County against Representative (now Sentator) John V. Tunney and was convincingly beaten, then moved five hundred miles north into San Mateo County. "Rent-a-Congressman," his opponents called him. Barry was one of the dozen candidates on the ballot in the 1967 election in which McCloskey defeated Mrs. Black, but he withdrew before election day and endorsed Shirley. His name remained on the ballot, and he received 471 votes after spending $51,155 on the election.

Mrs. Black had toyed with the notion of running again—indeed, some of her backers expect to see her try again in one of these elections—but it was too much, too soon. On February 1, 1968, she announced she would not be a candidate in June, although she left the door open for a future race. "Our electorate has duly dispatched Mr. McCloskey to Washington," she said. "We should continue his trial for one full term, not one month." That left the door open for Barry, whom McCloskey simply didn't regard as a threat. Few Republican officials took Barry seriously, either, but he soon was turning up everywhere, passing out red-white-and-blue nail files and mailing out, as "San Mateo County Republican news," a weekly newsletter that took on McCloskey for party disloyalty and for his *Pueblo* and Vietnam stands. McCloskey did not reply, believing at the time that he would make the best impression by staying on the job in Washington rather than answering Barry's attacks. "We had some early polls showing Pete way up and Barry way down," recalls Bob Thede, the admiralty lawyer who had directed the successful election-day vote-turnout effort in the first McCloskey election. "We had spent all this money just a few months before and the consensus was that Barry was such a poor candidate we ought to ignore him. Obviously, it was very bad strategy, but at that time it didn't look that bad. I was now in charge of the precinct organization, and we felt that even though we weren't going to have much of a campaign, it was a good opportunity for us to strengthen that organization and to generate some new leadership and some talent and give people some experience. So we decided to do some precinct work anyway, primarily as an educational experience and as a trial run. That's what turned out to save us, but that wasn't through any foresight and intelligence on my part." The "educational" precinct work, coupled with some last-minute warnings from Al Schreck, combined to produce a semblance of campaigning in the final week that may indeed have saved McCloskey. He defeated Barry by the narrow margin of 35,660 to 31,602 votes.

The closeness of the race against an essentially poor candidate was a reminder of how dependent McCloskey had been on Democratic votes and Democratic volunteers. But the Democrats could not vote for him in a Republican primary, and the peace-oriented volunteers had been immersed in the California primary contest between Eugene McCarthy and Robert Kennedy. The election also taught McCloskey a valuable lesson that others have learned only in defeat, i.e., that in politics no opponent can be taken for granted. He spent only $9,730 against Barry, who reported expenses of $29,214. It was a mistake that McCloskey would not make again.

There was another side to the 1968 campaign that did not reflect creditably upon McCloskey. In his race against Shirley Temple Black he had denounced a "last-minute smear attempt" by Mrs. Black's campaign leaders for issuing a letter declaring that he would "consign more than 1.5 million of our South Vietnamese allies to the threat of execution—a slaughter unparalleled since the days of Nazi Germany." The charge was so wild that its effect, if anything, was probably to further damage Mrs. Black's already sinking candidacy rather than to hurt McCloskey. But it was McCloskey who panicked in the last days of the 1968 primary campaign. Stung by a drumfire of accusations from Barry, some of which misrepresented his voting record, and finally aware that he was in a real contest, McCloskey accused two of Barry's campaign workers—Mitchell Paige of Redwood City and H. Richard O'Hara of Hillsborough—with being "Birchers." The two men, so described because they headed a veterans' committee against McCloskey, promptly responded with a $400,000 slander suit, and McCloskey issued a formal retraction of the allegations in a statement that appeared in newspapers on election day. McCloskey insists that he was using the description "Bircher" as a generic term indicating an ultraconservative viewpoint rather than accusing anyone of membership in the John Birch Society. It is a poor defense, especially considering McCloskey's subsequent criticism of colleagues who misuse the terms "leftist" and "Communist," and the Barry campaign was in many ways the low-water mark of McCloskey's political career. The near-loss revived McCloskey's conservative opposition, who now realized that he might be defeated by a strong Republican candidate in the primary. But the appearance of McCloskey weakness after the Barry campaign proved as deceptive as the appearance of strength after his defeat of Shirley Temple Black. McCloskey would recover from the nadir of the Barry campaign to swamp his Democratic opponent in November and decisively regain the nomination in 1970. He was too good a soldier not to learn a lesson from near-defeat.

There were other lessons to learn at the Republican National Convention, where McCloskey supported New York Governor Nelson Rockefeller. That convention, with its usual assortment of strange bedfellows, for a time put McCloskey and supporters of California Governor Ronald Reagan on the same side in their abortive effort to stop Richard Nixon. "Right up until the vote I had the hope we could defeat him [Nixon] on the first ballot," McCloskey says. "But as I went around the convention I had a growing sense that if we had stopped Nixon the convention would have turned to Reagan, not Rockefeller. When Nixon was nominated, I kind of breathed a sigh of relief."

With both his own primary and the national convention behind him, McCloskey turned to his duties as a congressman. He was probably better adjusted to the House in the final six months of 1968 than he would ever be again, and a friend remembers that McCloskey was even "hopeful" that Nixon did have a plan for ending the war in Vietnam. In any event, McCloskey was determined to be a good congressman. He became absorbed in environmental issues and in campus unrest. He started a series of informal meetings with his constituents at shopping centers, railroad stations, and libraries, almost always drawing some new people. The House, which he had worked so hard to get to, seemed a good place to be.

He remained a loner, a man who made friends well and easily but at the same time kept to himself. He demanded independence for himself and from others, even from his family. "He believes in independence for his children, and he gives very little guidance other than example to his kids," says Cubby McCloskey. "He has absolute faith they're going to be able to handle themselves from the time they come out, which is a perfect joke. He just has this belief in kids, that they're going to make it. He fortunately has four wonderful kids, so maybe this hands-off philosophy is a good one. He can stamp down very hard, of course, when the spirit moves him, and it's usually about something he feels very strongly about. Sometimes he's arbitrary, sometimes he's not, but they all know him for a very human father. He's not up on any pedestal as far as they're concerned." He was at his best in crisis. If one side of his personality reached out for attention—"like a moth to the light," says David Lennihan—the other side did quite important things for people that nobody ever read about. He saved people from alcoholism, and a close friend from a mental breakdown. "Pete and Cubby just wouldn't let me go under," says the friend. Cubby thinks that her husband's ability to help people in emotional crisis relates to a certain detachment he possesses. "Peter does not get emotionally involved, so he's able to help," she says. "He's close but not close to people. His friendship is not on a personal level."

A different kind of crisis occurred August 11, 1968. The McCloskeys were visiting at the Atherton home of Rodney and Polly Minott soon after completion of the Minott book, *The Sinking of the Lollipop.* It was a pleasant California afternoon around the swimming pool, where the children were playing. Then Rodney Minott, Jr., eight years old, was spotted deep in the pool by his older sister, who screamed and brought him to the surface. "We knew he was gone with the horrible realization that parents have," said Minott. But he asked Pete McCloskey to give mouth-to-mouth resuscitation, then ran to call an ambulance. "I just sensed that if anyone there had a competence that way, it would be Pete," recalls Minott. "When I returned, the boy was breathing."

McCloskey returned to Washington in January 1969 after a general election in which he defeated his Democratic opponent, Urban G. Whittaker, Jr., 166,250 to 40,957. The election again demonstrated McCloskey's popularity with Democratic voters; Whittaker received 16,000 votes less in the primary than in the general election, despite a voting turnout that was three and one-half times the Democratic turnout in the primary. This time McCloskey ran a full-fledged campaign, spending $71,892 against an opponent who agreed with him on most issues. Many of the voters who supported McCloskey also cast their ballots for

Hubert Humphrey, who carried the congressional district by 5,000 votes.

Some of McCloskey's friends soon showed up in Washington with the new Nixon administration, among them McCloskey's former law partner Lew Butler. He came at the request of Bob Finch, who was then hiring staff for the Department of Health, Education and Welfare. Butler originally planned to stay only three or four weeks, but he helped convince Finch to hire State Assemblyman John G. Veneman, one of the most capable California legislators in either party, as his undersecretary, and Veneman in turn persuaded Butler to stay on as assistant secretary for program planning and evaluation. During this period Butler spent his weekends at the McCloskey home and played basketball with his former law partner at the Langley High School gym. Once, McCloskey happily showed up at HEW headquarters with a plastic bag bearing Butler's laundered socks and athletic supporter and proudly delivered it to his desk, along with an orange for Butler's lunch. He was the same McCloskey as always, and he never allowed his friends to forget it.

Partly because of Butler, partly because of his natural sympathy for the underdog and his strong opposition to racial prejudice, McCloskey was saddened by what he regarded as the foot-dragging of the Nixon administration on civil rights. On June 21 he signed and sent to the President a joint letter opposing any extension of the school-desegregation deadline, and he subsequently called for President Nixon to exert "moral leadership" on the race issue. He was caught up, too, in the ferment of campus unrest, and participated in a tour of troubled California campuses along with Representatives Donald Riegle of Michigan and Jerry Pettis of California. They were on the Berkeley campus of the University of California on May 20, 1969, the day students were gassed from helicopters in an action that Riegle calls "a radicalizing experience for both myself and McCloskey." Back in Washington, McCloskey was one of twenty-two Republican congressmen of varying ideological hues who sent a thirty-seven-page report to the President opposing "repressive" legislation and favoring a lower voting age, draft reform, and student participation in politics. McCloskey also became a member of a special population-control task force headed by Representative George Bush of Texas. The testimony of various experts before that commission deepened McCloskey's view that radical measures were necessary. "I have come to the conclusion that probably the major need is for a national abortion law," he told a meeting of Zero Population Growth in his own district. The law, he said, should permit abortions upon medical advice, and the cost should be borne by the public treasury. "A girl ought to have control of her own body," he said to me subsequently in an interview. "If an individual can't control her own body, she hasn't got freedom. And I don't think a girl ought to be penalized just because in a moment of human desire . . . she makes a mistake and a child is conceived. I think the girl ought to have the right to end the pregnancy. And from all I can see, the child in most cases of such a pregnancy ought to have a right to come into the world with both parents wanting him. I'd give every girl an abortion free if she wanted one. It doesn't look to me from the girls I've talked to that an abortion is such a pleasant and happy experience that people are going to go out and deliberately take chances because they know they can get abortions."

The issue that attracted McCloskey most, other than the war, was the one that had brought him into politics. He had conceived of himself as a conservationist congressman, and he plunged into work on two House subcommittees that dealt with environmental issues, one a part of the House Government Operations Committee and the other of the House Merchant Marine and Fisheries Committee. Government Operations is primarily a report-writing and investigative body. McCloskey wanted a place on its Conservation and Natural Resources Subcommittee, and he received one, thanks to Bob Dole of Kansas and House Republican leader Gerald Ford. "I was about to become involved in a

Senate race," says Dole, who was elected to the Senate and is now Republican national chairman. "Jerry says, 'You've got Agriculture and Government, and we've got a brand-new congressman with no committee.' I said, 'Fine, I'll give him Government Operations.' McCloskey's told me it meant a great deal to him, and he's thanked me for it many times." McCloskey became a valuable member of the subcommittee. Democrat Henry Reuss of Wisconsin, the chairman, considers McCloskey "a superb congressman" and adds: "He's hard-hitting, objective, and well informed, and he's primarily responsible for our report on San Francisco Bay, which is one of our better reports." But McCloskey also indulged his capacity for tail twisting by filing a minority view to that report that cited solid scientific evidence to challenge the California Department of Water Resources and, incidentally, Congressman Chet Holifield, the chairman of the Government Operations Committee and one of McCloskey's main targets in the Woodside power-line fight. Holifield takes the traditional view of Southern California legislators favoring a massive exportation of water from the northern to the southern portion of the state, and he wanted no critical comments about the California Water Project in the bay report. McCloskey's minority report, also signed by the two other Republican members of the subcommittee, cited a U.S. Geological Survey study to show that diverting waters from the Sacramento River southward as planned by the state and desired by Holifield will damage the water quality of San Francisco Bay. Once again, McCloskey was out in front on a difficult issue. The Ralph Nader task force on California land use, in a 1971 report, cited the severe environmental hazards and dubious economics of the once sacrosanct water plan and called for the scrapping of the entire project.

McCloskey also raised other environmental issues. In December 1969 he proposed, to a Yale University audience, a federal cabinet office or commission for pollution and waste disposal. The new agency, he said, would have the power to tax industries for the pollution or waste they produce, a penalty that would give businesses an incentive to reduce pollution. McCloskey also worked with Senator Gaylord Nelson of Wisconsin and Stanford student Denis Hayes in the preparations for Earth Day. In an appearance on the CBS News program "Face the Nation" on April 19, 1971, both Nelson and McCloskey denied that Earth Day was a "fad" that would divert attention from the Vietnam War. And McCloskey also used the program to make another pitch for birth control. When David Culhane of CBS News asked McCloskey how many children he had, the congressman replied: "I am public enemy number one. I think I am pretty typical. I have four children."

The range of McCloskey's environmental interests is demonstrated by a July 1, 1969, letter he sent to John Ehrlichman asking the White House to elevate environmental quality to the same national priority as national security, economic affairs, and urban affairs. The letter, signed "Yr. obdt. sevt. Paul N. McCloskey, Jr.", suggested eight points for the President's forthcoming environmental message, among them national programs on land use, water and wetlands conservation, and a clean-up of junk automobiles. He also proposed tax incentives and penalties for container disposal, more air-pollution research, and a national environmental-science laboratory.

As always, McCloskey was unpredictable. For a time he helped delay Federal Housing Administration financing of a large, fiscally troubled housing project built on filled land in San Francisco Bay by Leslie Salt Company, the largest bay landowner. McCloskey questioned the safety of the project in event of an earthquake, which some scientists believe poses a serious threat to the development, known as Redwood Shores. But McCloskey backed down after homeowners accused him of being responsible for the FHA loan freeze, and Redwood Shores was ultimately approved for financing.

Some conservationists had thought that McCloskey would see Redwood Shores through. On the other hand, no one expected him to challenge his own House Republican leadership in April 1970, at a time that McCloskey faced still another interparty challenge in the forthcoming GOP primary. The issue was the threatened impeachment of Justice William O. Douglas, and the intensity of McCloskey's reaction surprised even his wife. "As much as I've lived with him, as long as I've known him, I don't know that anyone will really capture what it is that makes him react," says Cubby. "Some things you think would make him react, he doesn't react to. Other things you think he would react normally to, he gets very unhappy about. I knew he felt strongly about the Douglas thing, but I had no idea that he was going to stay up all night writing the way he did. It was something that suddenly just touched him." Cubby believes that her husband perceived a real threat to the Constitution in the attempt of 104 conservative congressmen, led by Ford, to create a special committee to consider impeachment charges against Justice Douglas. Some colleagues remember that McCloskey was particularly annoyed by Ford's assertion that "an impeachable office is whatever a majority of the House of Representatives considers it to be at a given moment in history." Whatever it was that set him off, it was the Ford statement that served as a point of departure when McCloskey arose in the House on April 21, 1970, to deliver a ringing defense of judicial independence. To accept Ford's view, McCloskey began, "would do grave damage to one of the most treasured cornerstones of our liberties, the constitutional principle of an independent judiciary. . . ." After declaring that Congress should not challenge a sitting judge except for the clearest showing of misconduct McCloskey returned to the Ford definition of an impeachable offense:

> If this concept is accurate, then of course there are no limitations on what a political majority might determine to be less than good behavior. It follows that judges of the court could conceivably be removed whenever the majority of the House and two-thirds of the Senate agreed that a better judge might fill the position. But this

> concept has no basis, either in constitutional history or in actual case precedent.
>
> The intent of the framers of the Constitution was clearly to protect judges from political disagreement, rather than to simplify their ease of removal.

McCloskey then called for both judicial and legislative restraint, reviewed the legislative history of impeachment as an offense, and discussed the cases of the nine federal judges who have been impeached during the nation's history. Ten months before he suggested a "dialogue" on impeachment of President Nixon, McCloskey declared:

> There is considerable evidence in the adoption of the Constitution itself that the Founding Fathers considered impeachment as analogous to criminal proceedings. The first full draft of a constitution, presented by the Committee of Five on August 6, 1787, contained a specific clause: "The trial of all criminal offenses (except in cases of impeachment) shall be in the state where they shall be committed; and shall be by jury."

He then examined in detail the specific charges against Justice Douglas, demolishing them one by one. He laid particular emphasis on the many ideological references in the eighteen-page anti-Douglas resolution prepared by Ford and the 103 other congressmen. "Liberal" and "leftish" were used pejoratively at several points in the resolution, McCloskey pointed out, and asked: "If political philosophy is not a proper ground for impeachment, then why is there need to mention it at all in a discussion of alleged judicial misconduct which is limited to less than good behavior and excludes the question as to whether a man is conservative, moderate, or liberal?" Indeed, McCloskey said, the references reminded him of Marc Antony's refrain that "Brutus was an honorable man."

In his midnight composition in defense of judicial independence McCloskey could not resist his old tail-twisting impulse. One section of his rebuttal dealt with Ford's charge that Justice

Douglas "apparently" gave legal advice to the Albert Parvin Foundation and that Parvin had allegedly associated with gamblers, and his attorneys with mobsters. These allegations, McCloskey noted, involved third-party associations instead of associations between Justice Douglas and underworld figures. "Where is there any legal or historical precedent for a charge of judicial misconduct against a judge for having questionable friends?" asked McCloskey. "Do we indict or think less of the speaker [John McCormack] because his friends are indicted?" In the light of day McCloskey deleted the latter sentence. But he promptly jumped into another controversy during the question-and-answer period when Representative H. R. Gross of Iowa, a friend of Reagan, questioned the ethical propriety of judges receiving any money from foundations. McCloskey responed that judges should not be punished on an *ex post facto* basis for violating a standard of conduct that Congress had not yet applied to itself. "I know it has been publicly disclosed that a U.S. senator has received twenty thousand dollars a year plus travel and expenses," McCloskey said. "We raised no questions about that."

The remark was an unmistakable reference to U.S. Senator George Murphy, then under fire from Democratic contender John V. Tunney for accepting a consultant fee from Technicolor. McCloskey's comment enraged Murphy, who was having enough trouble already with Tunney and with the opposition Republican candidacy of multimillionaire Norton Simon (whose campaign, incidentally, was managed by Weiner). Even without the anti-Murphy crack, McCloskey had asked for and received the enmity of the House GOP leadership as the first Republican congressman to challenge Ford's impeachment move on the House floor. He was not unmindful of the risk. Two days before his actual speech, McCloskey requested time for a special order in the House to make the challenge, and was told by a friend that any defense of Douglas would become an issue against him in the coming Republican primary. "It's not going to help the campaign," Mc-

Closkey responded, moments before leaving for Flint, Michigan, to address an environmental rally. "But, my God, if a guy doesn't speak up on this kind of issue, why is he here? Lawyers rise to the defense of the courts and do not sit idly by when judges are attacked."

9. *The Peace Lover*

He returned always to the war. War meant too much to him, perhaps more than he realized, and he returned to it again and again, seeking to square what was happening in Vietnam with his innermost convictions and his training as a Marine. He visited Vietnam for the first time in January 1968, a month after his election, identifying with the Marines whom he met there, and forming a negative impression of the South Vietnamese army. When he came back he was even more against the war than before, but he expressed regret, too, that he had been unable to fight in it, and he denied all attempts to label him a dove. "Did you ever hear a Marine officer called a dove?" McCloskey asked. "A dove doesn't want to fight. I believe in fighting communism whenever it rears its head."

But the Vietnam War was no longer a simple question of fighting communism. More and more it seemed to McCloskey, who was now a lieutenant colonel in the Marine Reserve, a classic question of the wrong war in the wrong place at the wrong time. Later he would say that he had distrusted colonels when he was a lieutenant, and distrusted generals when he became a colonel, but he now quoted generals, particularly General Douglas MacArthur and Marine General David Shoup, on the folly of committing American troops to a land war in Asia. "The traditional disregard for human life by the Asian warlord gives his army an immense advantage over the Western army, whose leaders value each human life under their command," McCloskey had said in the September 12, 1967, campaign declaration that he still quoted incessantly. The statement says more about McCloskey's own high concept of command than it does about what was going on in Vietnam, but it reflected his growing conviction that further commitments of U.S. troops would fail to stop the North Vietnamese. His maiden speech * in the House on the war objected to any further build-up and mildly insisted that the Congress shared responsibility with the President in approving any further expansion of the Vietnam commitment. McCloskey's one-minute presentation ended with a resolution declaring it the sense of Congress that U.S. forces not be increased in Vietnam without congressional consultation and that U.S. foreign policy recognize the goal of Vietnamese unification declared in the 1954 Geneva Accords. "This goal recognizes the fundamental principle that Vietnam is one country, not two, and that it remains the policy of the United States to obtain an early reunification of countries divided against their will, not to insist on the permanent establishment of a separate new nation of South Vietnam," McCloskey concluded.

March 1968 was a watershed month in the recent history of the United States. The Tet offensive the month before had shaken a lot of erstwhile supporters of the Vietnam War, and criticism was stirring in the Congress and in the news media. *Newsweek*, for instance, called for a reappraisal of the American effort and also objected to President Johnson's exhortations to White House visitors about the spirit of the Alamo. ". . . The analogy between Vietnam and the Alamo is scarcely encouraging," the magazine observed, "for all of the defenders of the Texas mission were ultimately killed." On March 12 Gene McCarthy surprised the press and the President by almost winning the primary in New Hampshire. Four days later Bobby Kennedy entered the presidential race.

It was against this backdrop that McCloskey arose to speak

* On March 13, 1968, pages H-1914 and H-1915 in the *Congressional Record*.

in the House on March 18, in his first detailed analysis of the war as a congressman. McCloskey's speech that day was part of an hour-long review of the war requested by Representative Paul Findley of Illinois, who had just finished an exchange with Chet Holifield of California about the dangers of Communist expansion. Findley had objected to the United States playing "world policeman"; Holified had supported the twenty-year American policy of "opposing Communist aggression whereever it takes place in the world." But McCloskey said the issue was not the wisdom of containing Communist expansion but the specific question of fighting communism in Vietnam. After another of his characteristic reviews of Vietnamese history McCloskey declared:

> We believed that the will to fight communism was stronger than the traditional apathy or antagonism by the rural farmer against a corrupt national government. We believed that we could cause, through advisers at every level, the central government to forego the corrupt practices which have been the trademark of most Asian governments. We believed that we could cause that central government to supplement military control at the province and district level with bona-fide honest and compact civil administration.
>
> We believed we could do this even though we would have to Americanize the fight . . . and, in effect, take over the direction of the pacification efforts through threats of pulling out unless our "advice" was taken by the very people in whom we sought to instill a sense of national pride and sovereignty.
>
> We believed that we could succeed where the French had failed, believing somehow that our good motives would be accepted. . . .
>
> These beliefs have not been borne out by the facts.

The Johnson administration had not faced facts, McCloskey contended. Instead of seeing what was actually happening in Vietnam, the administration had cited one statistic after another in behalf of its preconceptions. The military leadership, "being loyal to the commander-in-chief, as is expected of good soldiers," had likewise stressed facts that supported the administration's belief. Drawing upon his own pre-Tet visit to Vietnam, McCloskey said:

> In attending a series of briefings . . . I was continually impressed by how much time was devoted to conclusions drawn from the facts, rather than on the facts themselves. It seems that every loyal member of the administration desperately clings to the accuracy of those original beliefs which started us upon our present course.
>
> The time has come to call a halt. This country is big enough and great enough to recognize and admit mistaken beliefs upon which we predicated our present policy in Vietnam.

Except for this perceptive insight into the way in which U.S. policy-makers had deceived themselves, McCloskey's statement broke little new ground.* He repeated most of his September 12 statement, complete with the reference to the "Asian warlord's" lack of respect for human life. But the statement indicates that the Vietnam trip had clearly strengthened McCloskey's opposition to the war. He had discovered another truth that demanded at least equal status with "fighting communism whenever it rears its head" and that would in time supplant it. "The Viet Cong are nationalists as well as Communists," McCloskey pointed out. "'Vietnam for the Vietnamese' may be as inspirational an ideal as our own Monroe Doctrine of 'the Americas for the Americans.'"

Republicans found it easy to oppose the war in 1968, and McCloskey found it far easier to criticize Johnson's war policies than he would to challenge a Republican President on the same grounds. The war was a "Democratic war," after all, and there was room in the out-of-power party for Ronald Reagan, who wanted to win the war, and for Pete McCloskey, who

* And in any case would have made relatively little impression, because almost no one was present in the House to hear the speech. Representative William Hungate of Missouri, a Democrat and a war critic, afterward praised McCloskey's "most excellent, sincere, and thoughtful presentation," and added: "The only reason there has been no applause is that there are not enough members here."

wanted to withdraw from it. The differences, even in McCloskey's case, were blurred. In-depth polls showed confused and conflicting attitudes, sometimes shared by the same respondent, that embraced both the Reagan and the McCloskey views. "What the people want is for us to win the war and get out," said one political scientist, and he was not far wrong. It was this unfocused belief that the United States had either done too much or too little in Vietnam, or maybe some of both, that enabled Richard Nixon to campaign so successfully with an unspecified "plan" to end the war. McCloskey started out as an avowed supporter of Nixon, for all his long distrust of him. John Ehrlichman, the Stanford Law School colleague who had become a presidential adviser, arranged a meeting for McCloskey and other congressmen with Henry Kissinger to talk about the war. McCloskey left unconvinced that Nixon had any real plan to end the war, but he subsequently gave Ehrlichman the impression that his problem with the administration on the war was "almost casual." Says Ehrlichman: "He was almost diffident about the issue, and very assertive of his support for the President for the first ten or twelve months." This assessment in hindsight may seem to undervalue the depth of McCloskey's concern. But Ehrlichman's recollection is largely supported by McCloskey's friends and family. "There's been a big change in Peter between April of 1969 and now," says brother-in-law Charles McClung, who after doing much to influence McCloskey against the war in 1967 was still arguing with him about it. "The biggest fight Peter and I ever had—we were really yelling at two o'clock in the morning—was early in 1969. I was antiwar and he was pro-Nixon in those days. He was talking about the negotiations in Paris, about how Nixon was now the President and how we were working toward peace, and the old cliché about how there'd been no indications from the other side. We had a big beef, and I argued that the whole policy of supplanting white Americans with yellow Asians was immoral. Peter was against me then. I kept telling him, and I think he now agrees, that there's something cowardly about hanging back, saying, 'We won't have any Americans die, we'll just let you guys die and we'll push the buttons from back here.' Peter's patriotism insists to him that if the war is worth fighting, the United States Marines should be in the fight."

Some of McCloskey's hopefulness in those early months of the Nixon administration comes through in his first letter to the President about the Vietnam War. It may be too much to say that McCloskey was actually "pro-Nixon" at this point, but his letter, dated March 20, 1969, is respectful of the President's leadership role and at one point suggests a kind of suspended judgment about the course of the war:

> I take the liberty of imposing on your time only because I believe the solution of the Vietnam problem to be of such importance that even a junior congressman should not hesitate to communicate with his President when there is fear that one view is not reaching you.
>
> I would like you to know how much we junior Republican congressmen want you to succeed. Perhaps more than anything else, we hope that you will be able to restore the faith of the American people in their government and themselves. This can be accomplished if two conditions exist.
>
> First, the people must have confidence in the ability, honesty and candor of their leaders. You have earned this confidence, both from the public and those of us privileged to serve in the Congress.
>
> Second, our national policies must be *right*. They must reach through to the inherent idealism most Americans possess.
>
> In Vietnam, we are wrong. We were wrong to seek to contain communism through massive military force in this particular country. We were wrong in thinking we could build a new nation to serve our own purposes. We were wrong in thinking we could win, or that we can yet win.
>
> Vietnam is one country, not two. In my judgment the elements of terrain, history, culture, geography and human resources are just not present in a mixture which will permit a Saigon-based government to *ever* control the area called South Vietnam.

I, therefore, ask you to consider the merits of a public announcement admitting that we made a mistake in Americanizing this conflict in 1965 and that we intend to commence withdrawal in the near future.

Both you and the United States are big enough to admit past mistakes. I suggest that the credibility this will establish in the minds of our own people is far more valuable than the credibility we will lose abroad and which Mr. Kissinger has urged as requiring our continued involvement in Vietnam.

I have attached a memorandum setting forth my reasons for this argument.

It has been a little over a year since I was last in Vietnam. With the understanding that a change in conditions there may be making my conclusions no longer valid, I hope to spend the Easter recess in Vietnam to personally observe and question the basis for my views as well as those which I challenge. If I can be of any service to you while I am there, I would be pleased to try.

Regardless of any disagreement on this issue, it is an honor to serve under your leadership.

McCloskey did not carry out his intention of going to Vietnam during the Easter recess. The peace forces that would sponsor his subsequent trips were moribund through the Nixon administration honeymoon, and McCloskey's friends in government during that period focused more upon school desegregation than upon Vietnam. No one paid too much attention to what McCloskey had to say about the war.

The White House responded to the letter on April 16, nearly a month after McCloskey had written. The reply came from Kenneth E. BeLieu, deputy assistant to the President, and a member of the legislative liaison staff:

Dear Pete:

The President asked me to thank you for your letter of March 20 on Vietnam, and also to express his sincere appreciation for your gracious words of encouragement.

As I believe Henry Kissinger indicated during your recent discussion with him, we hope we have formulated a strategy for peace in Vietnam which will secure a fair and enduring settlement.

It is surely true as you said, ". . . our national policies must be right," and they should, in all possible instances "be made through the inherent idealism most Americans possess." One of the major problems—probably the major problem—stems from the need to change from conditions inherited to conditions conducive to ideal peace.

I must apologize for the delay in answering, but by the time your letter with its thought-provoking memo had been digested, the Easter recess was upon us and noting that you planned on visiting Vietnam during that period, I decided to withhold reply until your return.

With highest regards,

Sincerely,
Kenneth E. BeLieu
Deputy Assistant
to the President

The memo to which BeLieu referred was a digest of McCloskey's reasoning, expressed in his September 12 statement and his March 18 speech in the House, on why American assistance to South Vietnam had failed to create a stable government. It began with the premise that the Vietnamese war was a civil war, and, in what may have been an oblique reference to Kissinger, questioned whether American "experts" really understood the war. "Out of our experience thus far," McCloskey had written, "one principle seems absolutely clear. There is *no* known American expert upon whom we can depend for an accurate prediction, either as to the eventual ability of the South Vietnamese to go it alone, or the willingness of the North Vietnamese and Viet Cong to abandon the fight. I suggest that the Nixon administration accept this one principle: that there will *always* be doubt on these two points during the next two years."

McCloskey's own doubts grew as spring deepened into summer and turned to fall. "Vietnamization" had been announced by the President, and some troops were coming home, but McCloskey began to question the rate of withdrawals and the ultimate goal of Nixon's policy. "A plan to end the war" began to seem the bitter joke to him that it already was to some of the peace groups, now regrouping for the first time after the election. And McCloskey began, also, to doubt Nixon's leadership, the issue that was ultimately to become the most crucial of all. But these doubts were still a long way from any open break with the President. On October 23, when McCloskey spoke briefly in the House on behalf of repealing the 1964 Gulf of Tonkin resolution, he said: "It represents no lack of confidence in our President or his present policies for Congress to carefully reexamine its own role in the conduct of our Vietnam policy." The speech gave little offense to the Nixon administration in any case, because the President had been careful to point out that he did not base his own actions on the Tonkin resolution, and he would eventually agree to its repeal. However, the statement showed a change in McCloskey's own thinking. In his lengthy speech on March 18, 1968, he had declared that "Congress expressly granted the President the power to commit our armed forces in Vietnam under the Gulf of Tonkin resolution of August 7, 1964." Now he cited the same resolution as an abdication by Congress of its constitutional powers to declare war. "Under the Gulf of Tonkin resolution we now find ourselves bogged down in an infantry war eight thousand miles from home, where winning of that war rests not on American abilities, resources, or will but rather on the nationalistic spirit and will to fight of two competing groups of Vietnamese."

He wrote again to President Nixon about the war on December 23. He had participated in seven other letters or wires to the President since his April letter, and none of the seven had touched on Vietnam. Two of the letters had opposed proposals of the Nixon administration: extension of the school-desegregation deadline and the Amchitka atomic test. One had appealed for a continuation of the embattled legal-services program in the Office of Economic Opportunity. The others were routine advocacies for environmental or regional projects, none of them directly involving McCloskey's congressional district. Most were routinely replied to by Bill Timmons, the White House congressional liaison.* Such letters and such replies are the warp and woof of a congressman's existence. They are addressed to the President but never seen by him. The December 23 letter was something else again. McCloskey spent time and thought composing it, and he asked John Ehrlichman if he would call it to the personal attention of President Nixon. This letter maintains the respectful tone of the March letter, but it touches on economic arguments for the first time, and the tone of skepticism is more acute:

Dear Mr. President:

This is in response to your letter of December 17 to the House and Senate leadership.

You have asked for responsible congressional action on the dramatic spending and revenue issues now before us. You properly pointed out the dangers and problems of inflation and asked us to vote for balanced tax reform and lesser domestic expenditures in order to combat such inflation.

You have said nothing, however, Mr. President, about the reduction in expenditures which only you have the power to accomplish by ordering a more rapid disengagement from Vietnam.

The transfer of one division from combat in Vietnam into a training status at home results in a spending reduction of approximately $1.5 billion each year. The withdrawal of three divisions accomplishes the same result that you feel Congress should accomplish by cutting back appropriations for education, water pollution, and the elderly social security recipient.

I respectfully suggest that congressional actions in these fields have properly represented American public opinion and national priorities. Congress has acted on the assumption that the American people now put a higher priority on education, the environment and self-respect for older Americans than on preserving a perma-

* McCloskey's Vietnam letters as quoted in this and other chapters were provided by his staff. The replies were made available by the White House.

nent division of Vietnam. From your recent public statements, I suspect that you agree with this assumption.

As one of those who has thus far supported your efforts to obtain a just peace in Vietnam, I would like to express grave reservations over the chances of ultimate success of your program to terminate American involvement by the policy of Vietnamization.

Such success depends not on Americans but on the South Vietnamese, their will to fight and their willingness to support their own government. If the South Vietnamese are capable of preserving their independence, this capability will be demonstrated as easily in one year as it will be in three. Thus, I suggest that an accelerated withdrawal of American troops (perhaps at the rate of 30,000 per month) may have no more damaging impact on Vietnamization than the withdrawal of the 10,000 per month which you have already ordered.

The pursuit of an accelerated withdrawal policy should have at least as salutary an effect on our domestic economy and stability as the congressional actions which you have requested.

While the My Lai incident is not typical of American combat action, it *has* focused the attention of all of us on the fact that we have come to accept war by gunships, destruction of villages, the Phoenix program and other harsh anti-insurgency efforts as a necessary aspect of our involvement in Vietnam. The early abandonment of these methods of warfare by that country which must lead the world to peace in our time may be more important than the continued shoring up of the Saigon government by an American military presence which must resort to such methods to be effective.

In conclusion, I would like to express my respect for the manner in which you have served the nation as President during these past eleven months. Your leadership in the areas of draft and postal reform, minority employment, revenue-sharing, fiscal responsibility, anti-inflation efforts and the environment has made it a pleasure to serve as a Republican member of Congress.

Best wishes of the season,
Paul N. McCloskey, Jr.

Copies of the letter went to Ehrlichman and to Kissinger.

Ehrlichman promptly acknowledged the letter, on December 29, using the formal address of "Dear Congressman":

> Thanks very much for your note of December 23 and the enclosed letter to the President in which you urged a more rapid disengagement from Vietnam.
>
> I am sure the President is most familiar with your views on this issue; however, I will bring this letter to his attention.
>
> Best personal regards.
>
> Yours sincerely,
> John D. Ehrlichman

The reply did not satisfy McCloskey, who nonetheless thanked Ehrlichman for showing the letter to the President. McCloskey now went ahead with plans to visit Vietnam again, something he had wanted to do ever since Nixon took office. This time his trip was sponsored and paid for by Members of Congress for Peace Through Law, a bipartisan peace bloc, and by Harold Willens, the organizer of Businessmen Executives Move for Vietnam Peace and a McCarthy supporter in 1968. McCloskey spent a week in Vietnam, visiting both the northern provinces (I Corps) and the Mekong Delta, and what he saw there changed the outlook and the emphasis of his antiwar criticism.

"I flew over miles and miles of treelines where hamlets and everything had been destroyed," McCloskey told me the week after his return.* "I have real reservations that this policy is anything but a war crime. If you look back at Nuremberg and our policy in 1946, we insisted that it was a war crime to wantonly destroy villages. The only purpose of destroying these villages was that they gave occasional shelter to the Viet Cong that came into them or provided rice for the VC. For the United States to pursue a definite, specific policy of

* McCloskey's findings and impressions from his February 1970 trip were recorded by the author in an hour-long taped interview made with him immediately after his return. Portions of the interview appeared in Ridder newspapers on March 8, 1970.

scorching the earth of the civilian population because many of the civilians had relatives fighting in the Viet Cong—well, I'm not sure we can justify this policy over the long pull. To me it's exactly what we executed Germans for doing because they had harbored enemy units that had taken shelter there. This bothers me more than My Lai." McCloskey also tried to square what he had seen in February 1970 with what he had observed in January 1968 immediately after his election. The talk turned to George Romney, who had once damaged himself politically by declaring that he had been "brainwashed" about Vietnam. "Essentially, what Romney was talking about is that any American visitor, particularly a VIP, is shown the areas that reflect creditably on the United States. When I was there two years ago it was not apparent to me that we were pursuing a scorched-earth policy. No one told me, and I didn't observe it. This time the difference was immediately apparent." Most of McCloskey's comments about a "scorched-earth" policy concerned the forced evacuation of villagers to refugee centers in the northern provinces of Vietnam. Significantly, perhaps, in view of his later criticisms of the Nixon administration, McCloskey said even then that the policy of destroying villages in the northern and coastal areas had been largely abandoned because it had been "counterproductive." But McCloskey also maintained that one-third of the population in the I Corps and II Corps area was now in refugee camps and that the area would quickly go Communist if the Americans withdrew.

Though he was now raising moral questions that go to the heart of the U.S. dilemma in Vietnam, McCloskey still viewed the country with a military eye. In contrast to the I Corps and II Corps area, he said, the government and U.S. forces had made some "real progress" in the delta area south and west of Saigon. Here, he said, the South Vietnamese forces might be able to survive on their own after U.S. withdrawal. But even in the delta he saw a moral issue posed by the arming of almost every able-bodied civilian in the villages. "We're militarizing this country and creating seeds of warfare for the next generation," he said.

Nor could he abide what was happening to the Fifth Regiment of the U.S. Marine Corps, *his* Marine regiment. It seemed, though he did not say this explicitly, that in some way this bothered Pete McCloskey most of all. American casualties in the war had been steadily declining, and the Fifth Marines at the time McCloskey visited them in 1970 were sustaining far fewer killed in action than when McCloskey served with them in the thick of the Korean fighting two decades earlier. McCloskey, however, saw beyond the casualty figures and also beyond the hundred-and-one engagements reported almost daily in the press, battles in which several North Vietnamese or Viet Cong were killed for every Marine. The reports were misleading, McCloskey knew, because the enemy was losing its casualties in battle where U.S. troops could mass their firepower while the Marines in I Corps were losing theirs in "situations where no enemy is ever encountered or any battle fought." Statistics compiled by McCloskey with Marine assistance showed that the Fifth regiment had encountered 1,277 booby traps in 1969 and detonated 604 of them. It was a terrifying statistic. Ninety-nine Marines had lost their lives from these booby traps and another 1,135 had been wounded. "Can you imagine the morale?" McCloskey asked. Here was the underlying reality of free fire zones and villages such as My Lai, where (from McCloskey's point of view) undisciplined or poorly led troops had shot on sight. Many other war critics went to Vietnam during the first two years of the Nixon administration, and most of them said some of the same things McCloskey did about civilian casualties. McCloskey was the only one of these itinerant critics to go beyond the façade of so-many thousand "wounded" in an effort to determine the nature of the wounds.* The grim statistics of Fifth Marine

* He has been trying ever since to obtain detailed information about amputations arising from the Vietnam conflict. At this writing, Defense officials have declined to provide the information.

casualties in I Corps indicated to ex-platoon leader McCloskey that many of these wounds were amputations. McCloskey considered amputation as among the worst of a soldier's possible fates, equivalent almost to capture by the enemy. His earlier romantic notion of war, surviving and somehow flourishing in the hard reality of Korea, had accepted death on a battlefield, but never a postwar imprisonment as an amputee. McCloskey is a man who is constantly in movement and who values touch-football games and fishing in remote streams and climbing mountaintops alone. He had been emotionally overcome in 1965 when he visited his Marine friend who had lost a leg in Vietnam, and he had immediately after the visit sought recall to active duty. Amputation was somehow more than anyone should have to bear.

We talked about amputation and soldiers' wounds a year later, on the plane trip to Laos and Vietnam, and McCloskey told me war stories, one of them about a friend who had lost a testicle in Korea. It brought to mind Jake Barnes, the hero of Hemingway's unforgettable novel *The Sun Also Rises*, and McCloskey suddenly said with great emotion: "That was a horrible story. I was never worried about getting killed. I prayed to God I wouldn't be wounded." Now, in Vietnam, his friends had been wounded, and other Marines whom he had never known had been maimed for life by booby traps set by an enemy they had never seen in a war they did not want. McCloskey did not want the war either, and he would from this time on do everything in his power to end it.

Most of the people in South Vietnam, McCloskey now believed, had not benefited from American assistance or from American warfare. He still favored giving asylum to anyone who wanted to come out of the country, but he thought only the wealthy would leave. "I'd give anybody who wanted to leave the country the ability to come out," he said. "I don't fear the bloodbath as much as I did before I went to Vietnam. A lot of Vietnamese are working today on an accommodation basis. Their commitment is surface to the Saigon government." The North Vietnamese commitment, he had come to believe, was anything but surface. North Vietnam was determined to reunify the country, and the United States had done no favor to the Vietnamese people, North or South, by perpetuating the division. "We have stiffened the ability of a few people to resist the reunification because it served our purposes, but I don't think we've helped," McCloskey said. "I think when Nixon says that our policy is to let the South Vietnamese determine what form of government they want and that this is nonnegotiable, he's overlooking the fact that the great bulk of the people want peace at any price and are denied peace because of American assistance." Perhaps he had spoken this way before, but it is the first time that I remember McCloskey as a congressman talking about Nixon without referring to him as "President" or "Richard Nixon" or the "commander-in-chief." Despite McCloskey's advocacy in his December 23 letter of a speedier withdrawal, he accepted that the withdrawal would take a year and a half to accomplish. (McCloskey said that former Marine General Victor Krulak, the originator of Silver Lance and now the director of editorial and news policy for the San Diego *Union* and *Tribune,* had told him a complete withdrawal would take seventeen months.) What McCloskey now doubted was the President's intentions. And though he wasn't yet ready to go as far as his friend New York Senator Charles Goodell in fixing a withdrawal date—"It's a little presumptuous to direct the executive branch to get out in that way"—McCloskey clearly shared the developing apprehensions of Goodell and other antiwar senators that the President intended to leave a residual force in South Vietnam, perhaps as many as 250,000 troops. ". . . I suspect Mr. Nixon's policy is that we should get out at such a rate that the American people's concern is quieted, yet leave enough behind that the South Vietnamese military establishment is strengthened" McCloskey said. This policy was no longer acceptable to McCloskey, who had come a long way from his legalistic questioning and his advocacy of gradual withdrawal. Now he saw the Vietnamese war going on indefinitely because Saigon and the South Vietnamese generals had no real incentive to negotiate and form a coalition government. It was a point strikingly similar to the one made by Charles McClung at his breakfast speech four years before when he had argued, at the height of the war's popularity, that the United States should be honest enough to say that a Communist government, even an elected Communist government, was unacceptable if that was in fact our policy. McCloskey's own argument, far less theoretical, as his arguments always are, had been forged out of his own thinking since that time, out of his reading and his campaign position, out of his shouted discussions with men like McClung, now out of an inspection in the field that had confirmed the worst of his fears about the war. Looking ahead, he correctly foresaw (before Cambodia) that the renewed debate about the war would occur in the spring of 1970, and he saw, too, that "the great silent majority" was supporting the President on the war only because of the troop withdrawals.

McCloskey wanted something more, though he was still unable to fully verbalize it. He wanted almost a repudiation of the war and a recognition of what the war had meant to Vietnam, and he was operating on his own timetable, which had very little to do with the President's. "To me what we are doing in Vietnam is an immoral thing," he said during the February 1970 interview. "I think we have caused more Vietnamese deaths by our insistence that the country be non-Communist than would have occurred had we allowed self-determination. . . . There is nothing about the government in the North that is so harsh or repressive that it is worth [this] loss of life."

The Marine had come full circle now, and what was happening to his own Marines had helped him do it. It was not enough to argue that Americans be withdrawn and that Asians go on killing Asians, these Asians whose leaders McCloskey had long viewed as holding life so cheaply. Once he reached the conclusion that the war was wrong, such killing seemed shameful to him, and he was quite able to reconcile his basic belief in the necessity of militarily defending one's country with an advocacy of a Vietnam reunified under the aegis of the North. Perhaps McClung, who says always that McCloskey reached these decisions on his own, had been closest to the mark about his friend and brother-in-law when he spoke of the patriotism that made McCloskey a Marine in the first place. "I think," said McClung, "that he's enough of a militarist and a pragmatist to know the time may come when your government may say: 'You die for this cause. Don't question it. Die.' McCloskey can stomach a certain amount of hypocrisy, a certain amount of nationalist chauvinism, but one thing he can't stomach on behalf of this country he loves so much is what he perceives as a national cowardice."

McCloskey himself did not use the word "cowardice," but he certainly talked as if it would be dishonorable for the United States to abandon the field in a way that encouraged the fighting to go on. He was really on a different track than President Nixon, who also wanted the war to end, but who saw the preservation of a non-Communist South Vietnam as a milepost on the bloody road to freedom and a vindication of the national lives and treasure that had been poured into Southeast Asia. Nixon's and McCloskey's pronouncements and actions henceforth flowed from different premises and from a different understanding about the war's purpose and meaning. A conflict was inevitable, even though the forms of that conflict were undetermined and would be deeply influenced by events that would occur in the spring and fall of 1970. But McCloskey's position on the war and on American policy was now firmly cast. No one who knew him would ever think of Pete McCloskey as "pro-Nixon" again.

10. The Road to New Hampshire

The external question was the war in Vietnam and, later, the war in Laos and Cambodia. The internal question for the House of Representatives in 1970, the last year of Speaker John McCormack's reign, was House reform. It was an issue slow to engage the passions of the country. Some determined Establishment reformers like Richard Bolling of Missouri cared a great deal about it, as did some dedicated anti-Establishment Democrats like Donald Fraser of Minnesota, then the leader of the Democratic Study Group, and some Republicans like Barber Conable of New York. It was "a press thing," said some of the old chairmen contemptuously, and it was certainly true the reportorial interest in reform often was out of proportion to anything that actually happened to change the structure or customs of the House. But the time was right for reform in 1970, though not even many of the reformers realized it. The time was right for reasons that came together, one of them the scheduled consideration of the first legislative reorganization act in twenty years, another McCormack's age and the influence-peddling scandal (in which the speaker was not involved) surrounding a McCormack aide, another the willingness of a little-known California congressman named Jerome Waldie to challenge the speaker directly.

Pete McCloskey played a small but significant role in the reform movement, a conflict in which his instincts for the coming issue and his proclivities for tail twisting served him well.

On December 22, 1969, a day before he wrote his second letter to the President, McCloskey wrote Rogers C. B. Morton, a Maryland congressman who was then Republican national chairman, proposing selection of House committee chairmen "on the basis of administrative and management skill, rather than on seniority alone." The change would go into effect on whatever distant day the Republicans took control of the House, and McCloskey in his letter made what he considered a good Republican argument:

> The average age of the presidents of the 25 largest corporations in America is 57. The average age of the most powerful committee chairmen in the House is well over 70, and three committee chairmen will be in their 80s this year. In most cases, the most senior member may also be the ablest manager in the hard work of pushing bills through the legislative process. It is indefensible, however, that we be *required* to accept as chairman an individual who is *not* the ablest leader, merely because he has served the longest period of time on the committee involved. No profit-making organization in the free enterprise system could satisfy its stockholders on this point, and the Republican party, after all, is supposedly the party which provides and insists upon management excellence in the conduct of the complex problems of government.

Morton replied on January 19, 1970, and sent copies of the correspondence to John Ehrlichman and Bryce Harlow in the White House and to Bob Wilson, the California congressman who heads the Republican congressional campaign committee. The reply, much more than an acknowledgment, suggested to McCloskey that he formulate a specific proposal and present it to the Republican leadership of the House.

That was all McCloskey needed. He sent a letter to House Minority Leader Gerald Ford couched in bluntly partisan terms—"I believe there is a weakness of the Democrats which we should now exploit, and which would materially assist us in attaining majority status in November"—and outlined a plan under which committees would elect their own chairmen from among members with at least five years' experience. He also proposed an age limit of seventy and called upon Ford to pledge that the Republicans would discard the seniority system if they took control of the House. A firm Republican stand against the seniority system, McCloskey argued, might well "capture the enthusiasm" of young people, and would enable Republicans to "capitalize on the serious vulnerability of the Democratic leadership's age and unresponsiveness to the problems of the seventies." It was an indelicate suggestion to make to Ford, who depended on cooperation with the seventy-eight-year-old McCormack to make any points at all for his outnumbered party. McCloskey was relentless on the point:

> We might well characterize the election year challenge as "The Crisis of the 70s," pointing to the speaker, [84-year-old] Chairman (William) Dawson, et al. A few more nationally televised joint meetings of the Congress, with the President backstopped by the Speaker, will get the point across better than any written argument.
>
> I would add that the "unresponsiveness" of Congress is a major issue with the younger generation, and the seniority issue might well be the way to a new respect by them for the word "Republican."
>
> If this approach would embarrass you and our own leadership in working with your counterparts in the months of legislative action ahead, the burden of proposing it can easily be assumed by those of us in the 90th and 91st [Congress] who are so inclined.

McCloskey sent copies of the letter to eight members of the Republican leadership, plus Morton, Harlow, and Ehrlichman. McCloskey's proposal, coming at a time when Waldie was proposing a "no-confidence" challenge to McCormack in the Democratic caucus, played at least a modest role in the formation of a Republican task force on seniority headed by Barber Conable of New York. The Conable committee ultimately proposed an alternative limitation on seniority, and the plan was adopted by House Republicans in the 92nd Congress.

The McCloskey letter, however, probably had more effect

upon the Democrats than upon the Republicans. House reformers, long thwarted by a bipartisan leadership coalition, were in 1970 playing a double game of their own in which they met together, swapped documents, and made "Republican arguments" to the Republicans and "Democratic arguments" to the Democrats. (The Democrats, particularly, were concerned about the effect of the "senility and seniority" issue upon younger voters. Waldie, who had discussed the issue with McCloskey, had the perception to transform this concern into a direct challenge to McCormack that gained few votes but played a catalytic role in the reform process.) McCloskey's letter and subsequent Republican letters were leaked to the Democratic Study Group and used as an example of what the other party was doing. The same sort of thing, although McCloskey was not directly involved, was done in reverse early in 1971 when a Democratic task force under Representative Julia Butler Hansen of Washington met on its own committee-reform proposals. It was all a legitimate aspect of inter-House politics in which the younger and relatively powerless members attempted to do what had been done to them for years.

McCloskey supported the Legislative Reorganization Act and voted for most of the strengthening amendments added on the House floor. The act, often referred to in newspaper accounts simply as the "House reform bill," avoided the seniority issue both because the matter was being considered by the two task forces and because such reform leaders as Fraser and Conable did not want to jeopardize other far-reaching provisions of the legislation.* After the Legislative Reorganization Act was finally passed, many of the reformers returned to the attack

* McCloskey's most outspoken Republican critic in the California congressional delegation, Representative Charles Gubser, played a decisive role during deliberations on the Legislative Reorganization Act by co-sponsoring an amendment that virtually abolished anonymous voting in the House. Despite their political and personal antagonism, McCloskey has never ceased to credit Gubser for that amendment, which was far and away the most important provision of the bill.

on the seniority system. Among them was Pete McCloskey, who for once abandoned his trial-lawyer approach and spoke directly to the human issues involved. Strict adherence to a rule of absolute seniority "invites incompetence," McCloskey said, because all men are subject to the same temptations: "Who amongst us would not stay beyond our declining physical and mental capabilities if we are assured that survival alone will one day give us power? Who amongst us will willingly retire and give up power once it is attained through patient service? We suggest the retirement of elder justices such as Justice Douglas, but few of us choose to retire once the privileges of power are irrevocably in our grasp. It is not human nature to do so." Nor, as it turned out, was it "human nature" for a majority of congressmen to risk their own prerogatives in an all-out assault upon the seniority system. However, both parties did make the appointment of committee chairmen subject to ratification by the party caucuses and allowed criteria other than seniority to be considered in the choice of chairmen. These changes possessed a symbolic value to the congressmen who had waged the battle against seniority. Whether they are also harbingers of a more fundamental overhaul of the seniority system will be determined by a future Congress.

Pete McCloskey fought other battles in the House during 1970. One of these was in opposition to the equal-rights amendment, a position that reflects both McCloskey's old-fashioned view of womanhood ("He thinks of them as pets," Butler said once) and his accurate belief that the measure had failed to receive proper consideration in the House Judiciary Committee.* Only fifteen congressmen, individualists from all parts of the political spectrum, voted against the amendment. They were

* That was the fault of Judiciary Committee Chairman Emanuel Celler, who had obstinately refused for years to allow even a hearing on the amendment. It was finally pried from committee by a discharge petition initiated by Congresswoman Martha W. Griffiths of Michigan under a procedure that made amendment on the floor or any thorough consideration of its provisions a practical impossibility.

the targets of wrath from various women's groups, but they were far more forthright than many of their colleagues who criticized the amendment privately but were afraid to vote against it on the floor. The only organized opposition in the House came from a few labor unions that were concerned that the amendment would wipe out hard-won protection for women in industry. John Schmitz, an ultraconservative congressman who represents President Nixon's district in California, was one of the fifteen, and he came over to McCloskey and clapped a hand on his shoulder immediately after the roll call. "Well, Pete, that's your conservative vote for the year," Schmitz said. "And it's my labor vote." Cubby McCloskey, however, was less amused by McCloskey's stand. When he asked his wife what she thought about his opposition to the amendment, McCloskey said Cubby responded with "an eight-letter word beginning with 'bull.'"

McCloskey's independence on the women's-rights issue demonstrates the difficulty of trying to categorize him on issues. He is "liberal" on the war and the race issues, "conservative" on women's rights and the military draft, and eclectic on economic issues. The draft issue set him apart from many other young congressmen, who regard a volunteer army as a twin cause with opposition to the war. McCloskey, on the other hand, regards the draft as a staple of American citizenship. ". . . It has always seemed to me that the privileges and freedoms of being an American citizen justify two years of service in times of war or threat to the national security," he told the House Armed Services Committee on March 3, 1971. Civilian understanding of the military, and vice versa, is desirable, and repeal of the draft "may do further damage to one of our basic national concepts—that an individual should be proud to serve his country." But it was as a former platoon leader with a vivid memory of Korea that McCloskey made his most important contribution to the Armed Services Committee hearing:

> We no longer have the privilege of a year's preparation of an American expeditionary force, as in World Wars I and II. Combat readiness in the 1970s requires readiness to do battle instantly and this capability constitutes the sole reason for *having* a conventional army.
>
> To be ready to survive in combat, and to do a creditable job as a combat infantryman, an individual should have not less than 90 days, and preferably six months, of hard sustained training which includes arduous physical ordeals as well as a good share of the miserable weather conditions which usually characterize the areas where combat infantrymen are sent into battle.
>
> This means that a potential combat soldier should be running 20 miles a day, climbing a fifty-foot rope perhaps five times a day, and living a good part of his life either wet, cold and miserable or dehydrated, hot, and miserable. Troop leaders owe their men this kind of training. . . . Some members of this committee may remember the difficulties encountered by American infantrymen living the soft life of PXs and garrison duty in 1950 just prior to the Korean conflict. I believe it is fair to say that some American infantry units were butchered in the early days of the Korean War partly because of a paternal desire on the part of peacetime commanders to make Army life as comfortable for themselves and their troops. Comfort has no place in a combat infantry unit, particularly during training in peacetime.
>
> This being so, what reasonable young man is going to give up a life of drinking beer with his friends, enjoying drive-in movies with his girl and sleeping late on weekends in order to volunteer for the hard and rigorous life of running 20 miles a day, standing watch half the night, crawling through jungles, and generally being miserable?

If Pete McCloskey has a natural constituency, it is the young voters of this country, most of whom are outspokenly opposed to the draft. His stand on this issue again demonstrates McCloskey's willingness to take the unpopular side of an issue. He has never wavered in his support for the draft, despite a variety of criticisms, of which an article by Bill Evers in the Stanford *Daily* is typical. "Unfortunately, McCloskey in many ways leaves much to be desired," Evers writes after praising him for opposing the war. "He is the living embodiment of the military mind." *

McCloskey's "military mind" did not stand in the way of a close friendship with Allard K. Lowenstein, an opponent of the draft who in 1969–1970 probably was the least militaristic-minded member of the House. Lowenstein, the New York anti-war mobilizer who engineered the "dumping" of President Johnson, had crossed party lines to endorse McCloskey during the Shirley Temple Black campaign, and the two men renewed their campaign acquaintanceship after Lowenstein was elected to the House in 1968. But it was the reform fight, not the war, that forged their friendship. "The first area where we really discovered that we could work very close together was on the issue of party reform and building cooperation across party gaps," Lowenstein says. "You're used to spurious cooperation in such circumstances. It was at that point that Pete was better than he appeared to be. When the push was on, he became tougher, he didn't appear to crumble. I discovered in that period that he was honest, that his word counted, that he cared. There are so many congressmen who never care to begin with and become cynical or who care only about the trappings and the power. With McCloskey there was never a time he wasn't willing to be self-effacing about getting the credit. All the times when you have to handle politicians so carefully and sensitively just didn't exist with Pete. At no point was there any nuance of him wanting to take the credit. Pete will accept a minor role if that's the best way to be effective." Lowenstein's office in the Longworth building was next door to the office of Don Riegle, the only Republican in the House

* Evers, who correctly observed that "McCloskey's experience with the U.S. Marines appears to have had a decisive influence on the formation of his character," also criticized McCloskey for his stand on recapture of the USS *Pueblo*. The best potential Republican candidate against Nixon, concluded Evers, would be Oregon Senator Mark Hatfield.

who was considered more of a maverick than McCloskey. Riegle and Lowenstein became friends independently and started getting together regularly to discuss the war and what they believed to be the concerns of the young. "I can't recall anytime that the three of us did anything together socially, but we felt comfortable with one another," Lowenstein remembers. "It progressed from an alliance to a friendship. We began to feel that we didn't have to play close to the vest. The three of us would meet in one office or the other and talk about the drift of the country and the war."

The three young congressmen became, along with the capable Donald Fraser, the co-chairmen of a "Committee for a Vote on the War" that began mobilizing the House for test votes on cutting off funds for the U.S. presence in Vietnam. The effort failed, but it was an important assertion of congressional authority for antiwar forces in the House and a waystop of significance on McCloskey's road to the New Hampshire primary. A challenge to the President in that state's Republican primary was not then even dimly conceived by McCloskey or by Lowenstein, who a year later would be organizing dump-Nixon rallies all across the country. In the spring and summer of 1970 Lowenstein was preoccupied with his own upcoming election in a district that had been regerrymandered to favor the Republicans. He was under attack for, among other things, allegedly fomenting student violence, and both Riegle and McCloskey crossed party lines to come to his aid. "We've got to save the good guys," Riegle declared, and both he and McCloskey spoke out against the attacks. Lowenstein insists that the early stand of both his friends was somewhat misrepresented by hostile critics; McCloskey and Riegle had appeared at congressional forums in McCloskey's district, but so had various conservatives. McCloskey, however, characteristically met the attacks on Lowenstein head-on with a statement that "Al Lowenstein's leadership in convincing student demonstrators across the nation to forgo violence and law-breaking has been one of the greatest contributions to national welfare by any member of Congress in 1970." This statement, reprinted in Lowenstein's campaign brochure, triggered an angry response from conservatives in the House. One of them, Representative Sam Devine of Ohio, promptly launched a campaign of his own to deny Riegle and McCloskey Republican campaign funds. Devine wrote a letter to House Republican Committee members "deploring this type of shenanigans and suggesting that activities of this type are detrimental to the Republican party and that we are better off without this breed and that all campaign funds be withheld." Representative Bob Wilson of California, chairman of the House Republican campaign committee and a conservative, wisely decided against imposing ideological tests for the campaign funds, but Lowenstein (who ultimately lost the election) was concerned that his friends were in trouble because of him. He told Riegle that he would delete the offending statements from his campaign brochure, and Riegle, who never shrinks from combat, promptly replied that he would come to New York and campaign for Lowenstein if he did that. Soon thereafter, Lowenstein was pulled out of a meeting by McCloskey and asked with a grin: "Don't you have anything better to do than to phone people and try to get them to spend their time not saying things they feel?"

McCloskey in 1970 appeared to have a reelection problem of his own. He had narrowly averted defeat against a supposedly weak candidate in 1968, and he now faced a well-financed challenge in his own party from a candidate whose supporters included Henry Salvatori, the multimillionaire engineer and physicist who is one of Ronald Reagan's heaviest contributors. But McCloskey, who had been fortunate in his opposition before, was fortunate again. Forden (Skip) Athearn, the new hope of the county's conservatives, was a law associate of outgoing state Senator Richard Dolwig, a man who was deeply distrusted by conservationists and by progressive Republicans. "If they had run a youngish ex-Marine who followed a moderate line, we might have been in trouble even then," says a McCloskey supporter who thinks McCloskey is in real difficulty now. But San Mateo County conservatives have rarely distinguished themselves with the quality of their candidates, and Athearn was simply unable to rally the moderate support that a Republican needs if he is to defeat McCloskey in his own party. Certainly Athearn tried. He attacked McCloskey on every issue from the antiballistic missile (which McCloskey opposes) to his stand on Adam Clayton Powell (McCloskey had voted to seat him, with penalities). The campaign settled down to an issue-and-image exchange in which the candidates somehow came across sounding like a couple of rival gasoline advertisements. Athearn was "the Real Republican." McCloskey, answering him, was "the True Republican." ("And so are you!" read the kicker on one of McCloskey's most massive brochures, a 21½-inch by 16½-inch foldout that bore McCloskey's picture and the slogan: "What is a True Republican? McCloskey!" on one side and fifteen pictures and more than two thousand words of text on the other.) The McCloskeyites even held a "True Republican rally," an event that some campaign workers felt needlessly disinvited the many Democrats who had always supported McCloskey. The campaign, however, was a success. Robin Schmidt came out from Washington to run the campaign office. Rusty van Bronkhorst and Cubby McCloskey's other old friends mobilized the women, and Al Schreck and his fellow financiers raised more money than at any time since the Shirley Temple Black campaign. All told, McCloskey spent $102,436 in the primary, to $58,232 by Athearn.* He defeated Athearn by the convincing margin of 38,830 votes to 25,907.

* McCloskey's contributors included Mr. and Mrs. Leonard Firestone, major contributors to former Senator Thomas Kuchel and probably the most liberal big contributors to Ronald Reagan in 1966. Salvatori and Leland Kaiser, both heavy contributors to Reagan, supported Athearn, whose campaign reports were more detailed than McCloskey's. The law requires that the amount of contributions be listed in the general election and only the contributors in the primaries. But Athearn listed the amounts, anyway. Salvatori gave $5,000 and Kaiser $1,000.

McCloskey had problems other than his own campaign. He and U.S. Senator George Murphy had held each other in mutual suspicion since the defeat of Shirley Temple Black, and McCloskey's crack about Murphy's consultantship with Technicolor during the Justice Douglas debate had destroyed the last vestige of any relationship. McCloskey favored Norton Simon in the 1970 Republican primary against Murphy.* Simon at the time was engaged in a self-appointed kamikaze mission against Murphy, who handily won the Republican primary but was damaged by Simon's attacks and became easy prey for Democrat John V. Tunney in the general election. McCloskey personally preferred Tunney, a House colleague, but he had been advocating the election of a Republican Congress as the surest way to scrap the seniority system, and he had agreed that he would support the entire Republican ticket. Even "bad Republicans" were preferable to "good Democrats" in this cause, McCloskey told a press conference, but he retreated from this view under pressure from the San Francisco *Chronicle*'s Mike Harris and other reporters. When the press conference had ended, Harris had wrung a statement from McCloskey which suggested that he might vote for Tunney instead of Murphy. "That endorsement [of Murphy] was the most dishonest thing I've ever done in my life," says McCloskey in looking back at it. "I shouldn't have put myself in the position of ever saying something that I didn't believe." The statement at the time alarmed some of McCloskey's supporters, who thought it might hurt his credibility with young people. But there is no evidence of this in the voting results. McCloskey defeated Democrat Robert E. Gomperts by 144,500 votes to 39,188, and emerged from the election with the second highest winning percentage of any Republican who in 1970 faced a contested election.†

* Simon favored McCloskey, too, and contributed $1,294 to his general-election campaign.

† Gomperts' campaign emphasized the difficulty that Democratic congressional candidates have experienced in developing issues against McCloskey.

He also emerged from the election with a deep distrust of the President, Vice President Spiro Agnew, and the entire ill-conceived Republican campaign. What bothered him most was an emphasis on "law and order" that McCloskey considered misplaced, misleading, and unfair. "Are they trying to say that the Democrats are against the law?" he complained. McCloskey was particularly annoyed by a Murphy campaign advertisement that depicted Tunney as voting against effective law enforcement and concluded: "It is this kind of permissiveness that has made our streets, our schools, and even our courthouses unsafe." Robin Schmidt recalls that McCloskey was "deeply saddened" by the tone and tactics of the campaign. "Both of us thought that it seemed to be so contrary to what was needed in this country," Schmidt says. "Rather than unifying the country, the Republican campaign was pulling it apart." Schmidt believes that McCloskey's unhappiness with the campaign was a component in the decisions McCloskey reached in those last crucial weeks of 1970 when he took the first important steps toward a presidential challenge. My own notes from the day-before-Thanksgiving luncheon tend to support this view. Whatever weight is assigned to it, there is no question that the campaign deeply disturbed McCloskey at the very time he was concluding that the Nixon administration did not really intend to end the war in Vietnam.

The Cambodian "incursion" announced by President Nixon on

San Francisco *Chronicle* reporter George Murphy (who has since left the paper for a second tour of duty as McCloskey's press secretary) covered one McCloskey-Gomperts "debate" that he described as sounding "more like the cooings from an aviary." Unable to develop much difference on the issues, Gomperts ripped into McCloskey for his endorsement of other Republicans, citing in particular his backing of "two old-line hack politicians" for reelection to the Legislature and his support of John Rousselot against Mrs. Medgar Evers, the Democratic nominee, in a Los Angeles County congressional district. Gomperts' statement declared that "these endorsements have caused dismay and disillusion in the ranks of these idealistic and highly motivated young men and women to whom (McCloskey) has been a mentor and idol." A copy of the release was tacked up at McCloskey headquarters and initialed by McCloskey, who added the word "Amen."

April 30, 1970, had disturbed McCloskey even more. He questioned its military value from the first, and, as we have seen, he did not share the Nixon administration's view about the desirability of preserving the Saigon government. In fact, he seems to have regarded the whole affair as a betrayal of the administration's commitment to withdraw from Vietnam. Lew Butler remembers that McCloskey called Ehrlichman and asked to see him, and then the three of them drove into Washington the next morning with Ehrlichman and McCloskey arguing all the way. Butler remembers McCloskey hanging on the car door when he got out and shouting back and forth over the roof with Ehrlichman. "I knew very well I couldn't do anything for him," says Ehrlichman in looking back at it. "He had staked out a position that was contrary to the President's, and I'd been involved in some minor way in the development of the President's position. I knew the thinking that had gone into it. I knew from listening to him that McCloskey simply didn't have the facts, and I could tell it was an irreconcilable proposition."

McCloskey returned to his office and began composition of what became his third letter to the President about the war. This letter, dated May 7, 1970, and routed through Ehrlichman, shows how far he had come in his thinking about the Nixon administration. The first two letters had questioned policy and expressed respect for presidential leadership; the third is a direct challenge of Nixon policy:

> Dear Mr. President:
>
> Shortly after you took office, I wrote you a letter suggesting that the former Administration's Vietnam policy was mistaken and that it might be well to admit our past mistakes.
>
> You apparently never saw the letter, a copy of which is enclosed, although I did get a reply from one of your aides.
>
> I would like to again respectfully suggest that you consider the possibility of admitting that America and its presidents are capable of making mistakes and have done so.

A national war policy requires three things: military strength, the willingness of our people to pay the cost, and the willingness of our young men to fight. Is it not apparent to you that we have lost the latter two?

Your recent remarks and those of the Vice President on the campus situation are bringing this country perilously close to revolution, because it appears to our young people that you do not *care* about them, nor have you been willing to *listen* to them.

The young have a legitimate complaint. *They* are the ones asked to fight in a war in which they do not believe, against people they do not hate. Their friends and older brothers are being killed and maimed. In their view and in mine, tank commanders and air strikes destroying Vietnamese and Cambodian villages have little relevance to any ideological battle between freedom and communism. The plain fact, Mr. President, is that nothing you or the government can do is going to convince our young people that American purposes in this war are justified or that they should participate in the continued killing. Your policy of "no defeat, no humiliation" may have been justified in the 1950s and 1960s, but it is counterproductive today. Our first priority must be to reestablish the faith of our people in our government.

As a Republican who has tried to support your honesty and innovation in new domestic programs, I plead with you to abandon your intransigent attitude on Vietnam.

With over 470,000 men in its Army, 515,000 in its Regional and Popular Forces, and at least 215,000 in its People's Self Defense Forces and National Police, South Vietnam now has nearly ten times as many people under arms as the North Vietnamese have *ever* been able to put into the field against them. That American military forces and firepower can prolong this war for years is unquestioned; that we can win it is admittedly impossible. Only South Vietnamese can win their independence, and if they cannot do it in one year, I doubt that they can do it in four.

I therefore respectfully request, Mr. President, that you do three things:

1. Let the students of America know that you have listened to them.
2. Let them know you and this Administration cares [sic] about their thinking.
3. Order a continuing withdrawal of U.S. troops from the Asian continent, with all troops to be withdrawn by June 30, 1971.

Respectfully,
Paul N. McCloskey, Jr.

Though Ehrlichman had concluded that McCloskey's position was now "irreconcilable" with the President's, his own reply to the May 7 letter suggests that he wanted to keep lines of communication open as long as possible—and that he still valued McCloskey. The letter also suggests a presidential certitude that is equivalent to McCloskey's own:

Dear Pete:

I have discussed your letter with the President and he has asked me to express his appreciation for your concerns.

You may be sure that it is the President's intention to reduce and ultimately to end our involvement in the Vietnam conflict. We are doing this at a pace which we believe will give Hanoi a strong incentive to negotiate and will give the South Vietnamese time to assure their own defense. By this time next year, there will be only half as many American forces in South Vietnam as there were when the President took office a year ago.

Please also rest assured that the President has listened to the students of America and will continue to do so. He demonstrated this in his press conference of May 8. He will continue to listen to them, just as he listens to every element of American society.

Best personal regards.

Yours sincerely,
John D. Ehrlichman
Assistant to the President
for Domestic Affairs

By the time this letter reached McCloskey he was in California campaigning for reelection. He returned to Washington in

November, talking about the need for change, about the need to end the war. He talked about it to Cubby, to Robin Schmidt, to Lew Butler. He talked about it to me the day before Thanksgiving at lunch, and I remember him saying at one point that a political challenge was what Nixon really understood. The comment is similar to Butler's recollection from their dinner of the same period. Neither of us apparently attached that much significance to it at the time, although McCloskey was beyond question thinking heavily about a possible challenge in those final two months of the year and the first month of the next. First there was the memorable Thanksgiving letter (reprinted in the first chapter of this book) in which McCloskey asked the President to order U.S. troops to "cease participation in the killing as America's gift to the world this Christmas." Then came a San Francisco luncheon at the University Club on January 29 attended by McCloskey, Schmidt, Al Schreck, Ry Kelley, David Lennihan, Bob Thede, and Peter Sherrill.* Lennihan remembers that McCloskey brought up the subject then. "My reaction was just wildly negative," said Lennihan, "and so I spoke. And I finally agreed with outspoken reservations that this course of action could be considered reasonable if it was absolutely clear that McCloskey had no ambition or desire, no willingness to serve as President but was acting solely as a vehicle through which those who chose to tell Nixon that they were Republicans but didn't like his Vietnam policy could do so." Even before the luncheon, however, McCloskey had been talking presidential challenge. When he spoke at the First Presbyterian Church in Palo Alto on December 20 he publicly voiced what he had been saying in private: "I suspect if a grassroots organization was formed in this state to deny the President the Republican nomination, it might affect his thinking." He had crossed one important bridge on the road to the

* Schmidt says that the talk at the luncheon was sparked by Sherrill, a pollster, who was preoccupied with "the new moods and new concerns of the country."

New Hampshire primary, though he was a long way from burning it behind him.

While McCloskey was pondering a presidential challenge, Butler was trying to decide whether he should seek another troubled office. "I was seriously thinking about running for mayor of San Francisco, and I was going to take Robin [Schmidt] with me to do it. So Pete said okay, and he and Robin and I organized a dinner to discuss my running for mayor. And we got all the same guys we'd had for the dinner when Pete wanted to run. We had a replay with a few new actors. That happened to be the night after Pete was at Stanford and said, 'Let's impeach Nixon.' I got off the airplane with [Health and Welfare Undersecretary] Jack Veneman to go to this dinner, and here was McCloskey, and everybody was on him because he'd been on the evening news. So we spent a hell of a lot of time on it. But we had the dinner and essentially talked most of the time about Butler running for mayor. All the guys there were really out of McCloskey's campaign, plus Robin, his own staff man, and there was no suggestion that any of them would be busy running Pete for President. Robin was seriously considering coming out and trying to make a decision, and he *wasn't* [Butler's emphasis] talking about running out on Pete's presidential campaign. There was no suggestion of that. When we got back, Robin and I talked, and I just decided I didn't want to do it. But still it wasn't because of Pete. Right at that point, it seems to me, there was a shift. As a result of the impeachment statement, suddenly Pete started saying more and more things, and it finally came out: 'I am going to run.' It was kind of what he'd said the preceding November, but now people were writing it."

The "impeachment speech"—most of McCloskey's friends and all of his enemies remember it that way, although McCloskey continues to blame the press for taking what he said "out of context"—occurred February 11 at Stanford and gave McCloskey the national attention that had escaped his musings or his

December 20 speech at Palo Alto. The speech was covered by Jeff Littleboy of the Stanford News Service, who filed a detailed account the following day with an opening paragraph remarkably similar to the opening paragraph in the Palo Alto *Times* after the December speech fifty-two days before. The only difference was that McCloskey in February was emphasizing Laos, where the ill-starred South Vietnamese invasion known as Lam Son 719 had just begun:

> STANFORD—President Nixon might change his mind about Laos "if we [the college community] started a national dialogue to discuss his impeachment," Rep. Paul N. (Pete) McCloskey told a Stanford audience Wednesday night, Feb. 11.
>
> He also suggested that contacts made by college students upon the "friends and close advisers" of their own congressmen would be a means of increasing anti-war feeling in Congress.
>
> In addition, Western college campuses should send delegations to their counterparts in the Midwest, Deep South, and to the constituencies of "hawk" congressmen in Southern California, the Republican Congressman from Portola Valley (San Mateo County) said.
>
> McCloskey was invited to an informal seminar in Mark Twain wing of Stern Hall by Robert Grant of the Associated Students' Council of Presidents and other moderate students interested in seeking non-violent ways to stop the Southeast Asia war.
>
> . . . He emphasized that any student effort to bring about massive change in the country's foreign policy or anything else must be sustained. He pointed to the collapse of student interest between the Cambodian incursion of last spring and the November elections, when not all anti-war candidates received full student support.
>
> Rep. McCloskey explained that there are three possible ways to change the course of American policy in Southeast Asia—one to actually impeach the President, "but this cannot be done unless the House votes to do it."
>
> Second, Congress can vote to "cut off Nixon's money" for Southeast Asia, a proposal which now has the support of 154 congressmen, but 218 votes are needed.

Third, the "national dialogue" discussing possible impeachment which can serve as an attention-getter.

Voting to "cut off the money" cannot be done by the end of June. It would take from six to nine months between the presentation of the 1971–72 budget in May and its adoption in the fall . . . McCloskey said.

Turning to the war itself, Rep. McCloskey said:

"Nixon's plan to end the war has failed. The government's dilemma is that if the North Vietnamese demands for withdrawal of every American military man in Vietnam is granted, the South Vietnamese government will fall—which no one in Washington is prepared to admit.

"What we are doing in Laos is as great a crime as those we executed Japanese and German officers for in World War II," McCloskey . . . told the student gathering.

"People want out of the war, but they are not willing to challenge the President, and this feeling also pervades the halls of Congress," he said.

If other people were "not willing to challenge the President," McCloskey was. He had lost most of whatever respect he had ever possessed for Nixon. When I suggested to him, in a conversation the following week, that the President would change Republican political strategy because of its general failure in 1970, he replied: "That confirms almost every feeling I have about what moves our leader." * Most importantly, McCloskey was convinced by events that the United States was being drawn deeper and deeper into an immoral war. First, there had been Vietnam, then Cambodia, then Laos. The arguments that Nixon advanced on television in behalf of the latter two campaigns seemed, to McCloskey, so devoid of merit that it was "necessary to do something Nixon would understand," i.e., a political challenge. McCloskey was not the only man in

* And this disrespect, once surfaced, stayed there. At a meeting with Washington reporters on March 31, McCloskey said he was optimistic that the President ultimately would abandon his bombing policies in Indochina. "Everything I've ever perceived about Richard Nixon is that he will do whatever is necessary to get elected," McCloskey added.

public life to reach this conclusion. What made him different from other people is that he was willing to act on it.

McCloskey's friends could not at first believe their ears when they heard and saw the broadcast reports and the news stories on the impeachment speech. "Either Pete was misquoted or he's not serious about it," said state GOP Chairman Putnam Livermore, McCloskey's friend from the days when they were fighting repeal of the open-housing law together. McCloskey himself tended to minimize the importance of his impeachment statement at the subsequent dinner for Lew Butler when he was asked about it by Emily Pike, the San Francisco County Republican chairman. "McCloskey's reaction was sort of nonplussed," recalls Dave Lennihan. "He paused, and it was obvious that he was thinking, and then remarked, 'Yes, I did in the course of a talk there [Stanford] use the word "impeachment."' Now this goes back to McCloskey's quality as a lawyer and also to a vice that attaches to most every lawyer. Lawyers have labels for categories of thought, and the labels have lay meanings, and the lawyer's meaning and the lay meaning are frequently different. . . . The remedy for an excess of power by an executive, whether or not that excess involves immoral or otherwise punishable actions, is impeachment."

Lennihan's view that impeachment is a broad remedy for "an excess of power" has its disciples, perhaps including House Republican Leader Gerald Ford, who argued on behalf of his anti-Douglas resolution that impeachment was "whatever the majority of the House of Representatives considers it to be at any given time in history." But McCloskey had unequivocally and effectively challenged this position in his April 21, 1970, defense of judicial independence. He compared impeachment to a prosecution, traced its roots in colonial history, and declared at the time: "There is considerable evidence in the adoption of the Constitution itself that the founding fathers considered impeachment as analogous to criminal proceedings." McCloskey quoted from the first full draft of the Constitution to prove his case, a case he made so well that it is disconcerting to hear him contend (as he did in a post-Stanford interview) that impeachment "is not limited to high crimes and misdemeanors." The long incubation of McCloskey's decision also suggests that he was moving to some dramatic and attention-getting statement of his position. For these reasons, it always seemed to me that there was a certain artifice, unbecoming to a man of McCloskey's candor, in his repeated assertions that he had not advocated impeachment of President Nixon, "only" a dialogue on his impeachment, almost as if he were willing to accept the advantages of using the word while disavowing its negative implications. McCloskey was, after all, as Jeff Littleboy's stories and notes show, talking about impeachment as "an attention-getter," and he acted out his point by drawing the widest possible attention to his challenge. Even his conservative former law partner, self-styled "hawk" Roger Mosher, remained relatively undisturbed by the impeachment statement, though he is deeply disturbed by McCloskey's remarks on U.S. policy in Southeast Asia. "The impeachment statement was vintage McCloskey," Mosher says, and few who know McCloskey would disagree. Whatever interpretation is placed on McCloskey's motivations—"I'm sure I don't understand them, and he doesn't either," says Butler—there is no question that the use of the word "impeachment" gave McCloskey's willingness to challenge Nixon on the war national publicity which he had not experienced since his original campaign. The publicity also called McCloskey to the attention of men who wanted to defeat Nixon and who had taken no account of an intraparty challenge before. After Stanford, McCloskey would find it increasingly difficult to turn back.

McCloskey expanded upon his challenge the following week in a House speech that was perhaps his most carefully prepared document since the statement opposing impeachment of Justice Douglas. "He found himself halfway across a slough, and he either had to go back or go forward," says Lennihan.

"He chose to go forward, which is typical of McCloskey." McCloskey's going forward started with an advocacy of resolutions calling for an immediate end to aerial warfare in Laos and Cambodia and a halt to funding of troops in Vietnam after December 31, 1971.* "I would further urge that early consideration of these issues is the obligation of the Congress under our Constitution, and that we can no longer stand by in blind acceptance of the policies that the President is presently pursuing. . . ." McCloskey defined these policies as a withdrawal timetable "which obviously contemplates leaving American troops in Vietnam as late as 1973, if not indefinitely," and "massive bombardment and aerial invasion of Laos and Cambodia." He declared:

> A reasonable argument can be made that the President's recent decision to employ American airpower in support of South Vietnamese and Cambodian forces in the neutral countries of Laos and Cambodia exceeds his constitutional powers and is, *at best* [author's emphasis], a deliberate flouting of the will of Congress.
>
> The Constitution grants to Congress, not the President, the sole power to determine where and when we go to war. If war is to be waged in Laos, if Laotians are to be killed and Laotian villages and countryside destroyed by American firepower, then it would seem appropriate that Congress is the only body in our government to properly make that decision.

McCloskey argued that the President possessed the power to conduct the war in Southeast Asia as long as the Gulf of Tonkin resolution, with its far-reaching statement about "prevent(ing) further aggression" was in effect. "A clearer grant of authority to the President to wage war in Southeast Asia could not have been made," McCloskey said, with a perception that had eluded many congressional doves. But he argued that the action had deprived the President of warmaking power in Southeast Asia other than "as commander-in-chief to protect the lives of Americans remaining in Vietnam, and to take all steps reasonably

* The *Congressional Record,* pp. H-794–800, February 18, 1971.

necessary to this end." He went on to examine the improbability that American lives were being protected by the provision of close air support to Cambodian forces operating sixty miles from South Vietnam. And he also examined a series of legal cases involving the President's authority to commit emergency forces. "I have been unable to discover a single instance . . . where an American President ordered offensive operations in a foreign country immediately after Congress had specifically repealed a prior resolution authorizing him to wage war in such country." Finally, he turned to the question of impeachment:

> I do not suggest that the case against the President is sufficient to justify that extraordinary remedy of impeachment which the Constitution gives to the Congress in cases of presidential abuse of his obligation to "take care that the laws should be faithfully enforced." I do not advocate impeachment, but the question is certainly one which justifies a national discussion and debate, if only to bring home to the President the depth of despair many of us feel over his recent moves without the prior consent of the Congress.

McCloskey then quoted Edmund Randolph's view of the impeachment clause in the 1787 constitutional convention, unwittingly impeaching his own argument in the Justice Douglas case. But he shed himself of the impeachment issue as soon as rhetorically possible and asked the valid question about what the Congress should now do to exercise its leadership capacity. Quoting Lincoln and Alexander Hamilton along the way, McCloskey proceeded to the central difficulty that Congress has experienced in attempting to exercise its constitutional powers in the twentieth century:

> First. We have repeatedly allowed the administration to conceal from both Congress and the American people facts which were highly relevant to our own decision-making process and the support of our constituents. For years we permitted the administration to conceal the fact that we were bombing in Laos well beyond the area of the Ho Chi Minh trail; American ground combat

forces have been sent into Laos and told to conceal the fact . . . the wives of American pilots shot down over Laos were instructed by our Defense Department not to reveal that their husbands had been shot down over Laos; we have pursued the fiction that American combat operations directed by the U.S. ambassador and civilian employees of the Central Intelligence Agency in Laos did not really constitute American combat activity at all.

Perhaps, most amazingly of all, we have permitted the administration to conceal from most of us in the Congress the precise amount of the Defense Department appropriations necessary to conduct the war in Vietnam and Laos. . . .

Second. As a corollary to our acceptance of the concealment of Vietnam war costs during our consideration of Defense Department budget requests, we have permitted our strategic weapons strength and research and development to lag behind that of our real Communist opponent, Soviet Russia. Shortly before his death, our distinguished colleague Mendel Rivers made an impassioned speech in this chamber, suggesting that the United States had never been in graver peril because of the deterioration of our comparative strategic position vis-à-vis the Soviet Union. Mr. Rivers stated that the three basic reasons for this deterioration lay in our great expenditures in Vietnam over the previous five years . . . and in increased domestic priorities. In his remarks, Mr. Rivers made it clear, to many of us for the first time, that in order to conduct the war in Vietnam, this country had cut back many essential defense programs . . . particularly in the field of research and development.

The magnitude of Russia's gain from our Vietnam involvement is reflected by the fact that while we have spent well over $120 billion in Vietnam over the past five years, the Soviets have spent less than $10 billion. Since their defense budgets are roughly similar to ours in size, say in the $70 billion range, the $110-plus billion saved by them has presumably gone into missiles, naval vessels, submarines, and research and development, which last year surpassed our own.

Here was an argument, neglected in most of the press accounts of McCloskey's speech, that was the antithesis of the dove case for unilateral disarmament. McCloskey had voted against some other defense expenditures, notably the anti-ballistic missile, but he had supported research-and-development funds and naval expansion. In the course of challenging the Vietnam War, he had also made the best possible military case for its prompt conclusion. He turned from this argument to moral questions, and his remarks are an illustration of what Charles McClung means when he says that McCloskey can't abide "national cowardice":

> Third. We have tacitly permitted the United States to gradually adopt methods of waging war which are repugnant to our highest traditions of military history and honor. Having lost the stomach for fighting this war and suffering the casualties involved, we have grown to accept the idea of hiring mercenaries to do our fighting for us. We have paid the salaries of South Koreans, Thais, and others, failing to connect this with our own historic antipathy to the concept of the British hiring the hated Hessians to put down our own revolution against the British crown. Less than twenty-five years after Nuremberg, where we insisted that the wanton destruction of villages and the forced relocation of civilians should be considered war crimes against humanity, we adopted the same sort of tactics in Vietnam, forcing Vietnamese peasants to leave the villages and farmlands where they had lived for generations, and then destroying the villages themselves. . . .
>
> Fourth. We likewise seem to have fallen into the view, now so vigorously espoused by the President, that it is all right to destroy the villages and people of small countries like Laos and Cambodia, if only we do it through air power, rather than in head-to-head ground combat where those who pull the triggers actually see the killing.

The President had not, of course, said that destruction of villages in Cambodia and Laos by air power was "all right." The statement, however, illustrates McCloskey's conviction that, as he put it two sentences later, Americans all over the world "are thoroughly hated and condemned for the disregard of human life and humanity we betray by our use of sophisticated airpower, napalm, and helicopter gunships against the people of villages like Skoun in Cambodia and Sarabane in Laos." He went on to argue that the war had also damaged U.S. militray potential; jeopardized the fate of our prisoners of war in North Vietnam, and deflected federal budget dollars from various domestic priorities. All told, it was McCloskey's most encyclopedic and effective attack on American war policy in Southeast Asia.

The speech did not go unchallenged. John Schmitz arose to declare that the Laos incursion was "one of the real breakthroughs in the allied effort against North Vietnamese aggression." Schmitz, who is also a member of the Marine Reserve, quoted Senator Barry Goldwater's comment that "the operation should have been carried out long ago." "The truth is that the North Vietnamese Communists, heavily supplied by the Soviet bloc and Red China, have shown by word and deed that their protracted campaign to bring all of Indochina under their heel can be stopped only by removing the implements they need to continue the war," Schmitz said.

But the sharpest challenge to the premise of McCloskey's case came from a Republican congressman more favorably disposed to him than Schmitz—Republican Caucus Chairman John Anderson of Illinois. Anderson, who wrote a letter praising McCloskey for use in McCloskey's primary campaign, took direct issue with the notion that President Nixon had ever based his authority on the Gulf of Tonkin resolution:

> I would remind the gentleman that it was not this administration, but rather a prior administration, that regarded the Gulf of Tonkin resolution as the functional equivalent of a declaration of war. This has never been the position of the Nixon administration. Indeed, as I understand it, at the time . . . repeal . . . was before the other body the administration expressed some disinterest in whether or not it [the Tonkin resolution] was repealed at all, because the President was not resting his constitutional power upon what admittedly is a very fragile reed. I think it is

already clear that it is on his implied power that the President bases his action to defend American forces in the field, and to protect those lives.

Under Anderson's gentle questioning McCloskey reiterated that he did not favor impeachment of President Nixon, and conceded that the President's implied power as commander-in-chief might be used to justify the interdiction of the Ho Chi Minh trail in Laos. He continued to insist, however, that such powers were insufficient to support the intrusion into Cambodia.

The McCloskey speech in the House came on the same day that one of the first and foremost Democratic critics of the war, South Dakota Senator George McGovern, contended that President Nixon was "flirting with World War III in Asia." McGovern's statement also touched on the prisoners of war, and the senator, like McCloskey, insisted that Nixon-administration policies were prolonging their imprisonment. McGovern had been well covered on the issue of the war ever since he announced his presidential candidacy the previous December. But on February 18 McCloskey received better billing than McGovern in many newspapers. McCloskey had become a national figure to a greater degree than at any time since his defeat of Shirley Temple Black. His campaign, however, was just beginning. Before McCloskey finished, the President would have far more to answer than a letter composed at McCloskey's Thanksgiving dinner table.
provinces (I Corp) and the Mekong Delta, and what he saw

Part Four
Presidential Challenge

We cannot live our dreams. We are lucky enough if we can give a sample of our best, and if in our hearts we can feel that it has been nobly done.

—Oliver Wendell Holmes

11. *Mission to Asia*

The road to New Hampshire led also through Xuan Loc and Son My and Ban Na Nga. Pete McCloskey took this road during the 1971 congressional Easter recess on his third Southeast Asian trip in four years. It turned out to be the most emotion-laden and controversial journey of his life.

McCloskey went to Vietnam and Laos as very much a potentional presidential challenger. He had stoked the fires of that challenge ever since the "impeachment speech" at Stanford, which almost overnight converted McCloskey into a national news figure. Nothing that McCloskey said to reporters afterward did anything to lessen this interest. On February 19, the day following his speech in the House, McCloskey told Adam Clymer of the Baltimore *Sun* that he was looking for someone to challenge Nixon in the primaries, and added: "I would back any responsible, seasoned Republican." Clymer compared the effort to Al Lowenstein's "dump-Johnson" movement in 1968 and quoted McCloskey as saying: "There are two ways to end the war. Cut off the money, or change the President." On February 24 McCloskey raised the likelihood of a presidential challenge of his own. While still holding out for some other "reasonable Republican," McCloskey said he would consider running himself if Nixon continued "his unholy policy of widespread killing and devastation in Indochina." And on February 28, Thomas Foley reported in the Los Angeles *Times* that McCloskey would enter the 1972 primaries if the President's Vietnam policy continued and no other challenger emerged. "The whole thing is to make the fight, and this is the right fight to be in," McCloskey said.

As always, McCloskey prepared for his trip with a series of voluminous briefings on the countries he was scheduled to visit. "In any given lawsuit there may be one hundred facts and only five or six of importance," McCloskey said once during those hectic days of preparation, and he seemed determined that the five or six facts of importance should not elude him. John Wilson, the McCloskey aide charged with preparing the briefing notes (one for every participant, plus a special book for McCloskey and other books on the Vietnamese elections and Laotian refugees), came up with more than a hundred pages of background information, maps, and people to see in Laos and Vietnam. McCloskey was especially concerned about Laos. He had begun reading of the report prepared by Senator Edward Kennedy's Judiciary Subcommittee to Investigate Problems Concerned with Refugees and Escapees, and he had read also articles in *Life* and *The New Republic* that were critical of American bombing policy in Laos. The author of *The New Republic* piece was Carl Strock, a Laos-based reporter who would later become a figure in the controversy triggered by McCloskey in the village of Ban Na Nga. The information in the black, loose-leaf briefing books prepared by Wilson was also of a critical tone. Much of it had been supplied by Fred Branfman, a former official of the International Volunteer Service who became one of the most outspoken opponents of American policy in Laos. He visited North Vietnamese and Soviet embassies and wrote articles critical of American policy in Laos. "The United States has carried out the most protracted bombing of civilian targets in history in Laos," read the Branfman-supplied information in the briefing books furnished members of the McCloskey party. "Hundreds of thousands of Laotians are living underground. They have been living there for years, huddling together in caves, holes, and trenches. Targeting is under the functional control of the CIA; operational aspects are handled by the Air Force. The American ambassador has nominal control, and the present one, [George McMurtrie] Godley, allows as much bombing as possible to go on." Not all of the information in the briefing book was of this character. The notes prepared for McCloskey and his staff also suggested factual questions (e.g., "How many houses were left standing when you left your village") rather than attitudinal ones. And Wilson set up briefings for McCloskey with State Department and U.S. Agency for International Development (AID) officials on the refugee situation.

Mark Pratt is the "country officer" in the State Department for Laos and Cambodia. He responded to Wilson's telephone request by briefing McCloskey on March 28. McCloskey, according to the recollections of both Pratt and Wilson, brought up the writings of Branfman. "He mentioned that bombing was the principal cause of refugees in Laos, and talked about a survey," Pratt says. But it was not quite clear to Pratt whether McCloskey was talking about a survey conducted by Branfman or of a hitherto unpublished survey on refugee attitudes made by the United States Information Service. Pratt knew that both Branfman and the Kennedy subcommittee were aware of the survey, which he says had been delayed by USIS Director Frank Shakespeare, who was "unhappy" that his employees had been used in its preparation. Because of Shakespeare's view, and Pratt, the State Department had decided to make a summary rather than the full survey available to the Kennedy subcommittee.

"We were trying to get the summary to the Kennedy subcommittee," says Pratt, "but there was no suggestion of urgency, and it was moving along slowly without being goosed from on high. When I got back to my office to double-check, I said the summary had gone over [to the Kennedy subcommittee], had it not? And I was told it was still in clearance." Pratt informed Roderic O'Connor, the State Department's assistant administrator for Southeast Asia, that McCloskey apparently knew what was in the contents of the survey. O'Connor, along with Robert H. Nooter, State Department assistant administrator for Vietnam, briefed McCloskey the following day. Wilson says that Nooter was unable to answer McCloskey's questions and that O'Connor stepped in "and did somewhat better." But McCloskey, in his best trial-lawyer style, continued to press for more facts on Laotian refugees, and O'Connor produced the survey. He did so inadvertently, he would explain later, because the summary contained a note saying that the document should not be turned over to McCloskey. "It wasn't any big secret document, but it was background and had not been cleared," says O'Connor. "It was standard operating procedure not to dish out other people's documents. When I returned, I took a little bureaucratic flak, which was of no great moment, and I called McCloskey's office." O'Connor's request at that point, both he and Wilson agree, was to ask McCloskey to withhold publication of the document and to treat it as "an internal working paper." Wilson, who says he never presumes to speak for McCloskey, told O'Connor that he would make that recommendation to the congressman.

McCloskey now had in his possession, before anyone else outside the executive branch, the first official survey of any kind which purported to document the effects of American bombing in Laos. But he did not grasp the significance of what had been given to him. Wilson says he put a personal note on the summary stressing its importance and mentioned the matter to McCloskey twice. "This is the document we've been looking for," he said on one occasion. "I examined the summary after the meeting and gave it back to the congressman," Wilson recalls. "There were documents all over his desk. I put a personal note on his desk to be sure he looked at it. But it became progressively buried." Wilson believes that McCloskey—"He's very single-minded and doesn't want to let loose of an idea before he's digested it"—just became too involved in other issues and details. Immediately before McCloskey left, says Wilson, he tried again, telling McCloskey: "On your reading on the plane, this is one thing that you should take a look at." But McCloskey was not to read the document until he actually reached Laos.

The night before he left, McCloskey went to New York to raise money for his Southeast Asian journey. Cubby went with him, and so, too, did Charles U. Daly, his old comrade-in-arms from Korea, and Daly's wife, Mary. New York had been mostly Daly's doing. First there was a bar, with Jimmy Breslin and two wealthy industrialists whom Breslin introduced to McCloskey. One was Martin Fife, a plastics manufacturer who donated two round-trip tickets to Southeast Asia. The other was Martin Rubin, an investor, who donated another ticket. After the bar there was a party, hosted by an old Stanford friend, David Guyer, that raised $7,750 for the McCloskey mission to Asia.* McCloskey, always at his best before small groups, made a quietly emotional appeal against the war.

We left Washington from Dulles International Airport in a driving snowstorm the night of April 6. It was the last such storm of the year in Washington, and the huge white blobs of snow melted as they struck the runway. McCloskey was in an exultant mood. He responds to travel and change and challenge, and he was now heading back for another look at the war that he had not been allowed to fight and had learned to oppose. "McCloskey carried with him a long, rolled-up map with a marking for every village in the Laotian panhandle," my notes of that night indicate. "He is already in Laos and in Vietnam." McCloskey talked that night of his war days, read from the

* Robert B. Meyerhoff, who gave $5,000, was the single largest contributor. Stewart Mott, the son of a founder of General Motors, gave $500, as did Donald E. Weeden. (Mott contributed $110,000 to Nelson Rockefeller in 1968 and $210,000 to Senator Eugene McCarthy the same year.) Other contributors at the dinner, all of whom gave $250 or less, included William Berhard, John D. Weeden, Alan D. Weeden, Robert M. Pennoyer, and David and Carol Guyer.

Kennedy report on refugees, and answered mail, including a letter to Lee Kaiser, the multimillionaire pro-Reagan financier who had written a letter to a newspaper in McCloskey's district calling the congressman "a dirty dastard." Kaiser had been the first person to suggest that he enter politics, McCloskey wrote in reply, and said, with a smile that was almost an afterthought: "That will fix him." He wrote other letters on the plane, too, letters explaining why his opposition to the war did not also embrace opposition to the draft. "I share the general concern that the availability of a large standing army provides some encouragement to presidential decisions to engage in foreign conflict, but believe that Congress has the clear power (and duty) to control such conflicts in our annual appropriations process," McCloskey wrote. Even his enemies can scarcely fault McCloskey's letter-writing policies. He writes real letters to real people, not the sort of so-glad-to-hear-from-you pap that is the staple of many congressional offices. Once, he responded to the entreaty of some outraged constituents to inspect a bar in his district that featured topless waitresses. McCloskey visited the bar and wrote back that he had no moral objection to the waitresses but thought they might present a health hazard when they bent over to serve beer.

But his mind was on serious matters that night and the next night when he left for Saigon by way of Wake Island and Guam. He had held a press conference before departing, a few moments after President Nixon appeared on television. (They had made cracks about the President's forthcoming speech earlier that week in McCloskey's office, and a reporter asked McCloskey what he would do if the President announced a total and immediate withdrawal from Vietnam. "Cancel my trip," McCloskey replied.) Now he was en route to Vietnam, alternately poring over his briefing book and telling war stories and dozing. ("He can sleep five minutes and refresh himself for eight hours," says Cubby McCloskey. "As you probably know, he's the lousiest traveling companion in the *world*.")

With McCloskey were Daly and Paul LaFond, a former Marine colonel retired after twenty-nine years in service. In 1969 LaFond had commanded the Third Marine Division astride the demilitarized zone, but he was now a member of McCloskey's staff and assigned, among other things, to evaluating Lam Son 719, the South Vietnamese attack into Laos. Also along were Representative Jerome Waldie, an antiwar Democratic congressman who represents a suburban and industrial district east of San Francisco, and Harold Willens, a Southern Californian who was one of the first businessmen to organize against the war. Willens (like Daly, he had been made a nominal member of McCloskey's staff for a salary of one hundred dollars) had paid his own way. Another who had paid and come on his own, with McCloskey's permission, was Jerry Cook, a young Fresno, California, businessman and delegate to the White House Conference on Youth. John Dominis, a *Life* photographer, and I were the only news-media representatives, which was fine with McCloskey. "Facts, facts," he said once, repeating his aphorism about one hundred facts in a lawsuit with only five or six that amount to anything. "We're going after facts."

Vietnam is a land of graves and greenery, a land that reminds McCloskey of the Korean ridges where he was twice wounded and where he earned the Navy Cross. McCloskey flew over Vietnam for the third time, concerned about the facts and more than the facts, deeply troubled about a war on which he was already on record. He had denounced the American "scorched-earth policy" after his 1969 trip, and he declared then that the United States was doing "exactly what we executed Germans for doing." In his "impeachment speech" at Stanford he had said: "What we are doing in Laos is as great a crime as those we executed Japanese and German officers for in World War II." Now he was in Vietnam, his case already made, questioning U.S. officials about Nuremberg and war crimes under the greatest sort of internal tension. "We're doing exactly what we executed General Alfred Jodl for doing," McCloskey said on many occasions, in a comparison between the U.S. evacuation of refugees in the northern provinces of South Vietnam and the German relocation of 100,000 Norwegians during World War II.* The war-crimes charge sat uneasily with the Americans whom McCloskey questioned, and even with a member of his own staff. During a Saigon briefing on April 7, McCloskey argued the case with George Jacobson, the staff officer for U.S. pacification efforts. Jacobson, an effective spokesman who on most issues held his own with McCloskey, just shook his head negatively when asked if he had read the Nuremberg precedents. But Jacobson received some unexpected help from LaFond, who described relocation of civilians in the northern provinces of Vietnam as an attempt to protect them from the Viet Cong, and added: "I don't think that's a war crime." McCloskey, tight-lipped, responded: "See, we're not all doves in this group." The incident dramatized McCloskey's unduplicated willingness to employ people who are more than yes-men, but it also strained the relations between the congressman and his aide. "They don't like what you're doing, Pete," LaFond said later in the trip after an evening with Marine officers. "They say you're undermining the younger men. They say to me: 'How can you work for McCloskey after you've been a Marine officer for twenty-nine years?' " McCloskey did not take his criticism easily. He believed that LaFond, like the others, was refusing to consult the Nuremberg precedents, refusing to believe that

* Whatever the merit or morality of the U.S. forced evacuations in Vietnam, the Jodl analogy appears to be a dubious one. Jodl was convicted of command planning and conspiracy, crimes against the peace, war crimes, and crimes against humanity. The forcible evacuation of civilians from northern Norway on October 28, 1944, was one of the counts of the indictment, but it pales beside the others, which include ordering the plans for the invasion of the Soviet Union and signing the notorious "commando order" that permitted the killing of uniformed soldiers. Jodl maintained on the stand at Nuremberg that the order was not in many cases carried out, and the prosecution then turned to another accusation. The British historian Alan Bullock says that few lives were lost in the Norway evacuation in comparison to most other evacuations by the Nazis.

Americans as well as Germans and Japanese could commit war crimes. I thought then and think now that the strain and tension which showed itself in McCloskey at this time stemmed from the difficulty of reconciling his career as a Marine officer with his present-day role as the most outspoken challenger of a war in which Marines have played such a conspicuous part. The Third Marine Amphibious Force, largest brigade ever deployed by the Marines overseas, was deactivated the week McCloskey was in Vietnam, and both he and LaFond visited Marine units that were looking forward to their final days or weeks there. "They make you humble," McCloskey said on the return helicopter flight from one such visit. "They're better men than we are." These better men, according to an article by James Pringle of Reuters that was written the week of McCloskey's mission to Asia, had in 1967 evacuated 10,000 civilians in the five northernmost provinces, an action Pringle called "one of the most callous forced movements of population in the war." If there is any Nuremberg basis for McCloskey's war-crimes charge, it is this forced movement of civilians.* (McCloskey conceded, in a subsequent debate in the House, that the aerial warfare which many of us find the most repugnant aspect of the war is not a "war crime based upon Nuremberg precedents." This uncomforting exclusion gives little assistance to moral as opposed to legal judgments, since it was based on the knowledge of Allied bombing policy in Dresden, Hamburg, Tokyo, and other civilian centers of population.) In fact, the most significant incident of McCloskey's six days in Vietnam concerned such an evacuation, this one involving Xuan Loc hamlet of Ap Thanh village in Thua Thien province. The villages had been resettled in a hamlet known as Gia Long B, and McCloskey was interviewing the

* The moral and legal questions posed by U.S. evacuations and free fire zones in Vietnam and the difficulty of applying Nuremberg precedents are authoritatively examined in Chapter 6 of *Nuremberg and Vietnam: An American Tragedy* (New York Times Co., 1970), by Telford Taylor, the U.S. Chief counsel at Nuremberg.

village chief and the elders in the town street with American advisers standing all around. The chief and the elders, speaking through an interpreter, told McCloskey that their original village had been "burned down by the VC," and then responded politely to McCloskey's questions about economic life in the new hamlet. This ritual was interrupted by Ho Le, an assistant platoon leader with a Popular Forces unit, who unexpectedly stepped forward and told McCloskey that the U.S. Third Marine regiment (LaFond's old outfit, though this was before he assumed command) had evacuated the villagers and burned down Xuan Loc in June 1966. "If they don't burn the houses, the VC will use them for shelter," was the way Ho Le explained the American reasoning. Though McCloskey didn't know it, his interpreter in Gia Long B almost ideally illustrated the other side of the American dilemma in Vietnam. The interpreter's name was Nguyen Than Nhat, and he was a recently married twenty-one-year-old staff sergeant in the South Vietnamese army. I talked with him at the next stop after Gia Long B and found that Nhat regarded such evacuations as an inevitable part of a war he didn't want. Further, the interpreter readily conceded that U.S. and South Vietnamese artillery had sometimes killed villagers. "The VC take refuge in the hamlets," he said in slow but excellent English. "The VC always make the people the targets. If we don't kill the people, we can't kill the VC." Nguyen Than Nhat was neither as simple-minded nor as callous as these words might make him appear. He realized that this targeting of the people was the essential problem of the war, and he repeatedly expressed distaste for any killing. But Nhat doubted that the Communists—"They never change their policies" —would ever let the war come to an end without killing everyone who opposed them. This included Nhat and his family, Catholic refugees who had marched south from North Vietnam in the great refugee exodus of 1954. Nhat was then four years old. He had managed ever since to avoid as much warfare as possible, but he said he had killed two VC on March 7 when the Viet Cong attacked a supply center where he was stationed. "I don't want to fight," he said. "But I've got to kill the Communists or they will kill me."

McCloskey visited one hamlet where the VC had made the people the target. On March 29, a week earlier, a mixed force of 1,500 North Vietnamese army troops and Viet Cong irregulars had struck Duc Duc and its satellite hamlets. Jack Foisie, the veteran Los Angeles *Times* military correspondent in Vietnam, reported that one of two prisoners taken in the fighting (the other died soon afterward) said the purpose of the attack was to demonstrate that the invasion of Laos "had not spoiled anything for us," and also "to make a point with the local people that they should have heeded our warning to move away." To make this point the attackers killed twenty-one military defenders and 109 civilians. Thirty-five of these civilians were believed deliberately "executed" by the Communist troops during their nearly twelve-hour occupation of the hamlet. But the American forces, though targeted in on Duc Duc, had not used their artillery. "That just makes VC," explained Army Colonel John Chism, who by coincidence was from Waldie's congressional district in California. The South Vietnamese troops, however, had apparently killed some civilians while firing into the village. No one made mention of this in Duc Duc, but Foisie quoted a "Vietnamese cameraman friend of mine" who blamed most of the civilian casualties on government troops.

The civilian toll in Duc Duc was the nearest to us in memory and time. Most of the forced evacuations which McCloskey had objected to so strongly had been carried out from three to five years before under a policy which, whether war crime or enlightened protection of the villagers, simply had not worked. Though he asked repeated questions in his staccato trial-lawyer fashion, McCloskey uncovered no evidence of recent misuse of American firepower. This may have been because of a new defensiveness among military men, most of whom were aware on one hand of the Calley trial and on the other of the rising stateside tide of protest against the war. Perhaps McCloskey and the other Americans who had spoken out against the war had already won a larger victory than they knew. I suggested as much to McCloskey at one point, and he agreed that conduct of the war may have changed in response to criticism of the way it had been waged. But he clearly was annoyed at a subsequent question about whether he had found evidence of any war crimes that had been committed between his February 1969 visit and the present one. "This is a first-class American effort over here," McCloskey said. "From what I've seen, the policy of search and destroy and of calling in artillery and air strikes on villages has ended. There is nothing I've seen in the present policy that could be called a war crime." I quoted these words in a subsequent story filed under a Da Nang deadline,* and it seemed to me a remarkable and positive comment on McCloskey's capacity for truthfulness that he would say this at all. But he has not, as far as I know, repeated the statement at any time since his return.

McCloskey crowded many experiences into his third Vietnam journey, more than most people would have accomplished in twice the time. He has an almost insatiable capacity for work, and an equal intolerance for the cocktail-party–swimming-pool routine that so easily diverts lesser men. Such events were scheduled for McCloskey by his military and civilian hosts, but he soon scratched most of them from the itinerary and allowed no others to be substituted in their place. He roamed all over the five provinces of I Corps, usually by helicopter, asking questions of Vietnamese and of Americans. We traveled to the Ashau Valley, to Hue, to a mountain district with a largely Montagnard population, to refugee reception centers, to resettlement sites, and to the DMZ. We met also with some of the forty young combat officers who had, while waiting for embarkation to Vietnam, written President Nixon a letter as revealing as any of McCloskey's own. The officers, all of whom expressed a willing-

* Ridder newspapers, April 14, 1971.

ness to obey their oaths, nonetheless urged total withdrawal from Vietnam "at the extreme earliest moment." McCloskey had made the letter public in August but withheld the officers' names. "We . . . find the continuation of the war difficult to justify, and we are being asked to lead others who are unconvinced in a war in which few of us really believe," the young lieutenants had written. "There is a great amount of bitterness both towards the military and towards America building up within the military forces." McCloskey's motivation in seeking out some of these officers in Vietnam was twofold. He wanted to find out if they had been punished for their letter, and he also sought their evaluation of the war. The response on the latter point was mixed, though one officer suggested to McCloskey that ARVN (the South Vietnamese army) could end the war after American withdrawal either by winning or losing, "and they might just decide that losing is easier." But none of the officers had been punished for their letter.

The Vietnam mission that had explored the related fates of Xuan Loc and Duc Duc turned also to the emotional experience of My Lai. McCloskey had been shaken by it, and his comments reflected both military and moral distaste. We talked about it on the plane en route, hours after Captain Aubrey M. Daniel III, the prosecutor in the Calley case, had charged that President Nixon's intervention was damaging to the military justice system. "It's awfully hard for a combat man not to feel sympathy for another combat man who maybe shoots first and asks questions later," McCloskey said. "But that does not extend to the Calley situation, where you have helpless people in your custody or under your control and allow them to be killed indiscriminately or shoot them yourself. I don't think there's a professional Marine in the whole Marine Corps who believes that Calley shouldn't have been convicted." I asked him then how he assessed the public outcry against the military court's decision. "I think it shows that large segments of the American people have become so inured to violence, so accustomed to considering the terrible Communist enemy as a threat that they justify in their own minds the killing of men, women, children, old people, as a lesser evil than communism. It's just a terrible example of how far this country has moved toward a position that's really unconscionable if this nation is going to lead the world toward peace. . . . I'm glad the Calley trial has surfaced this debate, because I think the debate ought to go forward on this issue. Have we become as a nation so accustomed to violence, to justifying violence, to [justifying] the indiscriminate air war, and things like that? My God, if we can justify My Lai and say Calley was right in doing that, we don't deserve to be leading the world. . . . We're what the Russians have been saying, we're an imperialist nation that has a racist attitude toward other people." McCloskey finished off this point with a comment he has made before and makes today about some of his congressional critics. "Most of these people who have been howling for the blood of the enemy I don't believe have ever been in combat," he declared.

McCloskey went to My Lai the day after Easter Sunday. The area around the hamlet was as insecure as it had always been, and Regional Force and Popular Force patrols had prowled the countryside before the congressmen arrived, looking for Viet Cong. The report of this disturbed Waldie, who made it clear he didn't want anyone, American or Vietnamese, risking his life for the congressional party. The U.S. military adviser in charge assured Waldie that it was "a low-level operation." But there was a tenseness to My Lai that we had not encountered even at the DMZ. Looking at the shelled ruins that were once homes, walking carefully in single file after repeated warnings about mines, we felt a special sense of insecurity. Perhaps it was only imagination, but there seemed an almost extrasensory oppressiveness to the hamlet, of which everyone was somehow aware. But of course we knew what had happened there. McCloskey, unfurling his inevitable map and looking deeply through the humid gloom into the fetid ditch where children and women and old men had been shot to death, said nothing at the time. Later he talked about young men making love to young women and said that everyone should have a chance to grow up and make love. "And he said it was no big deal," McCloskey recalled in the words used by Lieutenant Calley on the witness stand. Waldie said nothing at all.

My Lai did not provide the only emotional moments. Waldie and McCloskey also visited two hospitals, one of which confined the surviving North Vietnamese prisoner from Duc Duc, apparently the same prisoner whom Foisie had quoted. McCloskey returned close to tears, talking about the young prisoner (my notes show him as eighteen) and about how he had marched for fifty days to become a part of that terrible, typical little battle. The Communists had killed the civilians at Duc Duc because the soldiers lived in the hamlet and the attackers regarded everyone as the enemy. McCloskey asserted that this made considerable sense from the North Vietnamese and Viet Cong point of view, because the villagers were supportive of the government troops. This explanation seemed to me an uncomfortable one, incorporating many elements of double standard and not a little of the widespread American excuse for My Lai and similar events. McCloskey, however, was responding emotionally, not analyzing the war or offering a defense for North Vietnamese conduct. The young prisoner had reminded McCloskey of his sixteen-year-old son, John, the McCloskey child who in looks and manner resembles most his father. The independence and courage of the young prisoner had touched McCloskey, who as a combat officer had always dreaded capture and who now envisioned his own son in similar circumstances. "All you can do is hope that he lives and prospers," McCloskey said in recounting the visit the day after he returned from the South Vietnamese hospital at Da Nang where the prisoner was confined. "To say that he's a Communist and wish him harm is to admit defeat in the whole world." It was not the last time that McCloskey was to see his sons in Vietnam. Two days later, at

Waldie's suggestion, he visited an American evacuation hospital. This was the way McCloskey summed up the two visits, in a Hong Kong interview with the author two hours before the return flight to the United States: "I've seen two people in this country that are exactly like my sons. The first was the prisoner from North Vietnam. He was scared, he was fearful, he was in the custody of the enemy. He'd been wounded in a terrible battle . . . and he sticks his chin out and says, 'I was captured, sir. He was trying to play the man. He behaved just exactly like my own son John under similar circumstances. And then we go to the evac hospital in Long Binh, and we went into this neuro ward and there is this American kid sitting there. He looked exactly like my eighteen-year-old son [Peter]. Good in every way except that he's a vegetable strapped to a chair and [will] never have a chance the rest of his life to do anything, because he's just going to be a guy without a brain."

All of the above suggests that McCloskey was in a highly emotional state during much of his visit to Vietnam, and so he was. But the account is incomplete without mentioning that he was also, on other occasions, the irreverent, ribald McCloskey of old, the McCloskey who flashed both the peace sign and the middle finger above the DMZ, the McCloskey who lapsed into a mock, thumb-sucking display of fear when a twenty-year-old Sikorsky helicopter jolted to a stop in a Laotian village, the McCloskey who relieved tension by a spontaneous, losing sprint with Chuck Daly during an air-base interlude. He was also McCloskey the Trial Lawyer, intent on gathering the "true facts" and the true statistics in a land where all statistics seemed suspect. ("A detailed history of what was destroyed by whom just doesn't exist," a province adviser told McCloskey at one point.) Above all, he was McCloskey the Adventurer. Some of the places he wanted to go were insecure, and others were attacked within a few days of our visit, but this did not concern McCloskey. One night two Vietnamese special police were killed by a grenade a block from the white, high-ceilinged former consulate office where we were quartered in Da Nang (McCloskey and Waldie had the "Lilienthal Room"), and Daly at breakfast the next morning steered the conversation into a discussion of security. McCloskey brushed aside this concern by saying that from a standpoint of arousing opposition to the war "maybe the best thing that could happen would be for all of us to get killed." Waldie, quietly eating his bacon and scrambled eggs, responded dryly: "Count me out."

In fact, Waldie played an important and largely unrecognized role in the McCloskey mission to Asia. So, for that matter, did the entire McCloskey staff. Daly, who displayed a deep and protective concern for McCloskey's safety, also taped most of his friend's inquiries and, on the one evening he was separated from the congressmen, interviewed former political prisoners in Saigon. Willens conducted a valuable inquiry into the then forthcoming South Vietnamese elections, and LaFond, who had friends in ARVN, performed a characteristically thoughtful investigation of Lam Son 719, the disastrous invasion of Laos. But it was Waldie who played the most significant support role. The Democratic congressman, once the number-two man in the California State Assembly and now a prospective candidate for governor of California in 1974, had come to know McCloskey during their mutual fight for House reform. Like McCloskey, Waldie is an attorney, a conservationist, an opponent of the war, and something of a political lone wolf. But he is by temperament more cautious, polite, and analytical than McCloskey, and the two men complemented each other perfectly on interviews. Waldie spent a good deal of his time sleuthing about the Phoang Huang (Phoenix) program aimed at destroying the Viet Cong shadow government and its spookier, more secretive counterpart in Laos. However, it was as a balance to McCloskey that Waldie was to perform his most valuable service.

The two congressmen flew from Saigon to the Laotian capitol of Vientiane on April 13, stopping first at the U.S. air base at Udorn, Thailand, where the Thirteenth Air Force flies missions over Laos and the Ho Chi Minh trail. At Udorn, McCloskey attempted to determine the routes flown by pilots over Laos. He asked to talk to an aerial reconnaissance pilot and was introduced to Captain Marshall L. Michel, who was still in his flight suit and had just returned from a mission. Michel, as McCloskey remembers it, pulled a flight map out of his boot and proceeded to explain that routes are flown along roads and river valleys known as "lines of communication," and McCloskey then asked about villages along the route. The pilot replied that he hadn't seen any villages, an answer that is verified in testimony he gave to Congressman Charles Gubser of California, the Republican who would subsequently challenge McCloskey's entire interpretation of the Laotian episode. McCloskey and Waldie then flew on to Vientiane and dinner at the home of U.S. Ambassador George McMurtrie Godley.*

Godley, an urbane, sophisticated New Yorker, and a Navy verteran, came to Vientiane in July 1969, replacing Ambassador William H. Sullivan. The new ambassador, reported Arthur Dommen of the Los Angeles *Times,* was "ideally suited" for the job because his Navy service from 1939 to 1941 had given him a grasp of military staff needs and "his subsequent service at the American embassy in Bern during the World War II years had familiarized him with undercover operations." Godley had also directed the use of American planes in another undeclared war, the suppression of leftist revolts in the Congo in 1964. In the Central Intelligence Agency's undeclared war in Laos, Godley—like Sullivan before him—is supposed to have complete direction of the bombing efforts. "Godley's war effort

* The U.S. military command, which had initially attempted to prevent Dominis and me from accompanying McCloskey and Waldie on their trip through northern provinces of Vietnam, declined to fly us or the McCloskey staff to Vientiane, and we followed the next day by commercial aircraft. No reasons were given, and the U.S.-government plane that left Vientiane three days later took us to Udorn and then to Bangkok without incident. I had the feeling they would have cheerfully transported us halfway around the world as long as we were going away from Laos.

is directed from his air-conditioned, windowless first-floor office in the embassy," wrote Dommen, "against as many as two North Vietnamese divisions in the north. The real enemy is Hanoi—what the Pathet Lao do or say counts for nothing—and his motivation is bluntly stated: 'I don't like to see the United States get beaten.' To prevent that, Godley has a most impressive array of physical power and personal discretion, so much so that Senator Stuart Symington (D-Mo.) once remarked he was acting as chief of staff and said 'perhaps it would be better to call him Proconsul Godley.' "

The dinner at Godley's home on April 13 was a strange affair. By everyone's account, the ambassador had already been cabled the copy of the refugee survey summary furnished McCloskey, a summary which Godley had seen before in a different form. Mark Pratt, the State Department officer for Laos and Cambodia, says that a copy of a New York *Times* article outlining McCloskey's pre-trip critical views of American actions in Laos and Vietnam also had been sent Godley. The ambassador and his deputy chief of mission, Monteagle Stearns, were clearly aware that McCloskey had the summary in his possession. Yet, according to McCloskey's account of the time, the personnel of the embassy "lied" to him—he was particularly critical of Stearns and former Marine Charles Weldon of the embassy staff—when McCloskey asked whether the embassy possessed any "hard data" on refugee attitudes. According to McCloskey, the reply was that the embassy had no such data. McCloskey did not challenge the point, he says, because he had not read the survey summary in his briefing book and did not read it until six o'clock the next morning. But embassy officials could hardly have been aware that McCloskey had failed to read a summary that had been given to him in Washington. It would have made little sense to deny the existence of information that they knew McCloskey already had in possession, and even Godley's fiercest critics have not accused him of lacking sense. Waldie's recollection, while basically supportive of McCloskey, offers another explanation for the apparent mystery. "The Godley dinner was a setup in which Godley was the teacher and all the underlings were instructed to lay it on to Pete. The man who could be the toughest on Pete would get the highest score. They all came there, not with the intention of assisting us, but of laying it on to Pete." But Waldie does not go as far as McCloskey. "I don't put the great big emphasis that Pete does on the failure to give him that report," he says. "We really didn't ask a precise question. It may have been as close as they could come to lying, but it wasn't actually lying. I anticipated when I went there that I wasn't going to get an answer without a precise question, and maybe not even with one. That's not so unique as to create a national incident. The practice is more common than that."

McCloskey flew into a series of rages the next day, perhaps conceived in the style of "Ambassador George Siboney" of Silver Lance, perhaps in actual emotional response to what he considered a deception. After reading the summary in his briefing book, he stormed down to the embassy and asked to see the survey. He staged a scene in Stearns's office during which he embarrased Waldie by attempting to have the deputy mission chief's secretary impeach her boss's credibility. He staged another scene after Stearns showed him the document, took it back to make a copy for McCloskey, and removed the heading showing that it was sent from a United States Information Service official to Stearns. "This report has been altered," charged McCloskey, who engaged in another temper display at the Vientiane airport when Stearns failed to keep his promise to have the copies of the report aboard two helicopters that were scheduled to take McCloskey on a tour of refugee villages at Nam Pot II and Ban Xon. McCloskey ultimately canceled the helicopters and waited out the duplicating of the report. It all made for a magnificent demonstration that was fully covered by the Vientiane press, this reporter, and Matthew Storin of the Boston *Globe,* but it was more sound than substance. The "altered" report, after all, had not been altered except for the heading.

"It's inconsequential," says Waldie, who gave McCloskey effective support on the substance of his accusations. "I never did understand why it [the heading deletion] was important and I don't now. It was not motivated by a desire to conceal. An alteration, as I see it, is a change in substance."

What was the substance of the refugee survey, and how did it compare with the summary? The survey was based upon interviews with 226 refugees from the Plain of Jars, most of whom had left their homes in 1969 and were now living in the Vientiane plain. After a brief discussion of life under the Pathet Lao, the survey summary had this to say about the bombing in Laos:

> Ninety-seven percent of the people said they had seen a bombing attack. About one-third had seen bombing as early as 1964, and a great majority had seen attacks frequently or many times.
>
> The Pathet Lao, 75 percent of the refugees responded, had taught them to dig bunkers to avoid bombing attacks. When bombs dropped, all the villages reported taking refuge either in a bunker inside the village (28 percent), in a bunker outside the village (41 percent) or in the woods (31 percent). Two-thirds had seen someone injured by bombs; in 80 percent of such cases the victim was a villager, in 20 percent the victim was a Pathet Lao. Somewhat fewer than two-thirds of those who answered this question had seen someone killed. Usually a small number of deaths had been observed; 32 percent had seen only one person killed by a bomb. This applied to troops as well. Only 18 percent of the respondents had actually seen Lao/Viet troops killed by bombing, and 25 percent had heard rumors of such deaths. Isolated atypical answers to the questions were also received; one man said he had seen 112 persons killed, other individuals spoke of strikes that had killed 80, 20, 30, and 20 Pathet Lao troops respectively.
>
> Ninety-five percent of the 169 persons who responded to the question said their villages had been bombed; 75 percent said their homes had been damaged by bombing. Most of these attacks took place in 1969. Ninety-nine percent of the people said bombing made life difficult for them; two-thirds holding that it made

> earning more than a bare subsistence living impossible in its intense periods. Eighty-eight percent said they had built a shelter in the woods. Seventy-one percent of those questioned said that the United States was responsible for the bombing; 17 percent laid the onus on the RLG [Royal Laotian Government]. Seventy-four percent of the people said they understood that air attacks were caused by the Pathet Lao's waging war, but 23 percent said bombing was directed at the people as well as the Pathet Lao. Thirteen percent said it was aimed at the people only. Six percent said the Pathet Lao had stored ammunition in their villages, while 11 percent had heard of this practice in other villages. Respondents divided evenly in saying that Pathet Lao troops were present or not present in the area of bombing. The refugees knew aircraft names [F-104, Skyraiders, T-28, F-4] and were remarkably articulate about types of aircraft.

This was the entire section of the summary under the heading "Bombing." The summary went on to declare that 49 percent of those interviewed gave fear of the bombing as the reason they sought refuge, 29 percent gave dislike of the Pathet Lao, "while 15 percent said the arrival of the RLG and its allowing or encouraging them to leave was the primary factor. . . ." "Fifty-seven percent said they would return to their villages if bombing stopped, but this seemed associated in their minds with a complete end to the war and the disappearance of the Pathet Lao," the summary said. "Ninety-six percent said they would not return if the Pathet Lao were still in control of their homes." The United States Information Service officer who directed the interview concluded that it was a combination of the bombing, the objections to the forced porterage imposed by the Pathet Lao, and the lack of restrictions in the Royal Lao zone that induced the refugees to move.

Both the summary and the full survey yield identical conclusions. The survey does contain one statement not reprinted in the summary—"The bombing is clearly the most compelling reason for moving"—but the statistics of the summary speak for themselves. McCloskey, however, made much of this sentence, which he cited as an important omission in a "carefully prepared" summary. Such an inference seems unwarranted, when it is considered that two other "omissions" actually give the summary more impact than the parent document. The survey, unlike the summary, goes into some detail about its own limitations—a point cited by Godley and Stearns, who question its conclusions —and the typicality of its sample:

> Bad weather and the usual travel impediments hampered the interviewers' movements and limited the scope of their findings. The lack of time and paucity of the interviewers' experience (only one of the four had ever been involved in such an exercise) were also limiting factors. Nevertheless, the relatively large number of people queried should give some degree of validity to the findings—at least enough to indicate general trends of thinking. This group of people is atypical when compared to other refugees in Laos—the length of time they spent with the Pathet Lao separates them from the mass of refugees here.

A more important omission from survey to summary was this qualification:

> . . . Given the period involved for most of the respondents (1964–69) the number of people seen killed by the bombing was extremely low—32 percent had seen only one person's death caused by a bomb. The only exception to this was one refugee from Mouang Soui who reported having seen 112 people killed during a bombing raid. (Unfortunately, the interviewer who talked with this man is now sick and had to be taken to a hospital in Bangkok, so it is impossible to get any more details about this case.) The other responses indicate a generally low casualty rate.

The picture given by this report, though cited by McCloskey ever since, hardly squares with either Branfman's claims or with McCloskey's own invocations of "war crimes." But neither does it square with the official embassy picture of refugee generation contained in a black, loose-leaf notebook (almost indistinguishable from a McCloskey briefing book) that was distributed to members of the congressmen's party. The report plows through twenty-six pages of text, twenty-eight photographs, six maps, and two well-written appendices on the North Vietnamese and Pathet Lao. Nowhere is American bombing even mentioned.

Having spurned an inspection of two refugee camps that the embassy wanted to show him, McCloskey and his party went on the CIA-leased Air America helicopters to the dusty village of Ban Na Nga on the Vientiane plain. In contrast to Vietnam, where he spent most of his time far away from the news media, McCloskey had by now attracted to him most of the Vientiane press corps and some other reporters. He and Waldie spent most of the morning interviewing refugees in Ban Na Nga, all of whom came from seven villages in Thasseng Kat, an administrative division of Xieng Khouang in the southwest section of the Plain of Jars. All, without exception, had experienced bombing. McCloskey, in his usual trial-lawyer style, confined his questions to the facts that concerned him. He did not, as far as I am aware, ask any questions about the North Vietnamese or Pathet Lao other than about the presence of soldiers in the village at the time of the bombing. He did not ask why the refugees had become refugees. He did ask many detailed questions about the bombing, of which the following, an interview with a Buddhist monk, is a fair sample:

Q: When did the bombing start?
A: '69 they bombed, '67 they bombed, '66 they bombed.
Q: Many, many bombs?
A: Many hundreds.
Q: Was the village destroyed?
A: Not a single house remained.
Q: How did the village live . . . where did they live . . . how did the people live?
A: He said they . . . in the jungle.
Q: Did you have bunkers in the camp?
A: Yes.
Q: How far from the village did you live?
A: One hour walk.
Q: Were there any soldiers in the village? Did any soldiers live in the village?

A: They only passed through.

Q: Were any of your people killed or hurt by the bombing?

A: Six killed.

Q: Were they relatives? Do you know their names?

A: Six male adults.

Q: Were there any children killed?

A: No.

Q: How far from the village was the closest soldier's camp?

A: He doesn't know. He just saw them going through his village.

The sixteen persons interviewed by McCloskey and Waldie included a sixty-two-year-old woman, Tian Di, who after first trying to run away allowed herself to be interviewed and bared her breast to show shrapnel wounds. Her husband had been killed in a raid. Another refugee, a ten-year-old boy, displayed leg wounds that both McCloskey and Daly, who have seen such wounds before, believe were caused by cluster-bomb pellets of white phosphorus. This is the way McCloskey summed up his Ban Na Nga interviews when he testified before the Senate Foreign Relations Committee on May 27: "The refugees were unanimous in describing the destruction of every single home in each of the seven villages where they had lived. They described both T-28 and jet aircraft, as well as the use of CBU cluster bombs and white phosphorus; in all but one of the villages, the refugees had seen people killed by the air strikes, the most numerous being the village of Ban Phone Savanh, a village of thirty-five homes where nine were killed and fourteen wounded."

Neither McCloskey nor any of the rest of us who had come to Southeast Asia with him spoke a word of Lao. We were all at the mercy of interpreters, and McCloskey had asked Ambassador Godley to provide him with some who were "unbiased." The four interpreters in Ban Na Nga were Father Matthew Menger, the Reverend G. E. (Ed) Roffe, both serving at Godley's request, plus Edwin T. McKeithen of the U.S. Agency for International Development (USAID) and a Chinese interpreter named Wong. Menger, who was initially with Waldie, had on the journey to Ban Na Nga already convinced the congressman of his bias. "The trouble with the American youth of today is that they are yellow," Waldie says Menger told him. "They are not willing to shed their blood for other peoples." Waldie replied that Menger, a Dallas-born priest who was a Lao linguist and had served with the Meo for more than twenty years, might be in touch with Laos but was out of touch with America. "Go to Vietnam, from which Mr. McCloskey and I have just come," Waldie suggested. "Go to the hospital we visited. Take a look at the Americans who have shed their blood for causes in which I do not believe and probably they do not believe." Waldie and McCloskey split up in the village, and Menger went with Waldie. The other three took turns interpreting for McCloskey. When McCloskey and Waldie met in the village after nearly two hours of interviewing they compared notes and found that the refugees who had spoken to Waldie had said that Pathet Lao or North Vietnamese soldiers were present in the village when it was bombed. The refugees interviewed by McCloskey had said there were no soldiers in the villages. Waldie, attempting to retrace his steps with Roffe, was able to find only one of the refugees he had already interviewed. "The man gave a response entirely contrary to that which he had given in Menger's presence," Waldie said. This finding and Menger's insistence that McCloskey was "not getting the true picture" produced a bitter clash between Menger and McCloskey which Carl Strock, the Associated Press reporter in Vietiane, freely joined. Menger, a tall, thin-faced priest, was calmly puffing on his pipe when the argument started, but he and Strock were shouting at each other before long:

Menger: "Let me tell you. I have lived with these people. They will tell you one thing. You go back to the same people. You sit down with them, you have lunch with them, you live with them for a couple of days, you will find the real story. You're not getting the real story."

Strock: "You don't think they were really bombed?"

Menger: "Look. Wait. You want the real story. The immediate

cause of their leaving was probably the bombing. But that is the immediate cause. But the ultimate cause—the real cause—is because they do not want to lose their freedom. . . ."

Strock: "Why didn't anybody tell us that?"

McCloskey: "Nobody has said that. These people—every single one of these villages has been destroyed. There hasn't been a village we've . . ."

Menger: "This is a very Communist area."

McCloskey then closely questioned Menger on just what points the refugees were "not telling the truth." The priest retreated point by point under McCloskey's interrogation, conceding that the woman with the shrapnel in her breast "probably" was telling the truth about her husband being killed, and that others who had shown their wounds to McCloskey were "possibly" truthful. Finally, Menger could stand it no more:

Menger: "Even though our American bombing has in some instances killed people—I don't care if it's hundreds or thousands—all I can say is, 'Thank God for the bombing.' Otherwise, this country would not be free today." *

Strock: "I will quote you on that. I will say that Father Menger said, 'Thank God for the bombing.' I will say that."

Menger: "You can say 'Thank God for American aid to this country. . . .' "

Strock: "I'm going to say 'Thank God for the bombing' and put it as a caption under a picture of one of these wounded people."

McCloskey had by this time turned his back and walked away. The argument between Menger and Strock continued on the way back to the helicopters, with others joining in. Strock made it clear that he thought the priest had not been truthfully translating. And Menger told me subsequently that Strock was one-

* Both Matt Storin of the Boston *Globe* and I, the only stateside reporters present in Ban Na Nga during the interviews, recorded Father Menger as saying "hundreds *of* thousands" rather than "hundreds *or* thousands." McCloskey used "or" when he put portions of the interviews in the *Congressional Record.*

sided in his accounts of Laotian events and "unconcerned with the truth." Neither man displayed the self-awareness to consider that "the truth" extends both to accurate translation and to unbiased reporting.

But it is too easy, too easy and far too unfair, to assume that the truth necessarily lies in some other-worldly middle ground. The legitimate objection to McCloskey in Ban Na Nga, and to Menger and Strock as well, is not lack of truthfulness but lack of perspective. The congressman and the priest and the reporter, each convinced of the rightness of his cause, were in this case not seekers after truth but advocates and true believers. And they were not alone. The same day that McCloskey visited Ban Na Nga a delegation of ministers who were attempting to secure the release of American prisoners of war toured some of the refugee camps which McCloskey the day before had declined to visit. The special assistant to this delegation was William Hecht, a pastor of the Lutheran Church, Missouri synod, and a political conservative who had been executive director of the Republican party in Missouri for three years ending in 1969. Hecht was impressed by what he saw in these camps but emotionally affected, as McCloskey had been in Vietnam, by his visit to a hospital. What he saw there was the aftermath of an April 13 ambush where a civilian taxi en route to Vientiane had been waylaid and eight passengers, mostly women and children, killed. One old lady and baby had survived uninjured because they were protected by the bodies of the others. Three other persons had been wounded, and it was these whom Hecht saw. "We were in the hospital in Bon Son, and we talked to the survivors of this ambush," says Hecht. "Who speaks for them? One little boy who was there had an eye shot out. And just a week before we came to Laos the base had been attacked by the Pathet Lao or the North Vietnamese, and they had killed eleven civilians. So actually there were more civilians killed in a two-week period than McCloskey and his friends saw."

Hecht, unlike Menger, made some distinctions between Communists. He was convinced that the North Vietnamese and not the Pathlet Lao had ambushed the taxi, because the refugees "seem to feel that the Pathet Lao don't operate that way, but the North Vietnamese do." But neither Hecht nor the group he was with made any inquiries about American bombing, as far as I could ascertain. Nor did McCloskey, once he had determined that the villages of the refugees he was interviewing had been bombed, ask questions about whether the refugees were fleeing either the North Vietnamese or the Pathet Lao.

Perhaps there are no neutrals in Laos. I doubt whether the Reverend G. E. Roffe, a Canadian minister with the World Missionary Alliance, could be so classified. Roffe, who has lived in the country for forty-two years and speaks the language fluently, interpreted on two interviews of my own with villagers (one of whom, I believe, was subsequently interviewed by McCloskey). The refugees in both cases, with no other translator present, said that they were (1) fleeing the Communists and (2) had seen their villages bombed by American planes in attacks that killed relatives and friends. Roffe, however, told Hecht that he detected no discrepancies between his own translations and Menger's, a statement that simply cannot be supported by the evidence. On the other hand, Roffe surely had a point when he wrote Representative Charles Gubser:

> One group of refugees [apparently the Ban Na Nga group, for Roffe was replying to Gubser's query about the McCloskey interviews] was accurately reported to have stated that they left their villages because of the bombing. That statement, in isolation, would seem unequivocally to condemn the bombing. But responsible reporting should take into consideration the context of such a statement. That would require asking, "What prompted the bombing?" And the simple answer would be that the presence and activity of enemy forces . . . required drastic measures, in part to make it possible to get planes in there . . . to evacuate the civilian population.

The refugees stated that they left because of the bombing, and

> that meant, at the very least, that they left because the bombing eventually made it possible for them to leave. They pointed out —and this was completely overlooked in the subsequent reporting— that their loyalties [and] ties were all with the royal government of Laos and they were happy to be able to rejoin those of "like precious faith." The bombing made it possible for them to flee an area which was under a repressive political regime, where religion was suppressed, and where they were subject to enforced labor. . . .
>
> If these people have any serious complaint, it surely is not that they and their villages were bombed, but rather that unfriendly forces imposed harsh conditions on them without warrant. The bombing was a direct result of the unjustified presence and completely unwelcome practices of these intruders.

If the USIS survey and the summary given McCloskey is accurate in any degree, the refugees have "serious complaint" both about the bombings and the Communists. It is convenient for case-making to ignore either the overwhelming number of people who saw bombings (half occurring in villages where there were no soldiers) or the 96 percent who do not want to return to their home areas while they remain under Pathet Lao control. But the Laotian refugees are, after all, human beings who wish to be neither invaded by the North Vietnamese nor bombed by the Americans. The truth is not achieved by proclaiming one of these conclusions and excluding the other.

I was in Ban Na Nga, and though I know not a word of Lao and far too little about the war in that country, it seems clear to me that the refugees were telling the truth about their own experiences. Wong, the Chinese interpreter, told me that he "certainly" believed the refugees were truthful. Three of the four interviewers who took the USIS survey were inexperienced by their own admission, but the findings in that document were overwhelming enough to support a fairly large statistical error without losing validity. If the findings are accurate, almost every refugee from these ninety-six villages had seen a bombing attack. The figure goes back to 1964, but by any measure far exceeds the eight villages that the U.S. embassy in Vientiane claims have been bombed by mistake.

There remains the question of what generalizations can be drawn from the evidence. Laos, a country the size of California, has a population of only 2.5 million and is mostly a country of 9,000 villages. Some 700,000 refugees have been generated in the country during the past decade, mostly by North Vietnamese invasion, and there are presently some 300,000 refugees on the rolls. Deputy Secretary of State William H. Sullivan testified before the Kennedy subcommittee that 20,000 of these come from the area around the Plain of Jars, from where the refugees questioned by McCloskey and the USIS interviewers also came. "There are some 9,400 villages, and it looks to me like we have destroyed thousands of them," McCloskey said on "Face the Nation" on April 18, the Sunday after he returned from Laos. Rarely has a broader conclusion been drawn from the available evidence. In the same broadcast McCloskey also said, and he has since repeated, that "meticulous steps" were taken to protect Laotian villages during Sullivan's term in Laos. He says he also believes Major General Andrew Evans, commander of the Thirteenth Air Force, who maintains that his planes are not bombing villages now. That narrows the time period for destruction of these "thousands" of villages to eighteen months in 1969 and 1970, a period that McCloskey refers to as the time when planes were diverted from Vietnam to Laos after the bombing halt there. But the bombing halt occurred in November 1968, six months before Sullivan left and nine months before Godley arrived. There is hardly any reason to believe that Sullivan protected villages during the first four years of his ambassadorship, while allowing them to be bombed during his final six months. Here is what Sullivan had to say about it, in his testimony before the Kennedy subcommittee; after first relating refugee generation to the military movements that have swept back and forth over the Plain of Jars:

> . . . It has been suggested that air attacks have been the primary cause of refugee movement, or even that air attacks have been deliberately mounted in order to create refugee movement and to deprive the North Vietnamese and the Pathet Lao of human resources represented by the refugees. It has, for example, been suggested that, as a result of the cessation of United States bombing over North Vietnam in November 1968, a vast increase of air power was applied to northern Laos and resulted in the increase of refugee movements in that part of the country.
>
> The facts do not bear this out. There was a significant shift of United States airpower from North Vietnam to Laos after the cessation of bombing in November 1968. However, this shift was almost exclusively to the area of the Ho Chi Minh trail, where sortie rates were very significantly and sharply increased after the cessation in North Vietnam. . . . There is no Lao population along the Ho Chi Minh trail, and therefore this augmentation of sorties . . . had no relationship to the generation of refugees. As a matter of fact, in north Laos the sortie level continued almost exactly as it was from November 1968 through February and early March of 1969. It was only in late March of 1969 and subsequently through the military campaigns which rolled over the Plain of Jars from then on until early 1970 that there was an augmentation of air activity in northern Laos. . . .

So much for the official case. It looked better when Sullivan said it than it looks now, though Sullivan clearly meant what he said. One does not have to presume that he is being untruthful or that Godley is untruthful, either, to harbor the suspicion that the control of the ambassador in Vientiane and his bombing officer over his planes is less secure than the ambassador believes. At any rate, the Air Force has been most reluctant to produce photos of supposedly bombed-out villages (which may or may not, as McCloskey's critics point out, prove anything—certainly it wouldn't "prove" that the villages were necessarily the victims of American action). Nor has either the American or the Royal Laotian government permitted firsthand inspection. The Vientiane press corps, hostile and subjective though it may be, has at least in part become that way because of secrecy restrictions wholly unlike those imposed on the Laotian reporters' counterparts in Vietnam. It is accurate to say that McCloskey claimed too much from too little, but it is not enough to say this and walk away. Perhaps the wisest words came from Waldie, who left Laos thinking that McCloskey had gone too far from the available evidence but became increasingly skeptical as the weeks went by and the answers were not forthcoming to McCloskey's questions. "The accusations made by the gentleman from California [McCloskey] are generally accusations based on hard facts," Waldie said in the House on July 12. "It is a tragedy that the gentleman has to speculate as to conclusions, because every fact necessary to end the speculation is within the executive branch of this government, and is available for understanding and information and study of the executive branch. But it has been denied us."

Waldie, it seems to me, has been more candid about his own biases than either McCloskey or his critics. He is a liberal Democrat, and he has made no secret of the fact, doubtless shared by other Democrats, liberal and illiberal, that he would like to have McCloskey take on the President within the Republican party. And Waldie also declined to use any verbal mumbo-jumbo to conceal his own outspoken opposition to the war both before and after the journey. "Sure, I had an opinion when I went over there," he said once. "Anyone who has lived in the United States for the past five years and doesn't have an opinion on the war is either dead or has his head in the sand." Looking back on that tumultuous journey, Waldie believes that McCloskey accomplished a constructive purpose on his mission to Asia. "I would not have done some of the things Pete did, but I would not have gotten the information either," Waldie says without artifice. "If Pete were as reserved as I pretend to be, nobody would pay any attention to him."

Both the State Department and the military paid plenty of attention to McCloskey, whose emotional search for the "true facts" in Southeast Asia did nothing to deter his willingness to oppose President Nixon. He showed this in two lighter moments of the trip, once when he stood up in khaki and addressed reporters who had gathered with him in Vientiane for a Chinese dinner. "I want to make my first presidential speech," he said with a grin. "If we meet in the White House, let it be in these clothes. This will be an administration of muddy boots." Earlier the same day he had spotted the shiny picture of President Nixon in a corridor of the USIS building and flashed a quick, irreverent salute. "There's our inspirational leadership," he said. It was the salute of a man who thinks he could do a better job as President of the United States.

12. *Republican Response*

The "other" Republican party, the party of Ronald Reagan, had distrusted Pete McCloskey from the first. McCloskey had come to Congress, after all, by defying the party establishment in his own county and by defeating Shirley Temple Black, a conservative and a friend of Ronald Reagan. On November 29, 1967, two weeks after that victory but before his actual election to Congress, McCloskey visited Washington and demonstrated his unerring proclivity for capturing national headlines, this time by suggesting that Reagan should stick to governing California rather than seeking the presidency. And McCloskey suggested in mid-1968 that he would not support Republican Max Rafferty (winner of a bitter primary battle against Senator Thomas Kuchel) against Democrat Alan Cranston, the ultimate winner. That was too much for Reagan. At a June 16, 1968, press conference the governor answered a question about McCloskey's reputed anti-Rafferty position by declaring that the congressman was violating the Eleventh Commandment ("Thou shall not speak ill of any fellow Republican"), a doctrine promulgated not by Jehovah but by the brilliant GOP state chairman of that period, Dr. Gaylord Parkinson. "I would suggest that maybe a young congressman has a little more to learn about party loyalty, and perhaps we can change his mind," Reagan responded.*

* Reagan's comments about McCloskey were overshadowed in California newspapers and elsewhere by the governor's gentle treatment of Alabama Governor George Wallace. The governor was about to embark on a Deep South political speaking tour that Republican national committeeman Tom

Reagan's attack alarmed McCloskey's supporters, who were still recovering from the shock of the near-loss to Robert Barry in the Republican primary. McCloskey responded to the concern in his own camp and the pressures of orthodox Republicans by issuing a statement in which he expressed unspecified disagreement both with Rafferty and with Cranston and declined to endorse either. At the same time, he pledged to support the Republican party. This hair-splitting failed to satisfy anyone except Cranston, who had based his campaign on Rafferty's extremism and appreciated the reminder of Republican division. McCloskey tried to explain what he meant in a letter to Holmes Tuttle, the Los Angeles automobile dealer who is Reagan's staunchest financial backer:

> I must confess to a considerable inexperience in politics. Governor Reagan was right when he indicated that I had a great deal to learn. I would like to think, however, that personal endorsement differs from party support. . . . I hope to work with the Republican party for an across-the-board victory in November. I see no inconsistency in doing this while declining to personally endorse a particular candidate.

As we have seen, the suspicion of party regulars about McCloskey's party loyalty was ratified by McCloskey's self-contradictory remarks during the 1970 Murphy-Tunney campaign. For many Republican partisans from both the center and the right wings of the party, McCloskey's February 11, 1971, call for "a dialogue on impeachment" came as the last straw. Reagan himself responded to this speech by declaring that a majority of Americans would want to impeach, not Nixon, but any President "who proposed to abandon an American prisoner of war." This response was mild in comparison to the anti-McCloskey mania

---

Reed (accurately, if jokingly) called "not a southern strategy but a southern solicitation," and Reagan was anxious to avoid any controversy with Wallace. When asked what views of Wallace's he disagreed with, Reagan replied: "Well, now, lately, on the basis of his speeches, this would be kind of hard to pin down, because he's been speaking a lot of things that I think the people of America are in agreement with."

that overcame many subordinate Republican spokesmen throughout the state. The comments of Royce Cole, a forty-year-old Palo Alto physician and member of the Republican State Central Committee, were typical.* In a March 4 speech to a Republican women's club titled "Impeachment: Nixon or McCloskey?" Cole said that McCloskey was trying to push himself ahead politically at Nixon's expense, and added: "If Congressman McCloskey's words prolong the war one minute or one life longer, then his actions border on treason." The California Republican Assembly (CRA), a once-liberal GOP organization that was taken over by conservatives during the Goldwater renaissance, stopped short of accusing McCloskey of treason but did, at its state convention in Los Angeles on March 22, invite him to "register in another political party." Directors of the same organization had, a month before, adopted a resolution declaring that small children had killed American soldiers in Vietnam and asking clemency for Lieutenant William Calley. The even more conservative United Republicans of California (UROC) went the CRA one better on May 3 by calling upon McCloskey to quit both the Republican party and the Congress. The tone of UROC's state convention in Fresno is indicated by the introduction of a resolution calling upon Republicans to "dump Nixon" because of the President's "left-wing betrayal" of the party. The resolution lost, but only by a vote of 153 to 206. Forden (Skip) Athearn, McCloskey's primary opponent in 1970, led the opposition.

McCloskey seemed at first amused, perhaps even pleased, by the frenzy of the response. He had never had the Republican right in his corner anyway, and the attention given him by arch-conservative opposition enabled McCloskey to broaden his case and make it somewhat more palatable to liberal and moderate Republicans who also had been unsettled by the call for an

* Cole was subsequently identified by San Jose *Mercury-News* political editor Harry Farrell as one of several potential conservative opponents of McCloskey in the 1972 Republican congressional primary.

impeachment dialogue. "I'm going to make this fight in the Republican party until they throw me out of it," McCloskey told me the day after the California Republican Assembly passed its register-elsewhere resolution. And he added: "The aim is not to run for President. It's to end the war."

McCloskey's problems with the "impeachment speech," however, neither began nor ended with the Republican right. The Republican who was most disturbed by the speech was McCloskey's neighboring congressman, Charles S. Gubser, and for a personal reason that transcended the impeachment suggestion. Stanford is in Santa Clara County, in Gubser's district. Though Gubser has been questioning the war for the past two years, he has consistently voted for military appropriations and is considered a "hawk" by many of the antiwar students at Stanford. At the time McCloskey spoke at Stanford, the antiwar coalition in the House was seeking votes to cut off funds for the war. McCloskey suggested that the way to influence congressmen was to reach the people they respect at home, especially their financial supporters and precinct workers. Asked about Gubser, he replied: "Go find his thirty closest friends and financial supporters. You might find that two-thirds of them are already opposed to the war." Gubser was so angry at McCloskey that he told Harry Farrell, political editor for the San Jose *Mercury-News,* that he might run against McCloskey in the reapportioned 1972 congressional district. "I think he [McCloskey] knows I don't respond to pressure from my supporters," Gubser said. "And I don't think he represents Palo Alto yet. I still do. We'll let Pete run his San Mateo County district, and I'll run mine."

Gubser, one of the most difficult-to-defeat congressmen in California, is an accomplished politician who at one time or another during his sixteen years in Congress has represented every point of view within the Republican party. Unlike other weathervanes in Congress, however, Gubser does more than point the way the wind is blowing. He gave decisive coauthorship to the important reform amendment that in 1970 eliminated anonymous voting in the House. And he insisted, as a member of the House Armed Services subcommittee that investigated the My Lai killings, on full publication of the subcommittee's valuable report. McCloskey gave Gubser credit for both the House reform provision and the My Lai report in his Stanford speech, but the two men have never really liked each other. Gubser considers McCloskey a "double-geared hypocrite" who has tried to use his opposition to the war to advance himself. The feeling of distrust is more than mutual. McCloskey admits that the charges he is a publicity-seeker "just drive him up the wall," but it is doubtful if he ever cared for Gubser anyway. "Charlie's made some bizarre changes," says McCloskey. "He told everybody he was going to vote against the supersonic transport, and then he turned around and voted for it. He was making noises like a dove when he was facing a Democratic opponent last year, and now [1971], he's voting for the war and making emotional speeches about a bloodbath. But Charlie is the consummate politician. He can turn on tears or anger or emotion at will." Some of that anger and emotion were turned on McCloskey when Gubser went into McCloskey's district on June 26 to address a California Republican Assembly meeting. In a speech titled "Neo-McCarthyism and the New Left" that challenged McCloskey's conclusions about U.S. bombings in Laos, Gubser said: "A large and influential body of Americans is aiding the cause of the New Left by besmirching the image of this great country with reckless conclusions based upon isolated facts. Some do this knowingly, while others are simply allowing themselves to be used. Unfortunately, the latter description fits the congressman who represents the district in which we are meeting today." * Gubser's oration prompted a challenge from McCloskey

* Gubser spoke in Burlingame. He distributed copies of his speech to the White House, and was aided in preparation of the press releases by Wagner and Baroody, a GOP-oriented Washington public-relations firm. The author was interviewing Gubser during this time period, and he asked me whom I knew at the White House who would be interested in what he was doing. I mentioned DeVan Shumway, an assistant communications director whom

for a House debate and produced an inconclusive series of speeches on the House floor. While these exchanges failed to resolve the questions about U.S. bombing practice in Laos, they did cement the bond of enmity between McCloskey and Gubser, with possible consequences in the 1972 congressional elections.

If Gubser and McCloskey are different in every particular, there are some surprising similarities between Reagan and McCloskey, the two most charismatic contenders for the soul of California's Republican party. Both are extraordinary communicators who use the word "politician" as a term of opprobrium while practicing good politics. Both are public men who value their own privacy and keep their inner selves from view. Both are men's men who appeal to women. Both derive sustenance from American history, and both are capable of justifying their least logical positions by historical analogy. Both Reagan and McCloskey attract good men but lack the ability to distinguish truly good men from sycophants. "He decides quickly, and the courage of his convictions when he is knowledgeable becomes the courage of his ignorance when he is wrong," * I once wrote of Reagan, and the statement could be made with equal validity about Pete McCloskey. Both men, in other words, possess the inner certitude to do what they believe is right, regardless of the consequences, and both launched presidential candidacies that began as limited-purpose crusades and became full-scale challenges to Richard Nixon, a man whom both of them have always underestimated.

Any comparison can be pressed too far, and it would be both misleading and unwise to ignore the differences between these two remarkable California Republicans. The most obvious difference is ideological, although Reagan has made many compro-

---

I had known as a political reporter in California. Shumway read Gubser's speech but suggested, perhaps seriously, that he omit the reference to "neo-McCarthyism." "The CRA will think that McCarthyism is something good," Shumway said.

* *Ronnie and Jesse, A Political Odyssey*, p. 321.

mises with conservatism, and McCloskey is far less liberal than some of his youthful followers believe. A more important difference is the way in which principles work upon each man: Reagan "proclaims a principle without commitment to a specific course of action," while a McCloskey principle often produces a direct action that develops into a commitment. There are important differences, also, in the way in which Reagan and McCloskey came to politics. Both men were hard-striving successes in their own professions, but Reagan was elected to office late in life and McCloskey early. One consequence, it seems fair to say, is that McCloskey has been far the more flexible of the two men and possesses a greater opportunity for growth or deterioration in office. Reagan, however, was elected to a position of real power, while McCloskey became a member of a body in which junior members lack virtually any power. This latter reality, if anything, has reinforced McCloskey's inbred willingness to dare, and, daring, to take large chances.

Considerations of party unity restrained Reagan from moving against McCloskey in previous elections, but the governor has now concluded that it is time for him to act. "The question isn't whether the Republican party is big enough for McCloskey but whether there's room in him for the Republican party," Reagan told me last July 1. At this time Reagan was unwilling to flatly declare that he would support a candidate against McCloskey in the 1972 Republican congressional primary, but the idea was clearly on his mind. "I won't rule this out at all, because I think there are times when a man removes himself from the umbrella of the Eleventh Commandment by his own actions," Reagan said. "And I just consider that he [McCloskey] has been very disloyal." Reagan maintains that his attitude toward McCloskey extends far beyond any ideological difference. The governor cites his own steady disagreement with Nixon over the Family Assistance Plan, the President's omnibus welfare proposal: "This certainly hasn't resulted in a breach. He [Nixon] respects my view, and this shows that no one in the party is asking for rubber stamps." However, Reagan insists on a different criterion for judging opposition to the war, a criterion remarkably similar to McCloskey's starting point in the 1967 election. The governor believes that the President deserves support on the war because he is the commander-in-chief, and Reagan further contends that what some of the war's critics (he implicitly includes McCloskey) have said about the Vietnamese conflict would be "treason" if war had been declared. "It seems to me that anyone who wants to take issue or criticize the conduct of the war has a responsibility to ask himself if he is in any way endangering the safety of the men over there fighting," adds Reagan. Fair enough, as far as individual responsibility goes. But the trouble with the "treason" argument, other than with Reagan's confusion between "sedition" and "treason," is that it imposes upon congressmen like McCloskey a responsibility which the nation's presidents, rather than the Congress, have eluded. McCloskey has always been willing to face the declaration-of-war issue squarely, and, presumably, to accept the restrictions on debate that the commander-in-chief is able to impose in wartime. Congressional critics should not be asked to accept a declared-war standard of free speech, while the executive branch reserves to itself the warmaking powers and declines to seek a declaration of war.

Reagan's position unquestionably commands widespread support in the Republican party. Whether he can effectively transform the Republican establishment's hostility to McCloskey into a "dump-McCloskey" movement without reopening the party's deepest wounds is another question. Despite his Eastern reputation as an all-out conservative, Reagan as governor has been more an all-out party man who has campaigned effectively for Republicans of all ideological persuasions. As a former Democrat (he was a party loyalist then, too, and campaigned for Helen Gahagan Douglas in the 1950 Senate race against Richard Nixon at a time that many Democrats were ducking Mrs. Douglas), Reagan has a keen awareness of the minority status of the

Republican party, which wins elections in California only when substantially united. Unlike Barry Goldwater and Max Rafferty, who excluded moderate Republicans from their campaign apparatus, Reagan held out the olive branch to liberals and moderates as soon as he was elected. He could lose while winning if he succeeds in dumping McCloskey while alienating the party's liberal wing.

The Republican most mindful of this danger is state Republican Chairman Putnam Livermore, McCloskey's ally in the 1964 fight against fair-housing repeal. Perhaps more than any other Republican functionary in California, Livermore suggests the proper association of the words "progressive" and "Republican." He is an outspoken conservationist and civil-rights advocate, and his reference to the "party of Lincoln" is more than hyperbole. Partly because of the acute political perils of division, partly because of his friendship for McCloskey, partly because he takes both constitutional precedent and Lincoln seriously and thought that McCloskey was misquoting both, Livermore became deeply involved in the Republican response developed after the "impeachment speech." Within two weeks after McCloskey's Stanford speech Livermore was swamped with letters from both sides. By far the preponderance of the correspondents wanted to eject McCloskey from the party or otherwise punish him; some letters, however, defended McCloskey as an asset to the party. Typical of the latter was a letter from Palo Alto attorney John E. Lehman, a former member of the San Mateo County Republican central committee and a 1949 University of California Law School classmate of Livermore's. Lehman praised McCloskey as an attorney and warned that the Republican party would lose all hope of attracting "the young, the disadvantaged, and the uncommitted" if it became incapable of encompassing divergent viewpoints. ". . . It would be a disaster if pressure groups concerned more with their personal ideology than the good of the Republican party as a whole were able to force Pete into another camp," Lehman wrote. "I know this, if there's not room in the Republican party for Pete McCloskey, then there's not room in it for me either. I hope that day doesn't come." Livermore's reply left little doubt that he wanted to "save" McCloskey, not expel him. He agreed that McCloskey had a right to express divergent views, pointed out that neither the state nor the county Republican central committees had censured McCloskey for opposing the President, and said that McCloskey would be welcome in the party as long as he desired to remain a Republican. "My concern is that Pete is associating himself with those whose real interest is the defeat of the President," Livermore wrote. "It is relatively easy to speak up negatively in a popular cause against an incumbent President who has a difficult job. It is much more difficult to work within the system day by day to influence the administration to wind down the war at a faster rate than it is doing." During this same period, Livermore was fending off anti-McCloskey Republicans who wanted the party to oppose McCloskey in the primary. "A primary contest against McCloskey would cost an enormous amount of Republican money, and it might result in electing a Democrat in the general election," Livermore said in one such letter. While attempting to soothe the private feelings of Republicans on both sides, Livermore was publicly denouncing the McCloskey challenge. On March 27, in a statement released in Los Angeles, Livermore declared:

> The reported plan of Congressman Pete McCloskey to become a Republican presidential candidate is, of course, ridiculous.
>
> He simply does not have the broad qualifications, experience, or the support of Republican voters that would be necessary to make his candidacy politically practical.
>
> Pete McCloskey has demonstrated, through his activities and his prolific publicity, that he is serving as a one-issue congressman. The American people demand more from a man who wishes to be considered for the presidency.
>
> Most people cannot believe Pete is serious. Many regard it as a joke. From a practical political standpoint I can assure you

> that—joke or not—Pete McCloskey does not and will not have the support of the Republicans of his own state should he embark on his political career.

Livermore's point of view was so widely accepted in California that even the San Francisco *Chronicle,* a staunchly antiwar newspaper whose editor, Scott Newhall, had contributed to McCloskey's first campaign, agreed with the Republican state chairman. In a March 30 editorial the *Chronicle* objected to the call for an impeachment debate and questioned whether a revolt against the national Republican leadership "would achieve a faster windup of the war than the President is responsibly attempting to bring off. McCloskey has been a vigorous and effective representative for his district, but he is, we fear, well on the way, not to the White House, but to a serious estrangement of his support in San Mateo County." McCloskey responded with a letter to the newspaper that conceded Livermore's main points but also renewed his challenge. "This is in response to your editorial . . . in which you concur with . . . Putnam Livermore's statement that for me to challenge President Nixon's renomination is 'ridiculous,'" McCloskey replied. "I agree. I don't want to run against the President; it is presumptuous to even consider such a challenge. The only thing that makes it necessary is the possibility that such a challenge might cause the President to reevaluate his present policies in Southeast Asia." The letter, which appeared two days before McCloskey's trip to Laos and Vietnam, went on to condemn the "unlimited use of air power" he said Nixon was using in Southeast Asia. "The unlimited use of air power means the continued slaughter of the rural villages of Laos and Cambodia," wrote McCloskey. "The massive use of cluster-bomb units, napalm, and Cobra gunships means the indiscriminate murder of children, women, and old people, since by their very nature these weapons do not distinguish between a few enemy soldiers and the local population where they seek refuge." The reply was too much for the *Chronicle,* long a source of antiwar articles for McCloskey and other Californians opposed to U.S. policy in Vietnam. "Representative McCloskey seems to have misread the editorial in question," the paper replied. "It did not remotely touch upon bombing raids, gunships, the slaughter of Laotian and Cambodian peasants, or any other horrors of the Vietnamese war which we have often deplored. Our editorial observed . . . that in calling for a national debate on impeachment . . . Representative McCloskey is contributing nothing toward a speedy end to that war but is most likely to estrange his political support in San Mateo County."

The White House reacted more slowly to McCloskey's challenge than the Republican party in California, and with less hostility than Reagan and less compassion than Livermore. Leading members of the Nixon administration, however, never regarded the candidacy as a "joke," partly because the White House is haunted by the specter of Eugene McCarthy and partly because the Nixon administration takes its politics (and just about everything else) very seriously. Attorney General John Mitchell spoke out against McCloskey on at least two occasions,* and Communications Director Herbert G. Klein said in San Francisco that McCloskey "appears to be the only candidate out to draft himself." But Klein said in the same press conference that the White House did not consider McCloskey a formidable contender. McCloskey's challenge had been discussed with the President by Mitchell, Klein, counselor Robert Finch, and domestic adviser John Ehrlichman, and the consensus viewpoint was that McCloskey was a "one-issue candidate" who would be deprived of his issue long before the 1972 election. Nixon and the men around him also agreed that the President should not help perpetuate the challenge by taking issue with it. "The President is not going to build up an opponent within his own party," says Finch. "That's a pretty

* The right-wing *Washington Observer Newsletter* on August 15, 1971, quoted Mitchell as saying: "If you can't get the GOP to listen to Nelson Rockefeller, you're not going to get it to listen to Pete McCloskey."

fundamental rule." By choosing to follow this "fundamental rule" of not advertising the opposition, Nixon left himself open to the charge that he was being unresponsive to dissent within his own party. The White House comforted itself with the belief that American troops would continue to be withdrawn from Vietnam and that the challenge raised by McCloskey would somehow go away.

Despite the President's decision not to dignify his opposition by recognition, some administration Republicans realized that any intraparty challenge, no matter how remote, was potentially harmful to Nixon. These Republicans looked increasingly to John Ehrlichman, McCloskey's old Stanford Law School classmate, to do something about this upstart congressman who dared to challenge the President. Ehrlichman, who says he had few illusions that he could talk McCloskey out of anything, did the best he could. He arranged two meetings for McCloskey with Henry Kissinger, hand-carried two McCloskey letters to the President, and urged McCloskey to soft-pedal personal criticisms of Nixon. "I told him once at a basketball game [at Langley High School] to shut up for his own good, but it didn't do any good," recalls Ehrlichman, who is fiercely loyal to the President. As all these efforts to quiet McCloskey failed, Ehrlichman became increasingly disturbed at what he considered "unproductive and destructive" attacks on the President. Ehrlichman was particularly annoyed by McCloskey's comment that if he were elected "there will be no more white-tie dinners at the White House, and I could get along with just one beach house." And Ehrlichman also resented McCloskey's oft-repeated statement that his letters to the President had gone unanswered. "This is a half-truth, given the context of the presidency and how the White House works—and Pete knows how it works," says Ehrlichman. "Here is a clean-limbed congressman who has been writing letters to the President, and McCloskey gives people the impression that nobody answers him, that they just tear these letters up and throw them in the wastebasket. I don't know what he means by 'unanswered.' If he were an autograph collector, I would assume that he meant the President didn't sign it with his own pen. Nobody around Washington really thinks that he's going to get a personal answer to every letter he writes to the President of the United States. . . . I would venture to say we have hundreds of letters from congressmen on every subject from pipeline projects to coffer dams—all addressed to the President by a congressman. Every one of them is answered by a member of the White House staff."

Outside the White House, other high-placed Republicans were almost as unhappy about McCloskey as Ehrlichman was. "I think that most people who can read must know that McCloskey is paranoiac to attack the President on the war," says Murray Chotiner, the longtime Nixon campaign associate who officially left the White House a year ago but is expected back for the 1972 campaign. "The President is winding down the war. How a man supposedly intelligent can find fault with that achievement is beyond me." Republican National Committee Chairman Robert Dole is more generous but equally anti-McCloskey. Dole, a Kansas senator, gives McCloskey credit for consistency in opposing the war, but adds: "I think the President has been consistent, too. He's kept his word to the American people on troop withdrawal." Like Ehrlichman, Dole believes that McCloskey's personal attacks on the President may make it difficult for him to be reaccepted by the Republican party. "It's a two-way street, and he can't have it all one way," says Dole. "If McCloskey, by constant criticism of Nixon and very personal attacks on the President, reads himself out of the party, that's his choice. But we don't have any plan to destroy McCloskey or purge him." As a matter of fact, Dole went out of his way for months to refrain from mentioning McCloskey, since he believes it improper for the Republican chairman to attack another Republican. Dole did, however, speak at a Republican fund-raising dinner in Burlingame, in the heart of McCloskey's district, and denounce the

Democratic critics of the President's Vietnam policy as "doomsayers calling on the most unselfish nation in all history to repent." Most of Senator Dole's remarks on the war could as easily have applied to McCloskey as to any Democrat. McCloskey, attending the same dinner, was booed when he was introduced.

While McCloskey seemed at this point as isolated from Republican thought and sentiment as any religious heretic from his church, he was not completely alone. Here and there around the country Republicans dared to praise McCloskey for his courage, or, less often, his advocacy. McCloskey's fellow maverick, Michigan Representative Donald Riegle, was outspoken in his defense. New York Senator Jacob K. Javits, while not personally subscribing to McCloskey's challenge, said on June 7 that the California congressman was "acting constructively" and added that ferment within the party was desirable. "If I personally believed that the insurgent movement would bring the best results and the most results, I would join it," Javits said. "As it is, I bless them." Perhaps McCloskey always had more secret supporters in the Congress than anyone realized. A politician does not lightly challenge a President of his own party, and McCloskey scrupulously avoided asking any Republican officeholder to back him. He said it would be unfair to ask Republicans to take this risk, and on occasion cited "White House pressures" he said awaited any dissident. A few Republican officials were able to see that McCloskey's challenge was not necessarily harmful to the party. Rudy Boschwitz, the Republican national committeeman from Minnesota, said the insurgency "had more pluses than minuses for the Republican party" and would provoke activity on the part of Republicans who otherwise "would be inclined to do little" before election time. But Boschwitz' perception was clearly the minority view. It was shared by some younger Republicans who saw, like Riegle, that the party faced permanent minority status and perhaps extinction unless it rallied younger voters. Many of these youth-oriented Republicans were grouped around the Ripon Society, that tiny liberal Republican organization that has often had influence far in excess of its numbers.

There were other Republicans, chiefly in the Congress, who did not fit easily into any of the categories of McCloskey opposition or support. Republican Caucus Chairman John Anderson of Illinois spoke for some of McCloskey's friends when he told me: "Pete's absolutely honest; he's not a Claghorn. I resist entirely the hypothesis that he's doing what he's doing for personal aggrandizement. This is an inner compulsion with him, and the one thing that I'm afraid of is that he will destroy himself in the process. He's a good man, and he should be saved for the party and the country." One Republican attempted to save both McCloskey and the party at the same time. He was Charles Wiggins, a Southern Californian, an attorney, and a friend of McCloskey's. On May 13, at a time that McCloskey was airing his Laotian findings and his presidential challenge on television talk shows and in the press, Wiggins wrote McCloskey this letter:

Dear Pete:

A couple of days ago, we spoke briefly on the floor about your recent political activities. Since I may not have stated my growing concern fully on that occasion, please take the time to reflect upon the views contained in this letter.

With every passing day, it becomes more and more apparent that you consider yourself as a serious presidential candidate. It is a high compliment even to be mentioned casually in this regard and any of us could have our common sense dulled by a steady barrage of encouragement and promises of support for this high office.

But, Pete, I believe you are too smart to believe these blandishments.

What party is going to nominate you as its standard-bearer? Surely neither the Republicans nor the Democrats are going to turn to McCloskey as their presidential candidate. You know this is a fact.

Your only practical options are to build a third (or fourth? or fifth?) party movement with you as its head; or to become a "spoiler" with the object of denying to Nixon the nomination, or, failing that, the presidency.

Although you personally may be excused for believing in the viability of your own candidacy, those around you are not so naïve. Very simply, Pete, you are being used. Your enormous talents and potential for our party are being perverted and misdirected by those who are not pro-McCloskey, but are anti-Nixon.

You are one of the many bright, young stars in our party. But you cannot long be so regarded if, by your actions, you are a willing participant in a strategy to elect the Democrat nominee for President in 1972.

Your differences with the President over the war are not unique. Many of our Republican colleagues hold similar views, but they have not permitted that opposition to be used as a vehicle for replacing the entire Republican administration with a whole new team of Democrats. This is the road you are following, and it leads in many directions apart from our policy in Vietnam.

Few members command the personal regard in which you are held in the House. I consider you to be one of my best friends in Congress (and will continue to do so, whatever course you pursue). It is because of this deep, personal affection that I am pained to see you being used by others who lack that personal affection.

Believing [that] many of your friends feel as I do, I am sending a copy of this letter to several of our colleagues in the hope that they will join with me in an effort to dissuade you from your apparent course.

Please reconsider the practical consequences of your efforts. It is not too late to change.

Pete McCloskey had no intention of changing, but the letter —and his reply to it—provide some insight into the emotional strain McCloskey was undergoing at this time. Earlier, when it was "just" the war, McCloskey always had a small but determined group of Republicans who sided with him and shared the criticism from on high. Most congressmen accept the right of any colleague to say what he thinks about an issue, and men like Wiggins would never personally criticize McCloskey merely for speaking out against the war. Later, after it became apparent that McCloskey intended to see his presidential challenge through, life would become easier and his friends and colleagues in the House would forgive him his candidacy or at least become reconciled to its reality. But in the late spring and early summer of 1971, when some of his best friends were arguing against him, it was not easy at all. McCloskey is always unpredictable ("He's the only guy I've worked for," says political campaign manager Sandy Weiner, "that I can't predict by looking at him what he's going to do"), but he was especially moody and tense during this critical period. He responded to efforts of friends, staffers, and reporters to draw him into "what-if" discussions by refusing to speculate on anything and by drawing up detailed registration and campaign organization plans for New Hampshire, Massachusetts, Rhode Island, California, and other states. At no time, however, did I ever observe the slightest indication that McCloskey had any intention of quitting. His determination—and his hatred of the Vietnam War—came through best in his handwritten reply to Wiggins, dated May 16:

Dear Chuck,

Your letter of May 13th brought tears to my eyes just now. I can't tell you how much it means to have friends like you, especially during the difficult times we now perceive. You do me great honor with your letter, and I will try to respond to your points in order—

First, you are certainly correct—the Republicans will not nominate me for the presidency—even should I win a few primaries.

Second, I intend to remain a Republican regardless—partly because of a hope that we will one day provide a decent balance to the American public, and that our system requires *two* strong parties—partly because of the belief that a third party would be destructive, but most of all because of the fact that the best people I know in politics—including you, Pete Biester, Don Rumsfeld, Clark MacGregor, Bob Packwood, Marlow Cook, Mac

Mathias—to name a few—are all Republicans. We have the ability to one day be a great party.

Third, you seem to feel that my course will lead inexorably to a Democrat victory in 1972. I feel strongly that if Dick Nixon is our nominee, there is no way we can *prevent* a Democrat victory—and that this time we will lose far more good men like George Bush, Tom Kleppe, Bill Cowger, and their like.* A party which cannot command the enthusiasm of young people is on the road to oblivion—just like a corporation, law firm, or any other institution which can't attract the highest type of young person into its employ.

Fourth, and most important. I believe, as strongly as I have ever believed anything, that the war, and particularly the President's clear and expressed intention of substituting bombing for American troops, are so devastating in their impact on America that I would be dishonoring a proud tradition of military and legal professionalism *not* to speak out in every way I can to try to end those policies. I have tried every way I can to reach the President, and without any result whatsoever. Before you condemn my actions too strongly, I ask that you read the enclosed copies of letters I have sent the President—all without reply. Also, I would value your critique of the February 18 speech which is enclosed. Am I wrong in the conclusion that this war and the President's policies are seriously undermining our greatest asset—faith in ourselves, our institutions and our laws?

Finally, whatever I do and whatever you do, be assured that it is your own quiet and thoughtful approach to the problems of the nation that causes many of us to have just a little more hope and faith that the country is sound, our people good, and that we may yet do the job we are capable of doing. Your friendship is one of the best things that has happened in this screwy business. Give me all the hell you want. . . .

* Bush, of Texas, and Kleppe, of North Dakota, were Republican congressmen who ran for the Senate in 1970 and were defeated by Democrats. Cowger, a Kentucky congressman, was defeated for reelection. McCloskey has frequently expressed the opinion that the "divisive" tactics pursued by the White House, and especially by Vice President Spiro Agnew, in the 1970 election campaign cost the Congress some of its finest Republicans.

Two weeks later McCloskey campaigned for the first time in New Hampshire. He was determined there, as always, to do a little more than he or others thought Pete McCloskey was capable of doing.

13. *New Hampshire and Beyond*

McCloskey spent the summer of 1971 in New Hampshire and California, trying to write and to plan a political campaign and to reconcile where he was in life with where it was he wanted to be. The writing of his book, on the theme of "faith and hope in America," went slowly and would not have gone at all except for the goading and professional assistance of his old Korean War buddy Charles Daly. "I want to say something about why young people who are turned off by politics should do something about changing the system," McCloskey told me in explaining the motivation for his book. But he was at this point unsure of exactly what it was he wanted to do himself, and it afflicted both his writing and his campaigning. He participated in Registration Summer, the youth vote-registration drive sparked by Allard Lowenstein, but young people in California registered overwhelmingly Democratic, and most of the non-Democrats registered "decline to state" rather than Republicans.* McCloskey's friends in San Mateo County, worried about the possibility of losing the district to a Repub-

* August 1971 registration figures from twelve of California's largest counties showed 106,097 eighteen- to twenty-year-old voters registered, many of them from Registration Summer's efforts. Of these 60,653 were Democrats, 23,129 Republicans, 17,150 decline-to-state, 4,645 Peace and Freedom party, and 520 American Independent party. The "decline-to-state" category is often misleadingly referred to as "independent." However, persons who choose this designation in California cannot vote in any party's primary election.

lican conservative, pressured him to decide if he would run for Congress again. Throughout June and early July McCloskey created a mild credibility gap of his own by talking about himself as a presidential candidate while refusing to discuss his candidacy. When he did declare, on July 9, he mumbled his way through press conferences in San Francisco and Los Angeles and seemed uncharacteristically evasive about his congressional plans. Recruitment of volunteers in New Hampshire also lagged, and McCloskey more and more took out his frustrations on his friends, notably campaign manager Robin Schmidt, and upon a hastily assembled and youthful campaign staff that at first failed to provide him with the detailed voter-registration information on which he proposed to base a campaign.

Much of the trouble was of McCloskey's own making. He possesses a vast store of technical political knowledge, and he insisted on building volunteer effort on the model he believed had gained him victory over Shirley Temple Black. A series of campaign memos, begun on May 10 and still continuing, demonstrates his grasp of the fundamental processes of registration, voter identification, and precinct organization. The memos shine with the acquired knowledge of California politics, where computer print-outs for precinct walking lists are readily available and virtually anyone can be designated a deputy registrar of voters. McCloskey would learn, slowly and painfully, that these same procedures were not easy to come by in New Hampshire, where registration practices vary from town to town and no standard list of voters is available. Some of the staff members thought McCloskey was asking the impossible, and the mutual frustration boiled over at staff meetings where McCloskey chastised volunteers whom he believed had supplied him with "philosophy, not facts." I attended one such staff meeting, perhaps the most acrimonious, where McCloskey insisted on "the transformation of this office from a lackadaisical, relaxed congressional office into a really hard, tough campaign operation." He objected to everything from the lack of voter-registration information in New Hampshire to the absence of bulletin boards in his campaign and volunteer offices. His objections were sound enough, but his manner of making them was not. Sooner or later, McCloskey obtained most of the information he wanted, but he lost volunteers in the process, a loss that could have been averted if McCloskey had realized that a candidate who acts as his own campaign manager often is equivalent to the lawyer who has himself for a client. Nonetheless, McCloskey's comments at this (June 18) meeting are eloquent testimony to the political intuition of this supposedly antipolitical man. "You can never predict that the great [antiwar] furor of today won't be the great apathy of three months from now," McCloskey told his staff. He called for reliance on volunteers in both New England and California ("I don't want to substitute mass media for bodies that want to work for me") and for a determined registration effort in his home district. "The only way I can get reelected to Congress if all else fails is to register thirty thousand people who aren't registered now," he said. "I would hate to lose a year from now because of what Common Cause does." This comment made it clear that McCloskey, whom many of his Republican critics mistakenly believe doesn't care about remaining in the Congress, was mapping his plans for House reelection even then. He made it even clearer later in the meeting. "I'd like to have the hedge of returning to the Congress if all else fails," he said.

I was struck, afterward, by McCloskey's sense that "all else" might fail and by his early realization that the Vietnam War might be a nonissue before the year was out. He was already wrestling with the question that divided his friends and advisers, the issue of whether or not he should be a "one-issue candidate." The feeling that McCloskey should not attempt an across-the-board challenge to the President was strongest in his own district. McCloskey's old friends, for the most part, had grown weary of defending him and of answering the question: "Just what does he hope to accomplish?" They had gone along, reluctantly, with the presidential challenge because they shared McCloskey's belief that the war was wrong, but they also expressed the hope that McCloskey would limit his candidacy to the posing of a Republican alternative who would prod the Nixon administration into quicker withdrawal from Vietnam. Some of those who had worked very hard to put McCloskey in Congress were appalled that he seemed to be throwing over his chances for reelection. "He was a cause, something everyone believed in," says Winky Lennihan. "And then we got Peter there, and we've had to work constantly to keep him there. And all of a sudden he kind of blows it. Which may be fine, if it's really worthwhile, and we all believe in the cause he says he's blowing it for, completely believe in the cause, completely believe in what he says, but we're not really sure it's quite necessary. I think a lot of people feel a little bit let down. He has a commitment to us—I don't mean a commitment to close friends, but to the people who elected him."

Others who were close to McCloskey felt differently, among them Norton Simon, the multimillionaire industralist who is McCloskey's chief presidential campaign contributor, and most members of his budding New Hampshire campaign staff, including campaign chairman Robert Reno. They believed that McCloskey needed to show where he stood on other issues to have credibility, and they shared McCloskey's opposition to Nixon-administration policies on school desegregation and judicial appointments. Newspaper reporters also drew McCloskey out on other issues, and the candor that their stories celebrated invariably led McCloskey into discussion of any issue that a reporter raised. Most importantly, the widespread public attitude that President Nixon was, however slowly, unalterably embarked on a policy of total withdrawal from Vietnam pushed McCloskey into a search for other differences with the President. This disappointed some Nixon presidential supporters who wanted the President reelected but welcomed the prodding of a Republican peace candidacy. "The McCloskey campaign is now proceeding on the basis that the peace issue is gone, and they've turned the whole thing into a presidential campaign for Pete instead of an in-house drill to change the President's policies," one prominent Republican attorney told me. "It's become an ego trip for McCloskey and a referendum on the President of the United States. It was supposed to be a referendum on the peace issue." McCloskey's indecisiviness during June about whether he would or would not be a one-issue candidate also damaged his credibility. Columnist Garry Wills, writing in the first week of July, called McCloskey a "kamikaze" who should "pick [his] smokestack and head right down it" without concerning himself with anything else. "All of McCloskey's eggs are in one basket, and he should be frank about that," wrote Wills. "Hedging just reduces his credibility. . . . Gestures toward a normal candidacy cripple his protest; they look like the promptings of ordinary ambition."

By the time of his official candidacy announcement on July 9, McCloskey had decided otherwise. "This will not be a single-issue campaign," he declared. "We seek, in addition to ending the war, to restore truth in government, to achieve a return to the historic Republican moral commitment on social issues rather than the present 'southern strategy,' and a restoration of judicial excellence and independence. We will seek to end CIA involvement in the internal affairs of other nations, and to limit that agency's operations to the field of intelligence gathering. We will seek a more responsive and effective economic policy, and a new set of priorities in the areas of rural and urban revitalization and the environment. Above all, we will hope to try to restore the faith of people in government and to stimulate their participation in the electoral process."

The McCloskey candidacy announcement attracted nationwide media attention, but it would be the last time in many months that he would be so favored. Six days later, on July 15, the President proclaimed his decision to visit Communist China and captured the political initiative both from McCloskey and from Nixon's numerous Democratic challengers. McCloskey greeted the President's statement on China by commending Nixon for changing with the times but by expressing doubts that "increasing friendship with mainland China will lessen in any way Chinese insistence that U.S. bombing and combat action on the Asian continent be terminated before peace is possible." Privately, the China action confirmed McCloskey's belief in the multi-issue course he had already chosen, a view strongly reconfirmed a month later when the President stunned the Democrats by proclaiming his new economic policy. Unfortunately, McCloskey for a time confused a multi-issue candidacy with the necessity of appearing an instant expert on subjects on which he was largely uninformed. Furthermore, he pooled his ignorance by issuing a torrent of press releases in a practice completely contrary to his pre-presidential campaign policy. Some of the press, then most of it, began to wonder. Before the campaign, McCloskey's staff had sometimes been slipshod about returning telephone calls, but McCloskey himself was totally accessible to reporters who came by his office or asked him to come off the House floor. He also answered tough questions without waffling, a trait rare enough to Capitol Hill to impress almost any reporter. Now, McCloskey was on the road much of the time, and George Murphy, his press secretary from the Shirley Temple Black campaign, had returned to put out press releases and field reporters' questions. In one New Hampshire appearance McCloskey extravagantly credited Murphy for the victory over Shirley Temple Black because "he thought up outlandish things for me to say." But outlandish press releases are free for the taking in the House gallery, where substantial numbers of the 435 elected representatives of the people daily compete among themselves for favorable press attention. McCloskey didn't compete very well. On July 30 he "respectfully disagreed" with the President that Spiro Agnew had done "a fine job" on his trip to Africa. Another release the same day extended "commiseration and sympathy" to Nixon for being censured over his China policy by the right-wing California Republican Assembly, the same group that earlier in the year had invited McCloskey to leave the party. On August 11 McCloskey expressed regret that John Lindsay had been "driven" out of the Republican party. On August 27 he informed no-longer breathless reporters that "the silence from the summer White House [about American prisoners of war] is deafening." On September 17, after Senator Ed Muskie's candid California blooper about the supposed unelectability of a black vice president, McCloskey said he would be "proud to have a man like Senator Edward Brooke as his running mate." He hadn't asked Brooke, who at the time was busily trying to discourage various Massachusetts Republicans from heading up a McCloskey ticket in his own state. On September 29 Murphy put out a release answering a dis-invitation to appear before a western-states Republican conference in these supposed McCloskey words: "I regret that, even in Las Vegas, the party leadership doesn't want to gamble on hearing my views. To use the parlance of that desert city: If the party doesn't take a chance on hearing dissenting views, it may 'crap out.' "

There were those who thought that McCloskey had done the same. He pounded away incessantly on the theme of "truth in government" and took to criticizing the press for not printing what he said and for speculating, usually negatively, about his chances. "They've got as much right to ignore you as they do anyone else, Pete," Schmidt said to him at one point, but it was less a problem of McCloskey being ignored than it was of his candidacy being outstripped by events. He had never quite realized that much of the attention bestowed upon him occurred more because he was "making news" than for any other reason. The press releases, most of them, were not news, and they made McCloskey seem desperate for his declining coverage. Los Angeles *Times* cartoonist Corky summed it up best in a cartoon in which a youngish-looking McCloskey in striped pajamas holds a press conference on his bed and declares: "I called this press conference to announce that I have showered, brushed my teeth, done some light reading, and will now go to bed."

McCloskey had other problems, equally serious. The worst was fund raising, which from the first failed to measure up to McCloskey's great expectations of the spring. Al Schreck, the financier and old friend who has remained staunchly loyal to McCloskey, came East in June and tried to set up a national finance committee that would raise $500,000 by the end of the year. He concentrated on progressive Republicans and "peace money" in California and New York and on solicitations directed to three issue-oriented mailing lists: opponents of the war, advocates of liberalized abortion laws, and conservationists. However, few Republicans, even those supportive of McCloskey's reelection to Congress, wanted to put up money to help him challenge a Republican President. This was especially true after Nixon announced the wage-price-rent freeze, an action which Schreck interpreted as a kind of buying off of the business community. "We felt the business community would be strongly responsive [to our fund-raising efforts]," Schreck told me six weeks after the freeze was launched. "We've been disappointed." And the "peace money" that Eugene McCarthy had tapped so successfully in 1968 was now dispersed among a half-dozen actual and prospective presidential candidates, notably George McGovern, but also (at the time) John Lindsay, Birch Bayh, Fred Harris, and McCarthy himself. In fact, McCloskey would have had no fund raising worthy of the name except for two men—Schreck and Norton Simon, the fabulously wealthy industrialist and art collector who dabbles in politics and has in recent years used his post on the University of California board of regents to question Governor Ronald Reagan's higher-education policies. Schreck did exceptionally well, considering the obstacles. He met with Simon early in June to discuss the financing of the McCloskey campaign. Simon promptly asked him what other businessmen would be involved in a McCloskey campaign. "I said it's something like the chicken and the egg," Schreck recalls. "Somebody has to go first."

The somebody turned out to be Simon. Of the $160,000 raised for McCloskey's presidential campaign by October 1, Simon, according to Schreck's calculations, contributed $85,000.* Schreck himself gave $10,000, and his brother-in-law Albie Wells another $10,000, as both had done for McCloskey's original campaign against Shirley Temple Black. Another $10,000 came from San Francisco clothing manufacturer Daniel Kashland. Reid Dennis, president of a management-investment firm and a McCloskey congressional backer, gave $5,000. Arthur Rock, a San Francisco venture capitalist, contributed $5,000, as did Cyrus Eaton, the eighty-seven-year-old Cleveland industrialist and long-time advocate of antiwar and left-wing causes. ("McCloskey is completely right in his views on international policy, and he obviously has a totally attractive personality," Eaton said after visiting McCloskey's congressional office September 21 and meeting him for the first time.) Stewart Mott, the grandson of a General Motors founder and a major contributor both to Nelson Rockefeller and to McCarthy in 1968, gave $2,000. New York stockbroker Donald E. Weeden contributed $3,000. Both Mott and Weeden had been among the select group of guests who had attended the Daly-arranged dinner that raised funds for McCloskey's 1971 trip to Laos and South Vietnam. The McCloskey campaign also received $3,000 in contributions through the mails from a Tertius Chandler of Berkeley, California, a contributor not personally known to Schreck. A substantial portion of the remaining $22,000-plus of the first $160,000 came from contributions of $500 or less, Schreck says. As expected, California and New York contributions predominated.

Schreck, who with some assistance from Schmidt and Lew

* All of the figures for contributors listed in this chapter were supplied by Schreck in a September 29, 1971, interview.

Butler had raised most of the money himself, hoped at this point to come up with another $250,000 before the New Hampshire primary, with Simon contributing $100,000 of this total.

"Norton has no strings attached to his money, but we don't want to be financed solely by him," Schreck said. "He's given us the running room and the seed money." Despite all of Schreck's efforts, the seed did not produce the expected harvest, and the McCloskey presidential campaign was forced into a painful and difficult staff cutback at the beginning of October, the very time that volunteer efforts in New Hampshire began to pay some dividends. Daly, still wrestling with the McCloskey book, had left Washington early in the fall to become vice president for community affairs at Harvard. Robin Schmidt, increasingly and unfairly blamed for the lagging recruitment of McCloskey volunteers, joined Daly as his assistant on October 1 after serving as campaign manager for three months. The parting was amicable, but the loss was great. Schmidt is a superb soother of ruffled feelings, of which there are many in a McCloskey campaign, and he had been a steadying figure amidst the predictable confusion of the fledgling presidential effort. He was replaced by Alvin E. Toffel, an energetic thirty-six-year-old former aerospace executive who knew Norton Simon and had served in the White House's office of management and budget before becoming McCloskey's issues chairman. "I'm not a complete political novice, but I'm the next damned thing to it," Toffel told me with McCloskey-like candor a week after he took over the job. In effect, McCloskey became manager of his own campaign.

Schmidt was not the only loss. In a series of meetings during the final week of September, decisions were reached to sever the relationship with California campaign specialist Sandy Weiner, who had been receiving a $5,000 monthly consultancy fee, and to fire scheduling secretary Richard Rykken, a onetime advance man for Senator Barry Goldwater and one of the few experienced regulars on the McCloskey staff. Neither was replaced. The staff-cutback decisions, all made personally by McCloskey but dictated almost entirely by financial pressures, slashed the monthly payroll from $21,500 to under $10,000 and left the campaign heavily dependent upon volunteers or paid workers who agreed to stay on at sharply reduced salaries. Almost all of the campaign effort was now directed to New Hampshire and its traditional first primary on March 7.* The new decisions were announced October 1 in a press release from the McCloskey office that for once contained an item of hard news. "Although we are building our strength across the country, we plan to devote almost all of our efforts to winning in New Hampshire," Toffel was quoted as saying. "We are strengthening our staff in that state, and the congressman plans to spend almost all of his time there campaigning among the people."

The "McCloskey for President" headquarters in Concord, New Hampshire, stares across Main Street at the nation's oldest state house and the statue of Franklin Pierce, only New Hampshireman ever to become President. The headquarters at one time was one of the best dress shops in New Hampshire and part of the Eagle Hotel, where the lobbyists drank and entertained before descending on the Legislature. Now it is filled with signs and posters ("It is a sin to be silent when it is your duty to protest") and the kind of well-scrubbed, hard working young people that the nation came to associate with the McCarthy campaign. Four doors away is the Republican

* Outside New Hampshire, the McCloskey campaign was reduced largely to a contingency effort ready to be revived if McCloskey performed well in the New Hampshire primary. Old friends Lewis Butler and Ryland Kelley were in charge of the effort in California, where they, like many of McCloskey's friends, were more concerned about McCloskey's reelection to the House than the presidential challenge. Lyndon A. S. (Tuck) Wilson, a Portland attorney, and Rodney Minott, author of *The Sinking of the Lollipop,* headed the contingency effort in Oregon, with an eye to that state's free-for-all presidential primary. Malcolm and Susan Farmer remained McCloskey's campaign leaders in Rhode Island.

headquarters, where a framed sign in the window uses Richard Nixon's words to celebrate "The party of the open door."

Bob Reno's law offices are across Main Street on the state-capitol side. Reno, a tall, spare, softspoken man long associated with peace causes and rarely with partisan politics, read about McCloskey in the New York *Times* and wrote him a letter offering to help in New Hampshire. Like so many who are attracted to McCloskey, he is a former Marine, in Reno's case from World War II and the South Pacific. The two men liked each other immediately, and Reno agreed to serve as campaign manager. He brought McCloskey into the state on the first weekend of June for a private reception at the civically important Snowshoe Club and for a public speech at the Unitarian Church. Speaking at the church against a red-walled backdrop with three white doves, McCloskey declared that "it isn't religion that keeps this country together; it's the law" before launching into a characteristically legalistic attack on United States involvement in Vietnam. McCloskey discussed the "Nuremberg precendents" and his own review of the Phoenix program in Vietnam ("in our zeal to stop communism, we're in effect imposing a police state"), and he established himself with a very dove audience as a man who hated the war and who spoke his mind. He dismissed one question about amnesty for draft dodgers with a blunt statement that this would be impossible while American fighting men were still engaged in Vietnam. The church was filled for the speech, and most of the audience warmly applauded McCloskey.

We drove back to Boston the same night. McCloskey was buoyed by the day's events, and he hummed snatches from "You're a Good Man, Charlie Brown," the title song of the musical then playing in Washington at Ford's Theater,* and declared exuberantly that he would win in New Hampshire.

* The McCloskeys had attended the musical and liked it so much that Cubby had spontaneously invited the cast over to their home the weekend before.

On the drive back he made plans to fish and climb mountains and take Cubby to New Hampshire and organize a volunteer effort there the way he had done in San Mateo County. We had a beer at the Logan Airport hotel, and a young Vietnam veteran and his bride recognized McCloskey and came up to him with offers of support. McCloskey chatted with him until he learned that his prospective volunteer had been married the same day. "Good God," he said. "What are you doing here talking politics?"

McCloskey returned to New Hampshire frequently during the summer and fall of 1971. While national press attention dwindled to the vanishing point, McCloskey's New Hampshire campaign forged steadily ahead. His staff office in Concord was directed by Michael Brewer, a twenty-eight-year-old Harvard Law School graduate who had worked both for Illinois Senator Charles Percy and New York Governor Nelson Rockefeller and who, he once told me, "tried to join the Marine Corps because I didn't have the courage to be a conscientious objector." The Marines rejected Brewer because of a bad back, but there proved to be nothing wrong with his mental equipment. He had thought about running McCloskey even before McCloskey thought of it, and with two youthful Republican friends late in 1969 launched the "Completely Unauthorized Committee for McCloskey for Higher Office of One Kind or Another." * Now Brewer was trying to run McCloskey for the highest office in the land against a Republican President who has always done well in New Hampshire. He began his task with the hope of attracting a sizable McCloskey vote from a prospective coali-

* The three friends printed "McCloskey for Higher Office" buttons at their own expense, advertised in the Ripon Society *Forum*, and tried to start a boomlet for McCloskey under the mistaken but widely shared belief that California Republican Senator George Murphy could be persuaded not to seek reelection. The stunt, of which McCloskey knew absolutely nothing, backfired when supporters of Robert Finch, the Nixon presidential aide who wanted to succeed Murphy, suspected that McCloskey was promoting the buttons. McCloskey promptly disavowed the "higher-office" intent.

tion of young people voting for the first time, Republican liberals, Democrats who might be induced to switch for the primary, and conservative Republicans who were dissatisfied enough with Nixon to cast a protest vote. Aided by twenty-three-year-old college Republican organizer John Field Reichardt and a small Republican-oriented staff,* Brewer set out to find GOP volunteers. The campaign strategy depended in part on the hope of attracting a significant number of the 64,000 potential eighteen- to twenty-one-year-old voters to McCloskey's cause. But it was not to be a duplication of Gene McCarthy's 1968 strategy. "I would estimate that we will need between 2,000 and 2,500 workers in the field," Reichardt wrote in an August 16 note to Reno and other top McCloskey staffers. "As much as possible, I feel these people should be . . . from the communities in which they work. A children's crusade, per se, will not be effective in 1972 in New Hampshire for McCloskey because the McCarthy novelty will have worn off, and because we would probably be competing with McGovern, McCarthy, Lindsay, et al. for the young workers, and may even be attempting to operate a competing effort with youngsters, something which would be confusing to all concerned, and probably counterproductive. A neighbor-to-neighbor program, with local known people involved, would be vastly superior."

During the summer of 1971 McCloskey campaigned in the sparsely settled north country of New Hampshire, climbing the Presidential Range of the White Mountains in a driving rain, shaking hands at county fairs, speaking to students at Plymouth State College and at the University of New Hampshire. He never wore a coat or a tie, and he made a point of asking for opinions as well as giving them. He began his formal

* The New Hampshire staff included John Mudge, the twenty-two-year old grandson of the attorney who founded the New York law firm of Mudge Rose, Guthrie, and Alexander. President Nixon was a member of that firm in the 1960s, long after founder Alfred Mudge had died. Another staff member was Nancy Payne, who worked for the Republican National Committee before joining the McCloskey staff.

campaign on June 26 on a stone staircase in the courtyard of St. Paul's School at Concord and recalled how McCarthy's performance in the 1968 election had led to President Johnson's withdrawal from the race. "At first I thought that anyone who would seek the presidency would either have to be an egomaniac or insane," he said. "But the more I look at the other candidates, and especially at the incumbent, the more sure I am that I could do as good a job." However, McCloskey's optimism wore thin as the events of the summer turned against him, and it began to show in his personal campaigning in New Hampshire. His speeches became listless and mechanical, and he resisted the efforts of staffers to gather crowds, preferring instead to spend five minutes or more with a single voter. A week after an unproductive afternoon of this at the Deerfield Fair on October 2, I asked McCloskey why he wasn't making an effort to reach more people. "If you want to know the truth of it, I'm a little bit timid," he replied. It was true enough, but I had rarely heard him talk that way before, and the self-doubt communicated itself to many of the New Hampshirites who heard him.

Despite these indications of personal indecision, political events in New Hampshire were moving toward McCloskey as surely as national events were moving away from him. Two of the movers were William Loeb, the hard-right publisher of the Manchester *Union Leader*, and Governor Walter Peterson, an embattled moderate Republican who has been the target of a Loeb vendetta for years. Peterson, who won reelection to a second term in 1970 by only 4,200 votes, realized that he had something to gain from a McCloskey campaign that would register young people and liberals in the Republican party. Accompanied by newsmen, Peterson strode across the street from his second-floor state-capitol office soon after the McCloskey headquarters opened, for what the governor described as a courtesy call. Loeb pounced upon the visit and editorially described both Peterson and McCloskey as "spoilers" who were destroying Republican unity. Loeb's own contribution to party unity was an editorial soon after Nixon's announcement of his visit to Communist China describing the President in terms far more savage than any ever used by McCloskey. "Mr. Nixon would do anything, even endanger the future of the United States, if he thought the fact of that danger would be hidden from the American people, especially if the overall effect might be to enhance the possibility of his reelection," Loeb wrote in reaction to the President's decision. The *Union Leader* is the only paper with statewide circulation, and it is a powerful force in mobilizing opinions both for and against its objectives. Many Republican progressives, particularly in such liberal strongholds as Keene and Hanover, automatically react favorably to candidates that the *Union Leader* opposes. There is little doubt that the drumfire of attacks the newspaper mounted upon Peterson and McCloskey was helpful to the McCloskey challenge, if only because it gave McCloskey the kind of name recognition he badly needed in New Hampshire. And Peterson rather liked McCloskey. "He's a progressive good guy in lots of ways," the governor told me.* "He's the kind of fellow our party needs. I probably should be considered a supporter of the President, but it's not a terrible catastrophe that McCloskey is a candidate. It will help to keep the party on a progressive course." Peterson also suggested that the McCloskey candidacy might even help Nixon by offsetting some of the right-wing pressure resulting from the President's China policy.

In New Hampshire most of this pressure is provoked by Loeb, who in October endorsed his pet candidate, Los Angeles Mayor Sam Yorty, for the presidency. The publisher set out his opinion of McCloskey in a letter sent to a McCloskey supporter late in September: "To put it bluntly, McCloskey is no damn good. He's a peace-at-any-price boy in the Vietnam situation. That's

* All of the quotations attributed to Governor Peterson in this chapter were obtained in an October 1, 1971, interview in his office. Peterson subsequently endorsed Nixon.

enough to make any sensible American refuse to vote for him. I think he is a completely dishonest individual." Three weeks later, in a signed front-page editorial in the *Union Leader* on October 13, Loeb warned Republican voters that the President's change of heart about China should not tempt anyone to vote for McCloskey. The editorial, titled "Paul McCloskey, Champion of Abortion," attacked the congressman for a statement at Plymouth State where he once again favored abortions on demand. It concluded:

> Whatever one thinks about President Nixon (and it is no secret that this newspaper is no longer his most enthusiastic admirer), it would be foolish for anyone, however disappointed in Nixon's performance in domestic and foreign affairs, to think that in McCloskey they have a sensible alternative!
>
> Regardless of our feelings about Richard Nixon, it would be of benefit to the entire nation if New Hampshire gave McCloskey such a licking that it would finish his presidential ambitions. It would serve as a clear indication that—at least here in New Hampshire—the "anything-goes" philosophy of McCloskey is something that is not wanted.
>
> Here in New Hampshire we have a golden opportunity to knock McCloskey out of the political arena once and for all. Let's try to do exactly that.

McCloskey also possessed a "golden opportunity" in New Hampshire, thanks in part to the *Union Leader*. Loeb's implacable hostility was less damaging to McCloskey than the refusal to take his challenge seriously that was characteristic of Republicans in many parts of the country. "McCloskey [is] looking less and less like Eugene McCarthy, more and more like Harold Stassen," commented the conservative *National Review*. But there is a presumption of seriousness about McCloskey in New Hampshire that may be his biggest unstated asset in the primary campaign. One reason is that the state was used to improbable-dream candidacies long before the 1968 campaign.* The open presidential-preference primary is peculiarly suited to New Hampshire's independent spirit and heritage, and voters are accustomed to making highly personal judgments about political candidates.

New Hampshire is in many other respects an ideal place for the kind of challenge McCloskey seeks to make. It is, first of all, a Republican state, and there are many liberals who would be registered Democratic or independent elsewhere who have remained Republican in order to participate in the primaries. McCloskey's concern with reclaiming the Republican party seems irrelevant, impossible, or both in other places; in New Hampshire it is a fundamental political question. The state, largely because of Loeb's unyielding opposition to education and to state taxation, ranks last in state expenditures for education, and its latest budget, according to one Republican official, is "a series of large and small disasters." The response of New Hampshire to the issues of education, taxation, and economic growth will be determined largely by Republicans, and McCloskey's call for a "remaking of the Republican party" is shared by thousands of progressives who wish to change policies rather than parties. McCloskey at his best could speak to all of them.

The McCloskey candidacy is also potentially benefited by a change in election procedures that will make it easier for the state's many independent voters to regain their independent status after voting in the primary of their choice.† The most

* The most famous of these challenges were made by Estes Kefauver in the Democratic primary in 1952, by Henry Cabot Lodge in the Republican primary in 1964, and by Eugene McCarthy in the Democratic primary in 1968. Kefauver and Lodge both won their primaries, while McCarthy received 42 percent of the vote. None of the three was nominated.

† At the time of the 1970 election in New Hampshire, 161,916 persons (42 percent) were registered Republican, 100,473 (26 percent) Democratic, and 124,505 (32 percent) independent. These percentages are expected to remain relatively stable in 1972, perhaps with slight gains for voters in the independent category. Though independents can vote in either party, they traditionally have participated lightly in presidential primaries. There are

significant new voting force in the state, the eighteen-to-twenty-one group, apparently has registered preponderantly independent. As elsewhere, these voters are generally more anti-Nixon than their parents. McCloskey is also valued by some regular Republicans because he diminishes the understandable tendency of the Nixon administration to take a small and solidly Republican state for granted. "Thank God for Pete McCloskey," commented Republican Congressman James Cleveland. "Now the White House is answering my telephone calls."

These advantages must be weighed against a significant series of obstacles facing the McCloskey candidacy in New Hampshire. Nixon has always done well in New Hampshire, and his only appearance in the state during 1971 was greeted by warm and enthusiastic crowds. Governor Peterson believes that McCloskey may be underestimating both the popularity of Nixon and the influence of the *Union Leader*. "George Romney campaigned well here in 1968 and never moved much in the polls," says Peterson. "McCloskey may have been misadvised about what he's up against." One of the things he is up against is the solid Nixon support among the courthouse regulars and local-government types known informally in New Hampshire as "the committee to do the right thing." McCloskey's search for New Hampshire volunteers has relied, with a few significant exceptions, upon nonpoliticians who are on the outside looking in and who have earned the suspicion of this cadre of government regulars.

Another possible obstacle to the McCloskey candidacy is the belated entry in the GOP primary of Congressman John M. Ashbrook of Ohio, who will carry the banner of Republican conservatism and help cast Nixon as the middle-of-the-road candi-

---

really two simultaneous presidential primaries, one for delegate selection to the national conventions and the other a "beauty contest" on presidential preference. Johnson allowed twice as many delegates as there were delegate candidates to file in 1968, thereby splitting his own vote and enabling McCarthy, who won 42 percent of the beauty-contest vote, to obtain 20 of the 24 delegates and create the impression he had won.

date. Ashbrook, the ranking Republican on the House Internal Security Committee, gives Loeb a candidate in both primaries and may siphon away the votes of some frustrated conservatives who conceivably would have voted for McCloskey as a protest against Nixon. He is, however, likely to take even more votes away from the President. And Ashbrook, by finishing third in a three-way race, could enhance the stature of McCloskey and weaken the conservative position rather than strengthen it.

McCloskey is also dependent upon events in the Democratic primary, where the presence of George McGovern will siphon off some youthful votes that would otherwise go to McCloskey. This siphoning could become a major diversion if either McCarthy or John Lindsay enters the Democratic primary. And the entire youth vote may be less significant in New Hampshire than in many other states because of a ruling that young people must return to their home precincts to cast their ballots.

This partial reliance upon the plans and contingencies of Democratic candidates illustrates McCloskey's general dependence upon events. Johnson was a sinking President in 1968, even though the press was slow to recognize it. Nixon appears to be near a peak of popularity, and despite some New Hampshire concern about his economic policies, is on solid footing with the voters there unless an unforeseen event—health, a Tet offensive that undid his Vietnamese troop-withdrawal schedule, or a right-wing challenge—shakes the confidence of Republicans in their President. The war, perhaps, is the most potentially volatile issue of all. "The President has to withdraw enough troops so that his policies are creditable by the time of the primary, yet not so many that his Vietnamese policies—and Vietnam—collapse by the general election," says Democratic Senator Alan Cranston of California. "McCloskey is the extra dimension of his problem. That's what his presence in the primary does."

Whether McCloskey is enough extra at this point to require the President to take cognizance of the challenge is an open question. McCloskey's early campaigning raised considerable doubt. His new campaign manager, Al Toffel, regarded McCloskey as a "management disaster" and wanted him to avoid the long, set speeches and a tendency to spend many minutes with each voter in favor of question-and-answer sessions with reasonable crowds, a situation in which McCloskey excels. Toffel, a former fighter pilot, also wanted McCloskey to separate himself from the Lowensteins and the Democratic doves and to speak more supportively of U.S. defense needs within the context of opposition to the war. Others in the McCloskey camp in New Hampshire objected to the candidate's insistence on advocating abortion, defending the draft, injecting himself into state-taxation issues or responding to the *Union Leader* in kind. But McCloskey remained his old, uncontrollable self both on substance and on strategy. When a young woman with a baby on her back approached him and asked what he thought about population control, McCloskey responded: "I don't think you ought to have more than two children." He continued to insist on more campaign volunteers than anyone could supply, to drone on at one speaking appointment in defiance of the next and to resist being pulled away from a conversation before he was finished. "McCloskey doesn't like to have his days divided up into bits and pieces," says Brewer. "He's a very strong guy and likes to have control over his own life. A guy like that is very difficult to turn into an organization man, but he has to become something of an organization man to win." Whatever happens to McCloskey in New Hampshire, he has shown that neither his head nor his style has been turned that much by presidential politics. If the Nixon administration is in the trough of a wave rather than on a crest, McCloskey may do better in New Hampshire than anyone expects.*

* It is uncertain, of course, just what "better" means. Louis Wyman, the more conservative of the state's two Republican congressmen, has predicted that McCloskey will receive only 5,000 votes. At the other end of the spectrum, McCloskey talks of getting 51 percent, about 60,000 votes. Governor Peterson believes he will be doing well to get more than 15,000 votes. And Congressman Cleveland, who probably knows as much about the Republican

What happens to McCloskey after New Hampshire depends in large measure how well he does in that first primary. "It's understood everywhere that I'll be running if I do well in that primary, but I can't ask people to support me on that basis," McCloskey told me in our final interview for this book. "If I'm just a goddam flash in the pan, I drop out. But meanwhile, I'm going to raise the issues and, hopefully, force the President to debate them." These issues were both more nebulous and more negative than the end-the-war position that had brought McCloskey into the race. McCloskey summed them up under the heading of "truth and faith in government," which was also the title of a dullish, scantily applauded set speech he made to the Kennedy Political Union at American University on September 15. But he afterward refined the explanation in an October 8 letter to supporters on the same theme. "First, I think restoration of faith in our system of government is our main goal today," McCloskey wrote. "Our young people are losing it rapidly; so are many of the rest of us." And he said that the Nixon administration should be held accountable:

> Faith requires candor and truthfulness on the part of those who lead—a willingness to admit a mistake when it occurs, and to respect truth, even when it embarrasses us.
>
> The Nixon administration has not been candid with either the public or the Congress. Concealment, deception, and news management have become commonplace. The examples are legion: the Vietnam war, bombing in Laos, the SST, now even the labor unemployment figures and the crime statistics. . . .

---

voters of New Hampshire as anyone, believes that the President is likely to win with 80 percent or more of the vote but adds that "the potential for an upset is always present in New Hampshire." How well McCloskey does, in Cleveland's view, depends upon whether President Nixon is a declared candidate for reelection who campaigns in New Hampshire. In this case, Cleveland believes that a 25-percent McCloskey vote would be a "storm signal" for the President. In the absence of a declared presidential candidacy and campaign, Cleveland thinks McCloskey would have to poll 35 percent to raise the same signal.

McCloskey also wrote that he had "felt increasing dismay over the immorality of some of the President's policies," among them the war, the political involvement of the courts, and the slowdown of civil-rights enforcement. In a sentence that William Loeb would have endorsed for other reasons, McCloskey declared:

> We are fast losing our most valuable source of strength—our faith in government—because it seems as if the President wants to do what will get him reelected rather than what is right, that he will attempt to substitute words and rhetoric for candor and affirmative leadership.

The trouble with all this was that it said too much and too little at the same time, rather in the manner of those earnest fundamentalists who tell us that the world would be made right if people would only follow the Ten Commandments. McCloskey started out by behaving as if President Nixon was the first chief executive ever to conceal information from the public. He later expanded this to include various deceptions of Presidents Johnson and Eisenhower (but never, as far as I am aware, of President Kennedy), and in one reference in his American University speech correctly traced the policies of national concealment to the "secrecy which arose as a necessity out of World War II, the development of sophisticated nuclear weapons and missiles and the continuing worldwide confrontation between the free world and the Iron Curtain countries." Given this history as the basis for deception, rather than some unexplained pathology of President Nixon, more is called for from McCloskey than a moralistic appeal to truth, decency, and just plain goodness. He had done better when his issue was the war.

Despite his difficulties in finding a new issue to equal the old one, McCloskey could pile up a respectable vote total in the California primary June 6 if he does well enough in New Hampshire to last that long. Ronald Reagan, now in the sixth year of his governorship, is experiencing the popularity decline that usually attends a long gubernatorial incumbency, and he will head Nixon's ticket in California. Norton Simon, hardly a candidate in McCloskey's personality class, received a third of the vote against Senator George Murphy, which comes close to being the irreducible liberal Republican minimum if the 1966 gubernatorial primary is excepted. Liberals who want to clip Reagan's wings would have every reason to vote for a McCloskey candidacy, particularly if it seems likely that Nixon would be renominated in any case. There is also the prospect of a primary challenge on the right, probably led by affable archconservative John G. Schmitz, whose district includes the western White House at San Clemente. Schmitz responded to the President's decision to visit China by canceling an already scheduled trip on Nixon's yacht and declaring that he was "breaking off diplomatic relations" with the President. He is a verbal match both for Reagan and for McCloskey and remains somewhat skeptical about the governor, whom he once accused of being an "Indian taker" for proposing budget cuts that he later rescinded. Schmitz says he would participate in a conservative challenge to the President only as part of "a collective leadership that based its stand on principles rather than personalities." Such a candidacy would cost the Reagan-led Nixon ticket far more votes than it would cost McCloskey.

The more difficult problem for McCloskey in California is the credibility question inherent in running for the presidency and the Congress at the same time. Secretary of State Edmund G. Brown, Jr. has ruled that such a dual candidacy is legal, chiefly because the man who heads a ticket of delegates to the national convention is not technically a candidate under California law. But it is questionable whether such a dualism would be politically acceptable to McCloskey's constituents, who might reasonably expect him to decide in advance whether he wants to be congressman or President. McCloskey also lacks the money to wage both a national and a congressional campaign, though this would surely change if he did well in New Hampshire or in the Oregon primary May 23.

McCloskey also will be competing in a new congressional district in 1972, though he is helped rather than hurt by the incumbents' reapportionment fashioned by the California congressional delegation and approved by the Legislature late in 1971. San Mateo County has too many people for one district, but not enough for two. The southern part of the county plus Stanford and part of Palo Alto in neighboring Santa Clara County will become a new district that extends into Santa Cruz and includes the University of California at Santa Cruz campus. It is a safe Republican constituency. A northern San Mateo County district will be 58 percent Democratic, but a district with this registration margin is not necessarily safe for the Democrats in California, especially against a liberal Republican incumbent who in the past has won more than 70 percent of the vote in the same area. "McCloskey has three out of four possible options," says San Francisco Congressman Phillip Burton, the Democratic reapportionment wizard who devised the redistricting plan. "He could run as a Democrat or a Republican in the northern seat or as a Republican in the new [southern] district. He's likely to win in any case." The most important benefit conferred by the reapportionment was that it denied conservatives from knowing where to concentrate their candidate-building forces. McCloskey took full advantage of this opportunity and concealed his political strategy by declining to tell anyone in which district he would run. (I have always thought, and still do, that he will try the southern district.) One probable result of this uncertainty will be an abundance of conservative candidates, a situation in which McCloskey would be virtually unbeatable. He may be unbeatable anyway unless the Republican regulars uncover a class candidate from somewhere near the middle of the road. Even a candidate of this sort might find that the "vengeance factor" created by a McCloskey defeat would mean a Democratic victory in November.

In one passage of his October 8 letter to friends explaining the new basis of his presidential candidacy, McCloskey discussed his objections to administration actions in Laos and the American South, then declared: "I would rather give up my seat in Congress than stand by in silent acquiescence in these policies." But he never had any intention of giving up his seat, as he made clear in campaign memos and exhortations to his staff as early as June 1971. He similarly reassured old friends who visited him in his congressional district or in Washington. One of the latter was Claire Dedrick, a plainspoken San Mateo County conservationist who had played a significant role in the McCloskey campaign against Shirley Temple Black. She visited McCloskey in his congressional office on September 28 while I was present and expressed concern that an anticonservationist would be elected to his congressional seat. "If you're not going to run, we want to know, because we've got to start building somebody up," Mrs. Dedrick said. McCloskey said that the Republican party wouldn't nominate him for President and assured her that he would run for Congress again. "I'm going to run like a striped ape," he said. "I'd rather lose than give up."

14. *A Soldier's Faith*

McCloskey met Daniel Ellsberg at a Princeton peace rally in mid-April, soon after the congressman had returned from Laos, and Ellsberg gave him duplicated volumes of what later became known as the Pentagon Papers. McCloskey read from the documents at his infrequent leisure, keeping most of them locked in his office safe, but he seemed not to have fully recognized their importance. When the New York *Times* began publication and subsequently fought Justice Department attempts at censorship as a First Amendment issue, McCloskey tried to force release of the Pentagon Papers to the Congress, then about to vote on a fixed date for Vietnam withdrawal. The legislative branch should be entitled to read the Pentagon Papers before being asked to vote any more funds for the war, McCloskey said. The issue became moot when the Nixon administration finally made the documents public.

On October 2, the day after Robin Schmidt was replaced as compaign manager and Sandy Weiner's political consulting firm was cut from the payroll in California, McCloskey flew from New Hampshire to Chicago to present a peace award to Ellsberg. Other peace advocates honored at a rally attended by 2,500 persons that night included Pablo Casals, Henry Niles, Coretta King, and Joan Baez. Miss Baez received her award immediately before Ellsberg. After announcing that the American flag had been disgraced by U.S. conduct in Vietnam, Miss Baez went to each side of the stage and, to the cheers of the crowd, laid the two American flags standing there on their sides. She then started to sing, and officials of the sponsoring peace group reraised the flags. Miss Baez stopped her song and lowered them again. At this point McCloskey came forward and, assisted by master of ceremonies Ramsey Clark, raised both flags. "Everything Daniel Ellsberg stands for is represented in the American flag," McCloskey said.*

Earlier that same day, at the Deerfield Fair in New Hampshire, McCloskey had been wandering about among the livestock barns when he encountered a young 4-H girl and her 900-pound black Angus bull. "He's named 'Senator,'" the girl told McCloskey, who petted the bull and remarked: "He's smarter than some." Both his casual irreverence for the institution of which he is a part and the deeper reverence for country epitomized by his spontaneous action in putting up the flags are typical of McCloskey. In this dualism of skepticism and patriotism McCloskey has chosen well for heroes in Oliver Wendell Holmes, for it was Holmes perhaps more than any other American of this century who combined zest for physical danger with a skeptical defense of intellectual liberty and a patriotic regard for country. McCloskey is a disciple of Holmes, quoting him at every opportunity, and it is worth examining him on the scale he has created for himself.

McCloskey is, first of all, a religious skeptic, who, like Holmes, is profoundly appreciative of nature and unconcerned with a hereafter. He is the skeptic and the soldier who needs no God or natural law ("that the private soldiers have not been told the plan of campaign, or even that there is one . . . has no bearing upon our conduct," wrote Holmes) to do the right as he sees it. It is enough, as Holmes has said, that we believe.

As lawyers, however, the McCloskey-Holmes comparison becomes a contrast, and a somewhat presumptuous contrast at

* "I wish congressmen could carry around on their shoulders the box of classified lies and brutality I carried around on mine," Ellsberg said in his acceptance speech.

that. Holmes was a teacher and a philosopher before he was a jurist, spending only three years in a law firm before moving to the battlefields of constitutional law at Harvard and then onward to the Massachusetts Supreme Court. McCloskey is a trial lawyer, always the advocate with a case to prove. Like other trial lawyers in politics, he is stuck with his case and the case he has made for himself. Holmes, the supreme rationalist, reached beyond advocacy to inner meanings and to what Max Lerner called a "philosophic universe." He was a relativist whose findings were a vantage ground, not points on a fixed compass, and he did not hesitate to let the life of law or the logic of life lead him to new conclusions. "Certitude is not a test of certainty," Holmes maintained, and his noblest opinions and speeches bespeak an awareness of the possibility of error that is the bane of true believers and of the simple-minded.

Candor does not preclude a capacity for self-deception. It seems to me that those who speak of candor or of blinding honesty or the like when talking of Pete McCloskey are right if they are speaking of an essence, a spirit, even a manner that describes his method of approach, but wrong if they stretch the "candor" to cover too much, and especially to preclude the kind of generalizations and half-truths in which all politicians, including McCloskey, engage. "For the most part, men believe what they want to," says Holmes, and this has surely been true of McCloskey. Though he is a religious skeptic, he sometimes acts like a man in possession of Revealed Truth, and while this certitude gives him the power to move people, it also contains an element of fanaticism that mixes oddly with his skeptical precepts. Worse still, McCloskey's failure to repeat at home his on-scene recognition that American military policy has changed in Vietnam and his selective use of information from Laos to bolster already formed conclusions suggest that McCloskey is not willing to examine his own self-deceptions in the manner he would recommend for others.

He is found far less wanting in other measures on the Holmesian scale. McCloskey's courage, both physical and moral, is undisputed, and this most fundamental of all virtues makes him a valuable force in a Congress in which the courage to lead one's constituency is all too rare. The most emotional I have ever seen McCloskey, other than when he talked about his own boys while we were in Vietnam, was when he read to me one morning from that splendid address delivered by Civil War veteran Holmes on Memorial Day of 1895, a speech usually known by the title of "The Soldier's Faith." Holmes talked in this speech about the failure of America to conserve its traditions, and the necessity for each generation to learn afresh the lessons of its day. These lessons, Holmes told the new generation of his day, are:

> That the joy of living is to put out all one's powers as far as they will go; that the measure of power is obstacles overcome; to ride boldly at what is in front of you, be it fence or enemy; to pray, not for comfort, but for combat; to keep the soldier's faith against the doubts of civil life, more besetting and harder to overcome than all the misgivings of the battlefield, and to remember that duty is not to be proved in the evil day, but then to be obeyed unquestioning; to love glory more than the temptations of wallowing ease, but to know that one's final judge and only rival is oneself—with all our failures in act and thought, these things we learned from noble enemies in Virginia or Georgia or on the Mississippi thirty years ago; these things we believe to be true.

It is McCloskey's favorite passage from Holmes, a man with whom he also shares a love for "rocks and boulders" and who is genuinely a source of inspiration. When McCloskey first talked of Holmes, I thought of him as something of a quondam hero, far too good to be true, but I realized, reading Holmes, that the fundamental spirit of the man, particularly in his response to challenge, is totally congenial to McCloskey. "A man is bound to be parochial in his practice—to give his life, and if necessary his death, for the places where he has roots," Holmes said in his celebrated comments on John Marshall. "But his thinking should be cosmopolitan and detached. He should be able to criticize what he reveres and loves." McCloskey measures up to the last demanding part of this standard, for he has been critical of those institutions—the Marine Corps, the Congress, and the law—that he perhaps loves better than all others. But his thinking, it seems to me, is rarely detached. "Pete McCloskey has the capacity to do anything except develop a capacity for passivity," says Robin Schmidt, in a judgment intended as a compliment. However, sound judgment and the capacity for fairness require enough passivity to think before acting and to measure one's actions in response to thought. McCloskey rescues himself from the perceptive difficulties that characteristically confront "men of action" by his superb intuition about people and places—he may be right, for instance, about Laos, though he did not prove his case—but he is adrift where intuition serves poorly as a compass. Most issues (one is tempted to say all issues) cannot be solved by the skill of the trial lawyer or the Marine platoon commander. McCloskey can lead men, beyond question. But on what issues shall he lead them, and whither shall he lead?

That judgment and this book might end here if McCloskey is viewed only as a presidential-campaign phenomenon who soared like a comet in the summer skies of Washington before vanishing from sight. He is much more than that. For one thing, he is a damned good congressman who takes the business of the House seriously and who has learned, for all his frustration with the seniority system, the mechanics of the committees on which he serves. His irreverence for authority is a tonic in the musty confines of the House, and he pursues his issues in committee with the same vigor that he advertises them in campaigns. A case in point occurred last September, at a time that McCloskey's campaign was particularly embattled, when he proved successful in the House Government Operations Committee with an amendment limiting the President's power to conceal information within the proposed Consumer Protection

Agency.* McCloskey's pursuit of legislative issues at least until the end of 1971 compared favorably with the legislative record of any other presidential candidate in the Congress.

Still, McCloskey may not be able to survive in the House. John Ehrlichman believes that McCloskey's drives don't square with the congressional system, and he may be right, although the comment says as much about the system as it does about McCloskey. Many congressmen, in McCloskey's words, "care only about maintaining high name recognition and a low profile in order to get reelected." Those that care about something more are frustrated by the inability of the legislative branch to compete with the executive and by the shocking, persistent inability of Congress to really do anything on its own. Perhaps even in the age of a nuclear terror, the era of the all-powerful presidency is out of date and the old Jeffersonian shibboleths about shared powers and the best government being the least government (McCloskey quoted this one in his first campaign brochure) deserve another chance. One of the reasons that McCloskey's drives seem so misplaced in Congress is that Congress, complaining all the while about the power of the presidency, has eschewed the notions of excellence and merit upon which the free enterprise system is supposedly based. Reform the Congress —and McCloskey is one of many who have tried—and choose men for leadership positions based on a yardstick other than seniority, and McCloskey would seem an almost ideal leader. Perhaps his lack of detachment would damage him here, also, but I suspect that in this setting it would be overidden by the qualities that come into play before the advocate takes over. He is, as his long-time secretary, Janet Brune, observes, "a tremendous arbitrator between parties." A man with this gift could be, in time, a legislative leader of a truly co-equal branch of government.

* The amendment deleted a provision of the bill which allowed information to be withheld "at the specific discretion of the President." In proposing it, McCloskey cited the administration's practice of refusing to make public a scientific report highly critical of the supersonic transport.

There are other courses for McCloskey outside the House. The seniority system is likely to stay far longer in the House than McCloskey, and I suspect that he will lose no opportunity to make his legislative contribution in the Senate if that chance arises. He would have difficulty at present in being nominated by the Republican party in his home state, and the only U.S. Senate election in California during the next four years (Alan Cranston, in 1974) is likely, but not inevitably, to prove beyond McCloskey's reach. He may also find a role outside the Congress, leading the Common Cause type of crusade in which McCloskey would surely do well, speaking to young people and fighting the good fight for the environment, as he did for years in San Mateo County. McCloskey detests this kind of speculation, preferring to go where his instincts lead him. They have served him well until the recent past.

It is possible, whatever happens to Pete McCloskey, that the battle he has waged within the Republican party may have been a more important fight than any of his fellow Republicans realized, a saving benefit not only to decent moderates such as New Hampshire's Governor Peterson but to the President and the party itself. The Republican party—before, during, and probably after Richard Nixon—remains a minority party. Its minority status in 1972 is almost certain to be accentuated by the presence of eleven million potential eighteen- to twenty-one-year-olds, a majority of whom have no use for Nixon. One does not have to sympathize with their views, or even with their grievances, to believe that the two-party system is seriously threatened if these young people choose the Democratic party in disproportionate numbers—and if they also vote. McCloskey, at least, has shown that a fight can be waged within the Republican party rather than merely against it.

It is impossible, now and perhaps ever, to assess McCloskey's impact on U.S. policy in Vietnam. There is no sign that any of the President's policies either in "Vietnamization" or troop withdrawal had anything to do with the McCloskey challenge.

Still, his presence in the race could act as a brake on any abrupt contemplated change. ". . . The very existence of the McCloskey challenge is a warning to the President of the consequences of any sudden zigzag or crisis in the war zone," Don Oberdorfer wrote in the Washington *Post* last September 19. "That does not seem likely today, but in this war unlikely things have often happened."

One of the most unlikely domestic products of that war has been McCloskey himself, coming as he does from an elitist military tradition to preach the values of peace. With all his imperfections, he has spoken for these values and stood for them, and he has, in this respect at least, met the test of his hero, Oliver Wendell Holmes. "I think that, as life is action and passion, it is required of a man that he should share the passion and action of his time at peril of being judged not to have lived," Holmes wrote. No one will ever be able to say that McCloskey withheld himself from the passion and action of *his* time. We have not seen the last of him in 1972.

Index

About the Author

LOU CANNON is a Washington correspondent for Ridder Publications. His book on Ronald Reagan and Jessie Unruh, *Ronnie and Jessie: A Political Odyssey*, was called by *The New York Times*, "the best book on state government that I have seen." In 1968, he won the American Political Science Association award for distinguished reporting of public affairs.